Cyber Rules

A Norton Professional Book

# Cyber Rules

## What You Really Need to Know About the Internet

Joanie Farley Gillispie

Jayne Gackenbach

**W.W. Norton & Company**

New York · London

For information about permission to reproduce
selections from this book, write to
Permissions, W. W. Norton & Company, Inc.,
500 Fifth Avenue, New York, NY 10110

Production Manager: Leeann Graham
Manufacturing by: Haddon Craftsman

**Library of Congress Cataloging–in–Publication Data**

Gillispie, Joanie Farley.
  Cyber rules: what you really need to know about the
    Internet/Joanie Farley
Gillispie, Jayne Gackenbach.
      p.      cm.
"A Norton professional book."
includes bibliographical references and index.
**ISBN–13: 978–0–393–70484–6**
**ISBN–10: 0–393–70484–X**
1. Internet. 2. World Wide Web. 3. Internet–Safety measures.
4. Internet–Social aspects. 5. Interpersonal relations–Computer network
resources. 6. Medical care–Computer network resources.
I. Gackenback, Jayne, 1946–II. Title.

TK5101.875.I57G52        2006
004.67'8–dc22        200604720

W. W. Norton & Company, Inc., 500 Fifth Avenue,
New York, N. Y. 10110
www.wwnorton.com

W. W. Norton & Company Ltd., Castle House,
75/76 Wells St., London W1T 3QT

1  3  5  7  9  0  8  6  4  2

# Contents

# Preface

Hanging out and hooking up in cyberspace: a powerful, transpersonal, transformational repository of good and bad, a cyber–collective unconscious. The urge to coalesce our experiences with children, youth, and families into a book has been percolating for thirty years. As psychologists and university faculty, Jayne and I have always been concerned that we teachers and mental health professionals are not as helpful as we could be, given the levels of distress we see in our patients and students: depression, chronic worries, addiction, unsatisfying relationships. Now these problems are creeping into cyberspace and we really don't know what to do about them.

It was difficult to create a literary product from such an amorphous and novel topic that would be both scholarly and practical. We did not want this book to be a tome of doom and dire warnings about how the Internet is corrupting our kids or contributing to the breakdown of the family. Nor did we want to succumb to a digital version of Internet Tips or Parenting 101 by promoting more of the same that does not work offline. How do we write a book about solving problems in cyberspace when we aren't solving the same ones offline? However, the Internet is as awesome (we collaborated on and wrote this book from two different countries) as it is awful (such as infant porn posted online using live Web cam).

The stakes are too high for knee-jerk solutions. We need a strategy that recognizes and understands the power of digital technology *or the power of digital technology will use us*. Internet media socializes people in new ways and will only continue to do this more, generating profound changes within ourselves, in our relationships, and in our communities. Here are some facts about our health offline: 20% of American children live in poverty in the richest nation in the world. Adults are a stressed-out bunch, ill from preventable diseases and bad habits. Many of us still are suffering from issues left over from childhood. We're unhappy and self-absorbed. Why do 50% of marriages end in divorce? Because we are confused and often ignorant or in denial about our issues, and now they are online.

Kids need help even more than adults because when they do not get their needs met at critical periods of development, they often spend a lifetime paying for it in one way or another, and so does society. Adolescents fare even worse. Our teens, at the cusp of adulthood, have the worst health of youth in developed nations and one of the poorest academic standings. Too many kids are depressed, obese, using drugs, and disconnected from their communities. Youths in the United States have more teen pregnancies, more STDs, more sexual partners, and a younger age of sexual debut than their European counterparts. Huh? What are we modeling? What is the message? What about their future? Do we care about the legacy of bad health and bad habits we are leaving behind (by default if nothing else)? Do we care about kids, do we care about each other? Questions about sex and relationships have always generated potent discussions and opinions. We're all looking for love and now we're doing it online.

While we can't seem to help young people handle the supersize pressures of growing up, the media is doing it for us. Cornell West, professor emeritus of religion at Princeton, says "we have it backwards. For 50 years we've been teaching our kids to be successful, be successful . . . when we should be teaching them to be great" (2004). What does West's philosophy have to do with *Cyber Rules*? The multimedia Internet experience makes kids feel great. Kids have power online and they know it.

Jayne and I do not claim that *Cyber Rules* is a panacea for everything that is wrong with cyberspace but we stand behind the information, problem-solving model, and advice in this book. We just can't ignore how Internet media is changing us. Communicating online enables us to be intimate and global, real and fake. Do we know the difference? Do we even care? How do we negotiate wellness through the maze of online interactive media effects that we have largely ignored offline?

We can use the Internet to close the gap between what we want young people to learn (which many do not learn well enough) and West's vision of greatness. Not success, not money, not stuff, but personal responsibility, concern for others, and a shared stake in the health of future generations. It's no accident that the title of this book is *Cyber Rules*. The Internet rocks and certainly rules the world for young people! Ask anyone who met a mate online or surfed the Web and learned what ambergris is at $200,000 per ounce. Children and adolescents embody the archetype of the Internet communication revolution: young, constantly changing, pushing boundaries, wanting control, rejecting the status quo, exploring identity, and searching for love.

This book is a guide for those who want to understand the power of the Internet media culture in order to use it in positive ways. If we are worried about the effect that media is having on our youth and culture then we need to become media literate *and* much more proactive about lots of things offline that we ignore or avoid. There is harm online. It's the same as offline but it *feels* bigger when projected into cyberspace because we can't control it: anger, racism, sexism, homophobia, greed, distractibility, impulsivity, consumerism, and deception are a part of the cyber collective, but so is altruism, cultural understanding, generosity, self-discovery, and concern for others. *Cyber Rules* acknowledges that few rules can be enforced in cyberspace from an authoritarian model. ("Don't do this because I say so" barely works on the ground.) As a result we need to convince people, kids especially, that there are some potentially harmful things going on in cyberspace that they need to be aware of and avoid, and which could hurt their development or hurt others if they choose to participate–a very tall order.

We need more information and skills for interacting online now, but we also need to understand it for the future, how cyber-human interaction will continue to evolve and change us. We already have wearable computers, neural implants, and computers that interpret your feelings and respond accordingly. Ironically, the government designed the first computers to decentralize knowledge and protect us in the event of a nuclear war, but now soldiers and F-22 Raptors use remote-sensing Internet technology to home in and kill. The Internet is the power that got away and generations of hackers young enough to be your children can get your password.

What can we do? *Cyber Rules* shares people's cyber stories, discusses the opinions of experts, and then gives the reader the criteria with which to measure and determine if cyber behaviors could threaten healthy development. Rather than a list of "do this or don't do that," *Cyber Rules* wants readers to practice evaluating cyber dilemmas using a problem-solving model and become experts about their own cyber use. This will not be an easy process. Healthy expression online or perversion? Isolation or meaningful connection? Cyber activism or a substitute for getting a life? We cannot be certain about what the psychological and social effects of Internet use will be, but hopefully this book will give you the information and practical advice you need to use the Internet wisely and "get it" about media.

## How to Use Cyber Rules

### THE AUDIENCE

This book is intended for a crossover audience because most clinicians, educators, and parents grapple with the same cyber issues. However, achieving the right tone for everyone is difficult. Not enough scientific validity and too much hype and clinicians will discount the material as unsubstantiated. Too much research and we will overwhelm the educator and the parent. Jayne and I have tried to find a balance but hope that the reader will find both the science and practicality useful. Clinicians, educators, and parents want answers, but no one is sure whether offline theories about behavior apply to cyberspace. California teachers are mandated to include Web-based curricula in their lesson plans but are not taught online pedagogy. Parents wonder if restricting, monitoring, or spying on their kids' Internet use is effective, while most teens know how to get around parental controls and are amused when adults think that they are in charge of their media diet.

*Cyber Rules* wants the reader to know what the research is on Internet effects, but also how to navigate data that can be contradictory because they are too broad or too narrow to apply to a particular cyber problem. Professional books tell therapists to expand their practice online but admit that there are no standards or laws (and few liability companies) that will protect them in cyberspace. More importantly, cyber dilemmas cannot be analyzed by uploading offline rules of psychology, or of law, economics, or politics for that matter, and expecting them to transplant effectively online.

## THE INTERVENTIONS

We want you, the reader, to solve the cyber problems presented in the clinical vignettes by imagining that you are the clinician, educator, or parent who must decide whether the cyber behavior is OK or not OK and why. Questionnaires assess knowledge and measure use patterns while the personal stories keep it real. The interactive exercises require you to conceptualize at least two different ways to organize your thinking about what's happening online. The exercises and vignettes test your knowledge and challenge your assumptions about cyberspace. They are designed to generate discussion with those whose opinions may be different from your own: therapists, teachers, colleagues, friends, and most especially young people. Certainly for every horrific cyber story there are an equal number of untold ones that are healthy and authentic. We want you to know the research, understand what potential problems look like online, and practice applying the advice in this book to a variety of scenarios and clinical vignettes so that you then know what to do in real life.

## HOW CYBER RULES IS ORGANIZED

The Introduction and Chapters 1 and 2 discuss specific problems encountered online and the ways that Internet communication affects identity. Personality and behavior in cyberspace are not constrained by face-to-face protocol, geography, and time. Is this a good thing? The exercises in Chapter 1, "Online Identities," illustrate that adults and teenagers explore different aspects of their identities online. Healthy Internet use is determined by comparing one's online and offline personalities.

The second part of this book takes the reader into the world of online relationships. Chapters 3, 4, and 5 address cyber social and sexual relationships via text, graphics, cell phones, and Web cams. What effects do these activities have on our offline relationships and well-being? The exercises that accompany these chapters help the reader to explore attitudes about what makes a healthy or unhealthy online relationship. Clinical vignettes and personal stories ask the reader to address the issue of harm online: whether cyber porn is developmentally healthy or a substitute for lack of social contact or whether a cyber affair is a real affair. Here the Internet appears to be redefining the games we play, friendships, dating, and how we look for a mate or a sexual experience. The final section of *Cyber Rules* explores health online: how to find the most accurate health information online and psychological treatment in cyberspace.

The societal problems that are so visible online give us an opportunity to craft a legacy of sustainable health for future generations. Should young people really listen to what we have to say if we leave things as they are? The digital age can help us connect more authentically with our children and make our relationships more meaningful. It's as easy to e-mail someone in the next room as half way around the world. Going global encourages us to appreciate diversity and to challenge our assumptions. But the Internet has forced us to rethink who's in charge, collaborate more when there's a problem, and negotiate solutions to digital dilemmas from a shared power perspective. It would be such a shame if we continue to keep our hearts and minds and actions disconnected, unconscious, and stuck as we log into a new world. We can use the Internet to become great. It is our hope that this book brings you at least partially there, wherever "there" is, for you and those you love.

# Acknowledgments

## Joanie

My first acknowledgments go to my family: to my husband, Mark, and to my children, Zoe, Gigi, Kellen, and Shane, for teaching me the most. Also to all the other kids who passed the 24-hour rule and became such an important part of our family: you are the lecture (share and don't whine) I never had to give. To my wise and loving father, Philip Farley, for his weekly communication the old-fashioned way, mailing me newspaper clippings because he didn't think I could get them online.

Thank you to all my students and patients over the last 35 years; I could not have done this without your willingness to talk to me about real stuff and to keep talking even when I didn't fully understand. Thank you for keeping in touch over the years. I am so lucky to have amazing friends and colleagues who put up with my steep learning curve with such good humor. Katherine Bang, Dekey Perez, Nicole Guide, and Josie Smith know all my bad habits and love me anyway. Thank you to Cindy Roby and Ginger Thomson for well-timed, laughter-filled cuz fests. And thank you Sandra Harner and Sue Hulley for your deep friendship and support. I appreciate that you listen so carefully but want me to remember that I am a work in progress.

Several universities have expanded and guided my thinking about online communication. Much appreciation to Stan Weisner, chair of the behavioral sciences department, University of California, Berkeley, for encouraging me to develop courses in media and Internet use. Also I am grateful to the University of Phoenix, California School of Professional Psychology, Alliant International University, and Dominican University, where I got to know a new generations of psychologists, teachers, and nurses.

As for the book, thank you to Lami Lapin for the connection and creativity in designing the cover. It provides a metaphor for what we want to convey to the reader and yet pushes a few status quo buttons in the process. Thanks also to Dr. Judy Kuriansky, media psychologist, for her right-on advice about the title. Most importantly, Jayne and I wish to thank those at W. W. Norton for their acceptance of our original proposal and willingness to publish yet another book about the Internet. We wish to especially acknowledge our editors Deborah Malmud and Michael McGandy for their helpful comments. Their publishing expertise helped us articulate our vision into a palatable read for a wide audience.

Finally, we are grateful to you, the reader. We really wrote *Cyber Rules* for you, hoping it will be a travel guide to cyberspace. If there is a clinician who first examines his or her assumptions about Internet communication before treating a patient with a cyber issue, an educator who models good and confronts bad netiquette, or a parent who really does talk (and listen more) to her children about cyber sexuality, Jayne and I will feel we have accomplished our goal. The Internet forces us to think deeply about the world we live in, especially the effects of media and the way we interact with each other.

## Jayne

I would like to begin by thanking Grant MacEwan College (GMC) and especially the department of psychology and sociology and the Grant MacEwan Faculty Scholarly Activity Fund. The Fund provided a grant for a research assistant to aid in editorial duties associated with this book. The grant recipient, Heather von Stackelberg, read and edited every chapter of this book as well as worked on the permissions clearances and other administrative duties. She has also offered insights from her communications background throughout this process for which Joanie and I are very grateful.

My interest in humans and computers emerged beyond the frequent user stage when Russ Powell, chair of the department of psychology and sociology at GMC, where I am now a full-time instructor, commissioned me to write an online course on dreams for GMC in the mid-1990s. Since then I have been writing and teaching introductory psychology online for GMC through ecampusalberta, a cooperative offering online courses (www.ecampusalberta.co). I would also like to thank Evelyn Ellerman, head of the communications studies program at Athabasca University, for her early and ongoing support of my work with human–computer interactions by asking me to write two courses for the program.

Many others have contributed to and supported my interest in computers, the Internet, and video games and they include colleagues (Brian Brookwell, Joan Preston, Jim Karpen, Storm King, Nikki Levi, David Lukoff, Steve Reiter, Harry Hunt, Richard Wilkerson, Jill Fisher), students (Grant MacEwan College, Athabasca University, and Saybrook Graduate School), technical support staff (Grant MacEwan College and Athabasca University), friends (Erik Schmidt, Peter Thomas, Wendy Pullin), and family (Mason Goodloe, Tony Lachel). Finally, I would like to acknowledge the eternal and special contributions of my children (Trina Snyder Lachel and Teace Snyder), mother (Agnes Gackenbach), and sister (Leslie Goodloe), without whose support and love no work could be accomplished.

# Cyber Rules

# Introduction

*Life arises from the endless interplay of polarity force . . .*
*heaven and earth, active and passive, light and dark, heat and*
*cold, dampness and dryness, contraction and relaxation . . .*
*The two forces attract and repel each other continuously.*
*Their interplay creates all energy, matter,*
*and the dynamic movement of life.*
(PECK & PECK).

## Getting It About the Internet

How do we *get it* about the Internet? What's *it* anyway? We wrote this book to help you learn about the Internet from both a psychological and a communications perspective. *Getting it* means digital media literacy: knowing how to use the Internet rather than being used by it. On the one hand we need to get it quickly, especially when there is so much bad press out there about kids' and adults' habits online. On the other hand, few argue that the power of digital technology has transformed our lives. Ask anyone what would happen if we suddenly couldn't use our computers, kids especially. Pulitzer Prize-winning author and New York Times columnist Thomas Friedman believes the Internet has flattened the world, "challenging hierarchical structures with a horizontal model of innovation" (2005, p. 103). Friedman describes what he means:

> Clearly it is now possible for more people than ever to collaborate and compete in real time with more other people on more different kinds of work from more different corners of the planet and on a more equal footing than at any previous time in the history of the world using the computers, e-mail, networks, teleconferencing, and

dynamic new software. But contemplating the flat world also left me filled with dread, professional and personal . . . . I realized that this flattening was taking place while I was sleeping, and I had missed it. I wasn't really sleeping but I was otherwise engaged. (p. 8)

Many of us can relate to Friedman's statement. The Internet has changed us in subtle and obvious ways and there is no end in sight to the fecundity of human-digital intercourse. Wear or cuddle with your computer? Step into the screen? Fascinating. Online love and hate? Confusing. Live-cam sexual exploitation of infants? Horrific. Where to turn for guidance in terms of kids' online lives? Here, for a start. This book is our effort to wake you up, so to speak, so that you can be in cyber-space consciously and meaningfully and your young ones will listen when you talk to them about harm online and not just tune you out (like they do offline). However, we want you to resist the need to be told what to do. The human effects of Internet use are complex. There's a lot at stake and a lot we don't know. We do not begin with what kids are doing online on purpose. We start, rather, with an overview of identity in cyberspace and the ways these cyber identities connect with others. Cyber Rules analyzes how our online identities and personalities compare to who we are offline. The cognitive and social mechanics of being plugged in electronically appear to be changing our neuro-anatomy. Take writing, for example. Keyboarding, as opposed to writing with our dominant hand, fully engages both hemispheres of the brain at once. This simultaneous dance of information processing allows right-brain functions, primarily nonverbal and spacial, to tango with the left's expertise in decoding verbal meanings. Of course this is reversed in left-handed people. Interestingly, our left hand types more words on the keyboard due to the way the letters are positioned. This forces our right hemisphere to expand verbal processing capabilities. Because young people's brains are still growing, these new, more interconnected ways of communicating will certainly have more profound effects than writing the old fashioned way.

IQ scores appear to be going up, indicating that we are able to process information faster. Many attribute this to the digital age (Johnson, 2005). We may also be more socially focused online. How? A quarter of the motor cortex, the part of the brain that controls all movement in the body, is devoted to the hands. Our fingertips are adept at communicating, as signers and lovers will attest. Even Freud understood the power of our hands: "He that has eyes to see and ears to hear may convince himself that no mortal can keep a secret. If his lips are silent, he chatters with his fingertips" (Freud, 1932, n.p.).

Is there a down side to being online? Perhaps. Social scientists believe that our online interactions are expanding identity, but also redefining the way we interact and socialize with others (Bargh & McKenna, 2004; Warschauer, 2003). What's happening to the power of in-person communicating online? Is it shallow or deeper, transformed in some way that we won't fully realize until our grandchildren are adults? How do the subtleties, nuances, and reciprocity so essential to offline relating manifest in cyberspace? Media psychologist Lilli Friedland is concerned but hopeful:

> Is it possible that we have become a mass of electronic hermits, not able to work or play well together? The traditional institutions of "civilizing" people, family, school, community, church/synagogue are challenged by trying to serve people whose loyalty is almost entirely to themselves. Will some people prefer to live in a fictitious world created almost entirely by the entertainment industry? As electronic media absorb more and more time, people may become less motivated to care for things and do anything for anyone but themselves . . . The younger generations are techno-savvy and prefer to communicate via Internet than face-to-face. The new media may dis-socialize people . . . but perhaps we should really look at technology as instruments that can make our lives easier and faster and give us the opportunity to focus on personal meaning. (2005, pp. 2, 6)

Attachment theorist Daniel Stern (2004) believes that socialization is the primary mechanism that brings meaning to our lives. He suggests that the language and sensory areas of our brain direct this process and becomes

> an intersubjective matrix where mechanisms such as mirror neurons may be the center of conditions for synchrony, imitation and

attunement (which) could be factors in controlling empathy and resonation with the other. (Klien, 2005, n.p.)

Mirror neurons fire away when we are engaged with each other online and with media. Neuro-scientist Marco Iacoboni at UCLA believes that these neurons may contribute to violent behavior offline because they are activated more easily after viewing violent media or engaging in combative, angry chat. Iacoboni believes this may predispose one to act more aggressively (Goldberg, 2005).

There's a lot of research *and* speculation about how the Internet affects us. Fortunately, gathering information from around the world, talking to experts online, and hearing people's online stories is easy to do in cyberspace. But the purpose of this book is more than an intellectual exercise or the need to give advice. We want the reader to learn how to use the Internet and consume media in more positive ways, to improve our relationships and our world so that our kids won't fall into the same old potholes we did. Are we for real? Why not? We have the technologies now to reach and teach almost everyone on the planet. This book is divided into three sections to make cyber culture more palatable. We discuss research, talk about projections of the self online as well as loving and playing in cyberspace. But we also include personal stories and mini vignettes so you can learn about others' experiences and thus gain perspective about your own. One of the most exciting aspects of our digital world is that it allows us to appreciate people who are different from us. Here is what Xiang, a high school student, writes from Malaysia:

> I have heard people tell me how unhealthy they think the Internet is, how information on the Internet just isn't reliable or accurate, how it results in dehumanising relationships. I listen to all of this while stewing inside. I am adolescent. Of course, you will say that my reaction is to be expected. Since adolescents love to argue and disagree and fight and talk back. Since adolescents love spending hours online chatting and playing games. But what I feel is relevant, is that I am also profoundly deaf. I am fully oral now but only beginning to learn sign language; but even my hearing aids do

not give me normal hearing. I have to concentrate intensely just to understand what someone is saying. I get most of my information from written words, books, journals, and the Internet. The Internet enables the deaf community to communicate without fear of being misunderstood. When I am told not to spend hours chatting, the fact is that while chatting, I am understanding far more than I normally do face to face. I am not 'wasting time.' It is not chatting for the sake of chatting but rather chatting for the sake of understanding, for the sake of a brief respite from the mental strain of looking, hearing, lip-reading. No hearing person I've met has any idea how immensely rewarding, how satisfying, how wonderful it is to understand someone else immediately through his/her words. It's exhilarating not to have to stare at lips, concentrating intensely, turning here and there to look at people's lips, adjust to different people's voices, and strain to hear. It's amazing to be able to finally *understand* what someone is saying without having to put in so much effort.

People may nag me to get out, to socialise, to talk. But what is 'to socialise' for me? I stand at the fringes of a group, neither outside nor inside, trying desperately to be 'in.' I'm looking back and forth as different people interrupt or cut each other off or intuitively talk all at the same time. They can react instantly to what someone else has said whereas I have to stand there, digest and process information, before I can understand. I can never understand what they're talking about if I come in the middle of a conversation. My mind has to connect body language, lip-reading and the fragments that I actually hear through my aids, and somehow solidify the whole into a message that tells me what the person is trying to say. Often I just walk away, feeling desperate and alone. The only situation where I've ever been able to take a full, engaging part in the conversation is when I'm online. Because, online, everyone is equal. Hearing takes a back seat and all that matters is how fast you read and type. And because of my deafness and inability to take a full part in conversations, I spent a lot of time reading. Now I read faster than many of my friends. So when online, I'm the same as everyone else. We all have to read the text, whether deaf or not. That's when I feel equal and able and that's when I participate to the fullest.

As with much scientific research, it is often the experiences of individuals like Xiang that help us to really understand a phenomenon. With the Internet, an expert can be a computer hacker fiddling in his parent's garage, a group of high school students who write for political blogs, or university research organizations. All inform the debate and will continue to do so. Because we acknowledge both the validity and the limitations of current scientific thinking as well as individuals' stories, guidelines and information are presented here to help you with Internet use now and as the media technology continues to evolve.

## How Do We Use Internet Media?

In 2005, the PEW Internet and American Life Project reported that 70 million adult Americans are online every day, up 37% from 2000 estimates (Rainie & Horrigan, 2005). In addition to spending more time online we are doing more too. Even the meaning of *online* has expanded. Some are connected 24/7. We now multitask, using different systems of online media simultaneously. Doing several things online at once is now the norm, so it is difficult to measure how many hours one is actually just using the Internet or consuming media, much less tease out the interaction effects.

As you can see in Figure I.1, the areas of the world with more money are the areas with more Internet usage. This digital divide reflects general cultural differences as well. The world's cultures can be conceptualized along the dimension of collectivism, where people perceive time, tasks, and relationships using polychronic models of relating versus individualism, which thrives on monochromic processes. Some emphasize the individual's rights while others emphasize group responsibilities. Western, industrial, and Internet-connected cultures in general tend to be wealthy and individualistic while Asian, Middle Eastern, South American, and African cultures tend to be collectivist. The most extreme individualist culture is the United States.

In addition to a national digital divide, University professor Janet Morahan–Martin noted,

**Figure I.1**

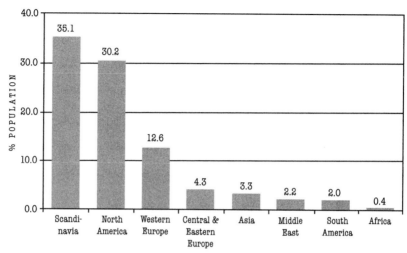

*Note.* From *Digital Divide?* (p. 22), by P. Norris, 2000, Cambridge, MA: Cambridge University Press. Reprinted with permission.

a gender gap in Internet use . . . from childhood on, males are more experienced with computers and have more favorable attitudes towards computers than females. These gender differences in computer experiences and attitudes as well as the masculinization of the computer culture may be transferred to Internet use and attitudes. In fact, the Internet culture was developed by its earliest users, primarily male scientists, mathematicians, and technologically sophisticated computer hackers. This culture can be discomforting and alien to females (1997).

While Morahan-Martin (2004) argues that differences in patterns of use continues, there is now gender parity online (Cole et al., 2003). The ethnicity of online users is also changing, as the following excerpt from an article from NUA Internet Surveys indicates:

• The number of home Internet users in the US increased by 33 percent in 2000, with African Americans leading the online growth.

• According to figures from Nielsen/NetRatings, the African American online population increased by 44 percent to 8.1 million between December 1999 and December 2000.

- Internet use among Hispanics grew by 19 percent to more than 4.7 million people, while the number of Asian American Internet users reached 2.1 million, an increase of 18 percent.

- Caucasians remain the largest ethnic group online, currently accounting for 87.5 million of America's home Internet users.

- NetRatings attributed the growth in Internet use across ethnic groups to the lowering cost of PCs and cheaper Internet access. (www.NUA.ie)

In spite of these improvements, the Internet remains a relatively privileged environment, but that may be changing. The Internet, as a failsafe, decentralized communication network, was initially invented by the military but it is now available virtually everywhere. As the world becomes more wired, Internet use by remote or economically disadvantaged populations will bring more personal power as well as business opportunities (Bier, 1997). Even in the poorest countries, 40–50% are able to use the Internet (Cole et al., 2003; Lebo & Wolpert, 2004). The Pew Internet and American Life Project, which studies the impact of the Internet on families and communities, discovered some differences in the ways men and women are online in the United States:

- 55% of Internet users say their email exchanges have improved the way they communicate with family members (60% of women; 51% of men).

- 59% report they communicate more often with significant family members now that they use email (61% of women; 56% of men).

- 66% of Internet users say email has improved their connections with significant friends (71% of women; 61% of men).

- 60% report they communicate with significant friends more often now that they use email (63% of women; 54% of men).

- 49% of email users say they would miss email a lot if they could no longer use it (56% of women; 43% of men). (Rainie & Kohot, 2000)

In 1996, psychologist Kimberly Young coined the term "internet addiction". At that time, Young determined that four to eight hours of Internet use per week indicated the presence of an addiction. But in 2005, investigators from the Kaiser Health Survey believed *six or more hours per day* suggested heavy Internet use. Paradoxically, the Kaiser survey results revealed that youngsters and adults who were classified as heavy Internet users reported more time with friends and family and more satisfaction at work. The children in the Kaiser survey reported doing better in school as a result of their time online (Roberts, Foehr, & Rideout, 2005). In contrast to early studies, the more we do online the more we appear to like it, so the more we do online (Rainie, 2005).

Perhaps the most urgent question asked about the Internet concerns the effect that freedom in cyberspace is having on our children and teenagers. Any adult who wants to know what kids really do online can now peek into their not-so-private cyber world for an eye-opening view of their loves, their losses, and what they don't want their parents to know about their lives on- and offline. (Check out adult-controlled blog sites like MySpace.com and FaceBook.com and compare with youth-controlled ones like YouthNoise.com). The smut-checkers recently hired by MySpace (Angwan, 2006) to mollify parents and advertisers will backfire. What do we think will happen if MySpace becomes censored, e.g., no more than 12 photos to start a site and no nudity? Right, they'll hide what they are doing. We should be glad we can see what's up with kids even if we don't like it, because then we can deal with it rather than keep our heads in the sand.

*New York Times* writer Emily Nussbaum calls Internet chat madly contradictory, anonymous but traceable, instantaneous but permanent, and a place where distinctions between healthy candor and too much information abound. She poignantly describes a fifteen-year-old's blog: "He wanted his entries to be read but feared that people would read them . . . he wanted to be included while priding himself on his outsider status" (2004, p. 3).

For families, kids' online lives are the conflict du jour. Parents bemoan the fact that their children are more connected to their online friends than to them. Kids surf in a larger world than most adults could imagine. Parents install NannyWare or find themselves secretly scrolling through their kids' instant messages (IM), e-mails, or Web site histories. Some experts insist that parents should monitor everything their children and teenagers do online. They advocate placing the computers in the living room, spying on their kids, and restricting the amount of time online, (Greenfield, 2004a; Thornburgh & Lin, 2002) (see also Chapter 2, "Children's and Teens'

Media Lives"). However, others insist that this authoritarian approach doesn't even work on ground and does little to teach kids how to learn healthy cyber habits (Heins, 2001; Tapscott, 2005, 1998).

What's a parent to do? Ask the experts? One mom read her son's instant messages and found this: "French p.96 lunch? 8) POS!" What's her son really saying? It's an online booty call for oral sex during lunch with a warning that his mom's watching the screen. Educators are also confused. In any one day they might come across more digital issues than parents or clinicians see in a month, from IM bullying to terrorist threats and covert cyber sexuality. A school counselor tried not to look shocked when 13-year-old Courtney pulled out her cell phone and nonchalantly scrolled to a picture of herself in thong underwear. She added the caption "cum at 5:00" and hit SEND to her blog site, complaining "my parents are just *so* annoying."

Research findings are important, but provide only part of the story. Social scientists took almost 30 years to tell parents and the public about television's ability to influence children (O'Keefe, 2000). Such is not the case with the Internet. The developmental implications of being online, as well as the effects of other interactive media, have burgeoned, but the results are contradictory. We do know that our use of Internet media flows through and to each other in multiple, integrative, and interactive ways. But this happens so quickly that making sense of the effect at any one point in time is problematic. By design and intent the Internet piques our interest and makes us want to explore. That part's easy. An unusual experiment by the Indian government was conducted to see if computers could be used to help illiterate children learn. Computers were placed where children had easy access, with no instruction and no instructor, yet within minutes the children discovered that if you touch the mouse pad for this strange "TV" the white arrow on the screen moved in the same direction. Within eight minutes these children had uncovered the magic of hyperlinks and were surfing the Internet. Soon they were downloading songs and games, but still needed to be taught how to harness the power of the web for uses beyond entertainment (BBC News, 2001).

The other part of the story concerns kids. They are the experts too. Listening to them and especially watching how seamlessly Internet and media are integrated into their everyday world is awesome. The PEW Internet and American Life research study discovered that nine out of ten kids are online every day. This is triple the number online in 2000, largely due to increased access via broadband and larger storage capabilities, which allow for more satisfying real-time audio and graphics in addition to text (Lenhart, 2005). This critical mass online cannot be ignored and what kids are doing tells us a lot. Take youth blogs for example. These are public forums. Students are usually surprised to learn that school admissions counselors visit MySpace (along with 75 million others) to see what applicants may have posted about themselves. Prospective employers do too. It's a good way to find out what else a young job applicant may be involved with that may affect their reliability on the job. Sixteen-year-old Shawn found out the hard way when a church elder told his father about a blog entry on his MySpace site. Both Shawn and Dad were surprised to see "throbbing member" as a caption under a photo. The posting was supposed to be a joke from a friend. Needless to say, as communication opportunities expand online, young people will be the first to embrace the new technology and find out later that cyberspace is a largely unregulatable scrapbook.

Donald Roberts and colleagues from the Kaiser Family Foundation (Roberts, Foehr, & Rideout, 2005) surveyed over 2000 elementary and secondary school students. Their survey included questions on a wide range of electronic media, including: TV, VCR, DVR, radio, CD/tape, video games, computer, cable/satellite TV, premium channel, Internet, cell phones, land-line phones, instant messaging, portable CD/tape player, MP3 player, handheld video game, personal digital assistant (PDA), and handheld Internet devices. Here's what they discovered.

The Kaiser survey revealed that most American homes are media saturated. For instance, 73% of homes in 2004 had three or more TVs. It is well known that television and radio have reached almost complete population saturation and now these venues are in sync with digital media and the Internet. Ninety-five percent of us also have VCRs, DVDs, and CD players and a majority of households in America have video-game consoles (83%), computers (86%), cable/satellite TV (82%), the Internet (74%), and Instant Messaging programs (60%). In the last five years media use and Internet access have steadily increased in homes, schools, and communities so that in Canada and the United States virtually anyone can be online. Interestingly, Internet users five years ago used to be predominantly white, young, and male. Now there are few gender, age, or ethnic differences in terms of overall access to media, but there are differences: girls are less likely to have video games in the home, younger children, African American, and Hispanic children are less likely than Caucasians to have the Internet or instant messaging in the home.

The majority of children in the Kaiser research study were fully wired from the convenience of their bedrooms with computers, TV, VCR/DVD, radio, CD/tape players, and handheld video-game players. Half had video-game consoles in their rooms. Cell phones were owned by the majority of 15- to 18- year-olds and 20% of the 8- to 10-year-olds they interviewed also have cell phones. Gender differences in personal ownership of various electronic media were wider spread, with boys more likely to own a TV, VCR/DVD, video-game console, computer, and Internet connection than girls. But there was one notable exception: girls had more cell phones.

All Internet-generated media activities have increased continually since 1999, even though total computer use comprises one-third the time consumed by screen media. Playing computer games and instant messaging are the most frequent computer uses now but this wasn't even asked about in 1999. The Kaiser survey also found that Internet habits change as children get older. The average age of first computer exposure is 9 months old. For younger children, games and recreational Web site use are the most frequent activity, while teenagers use e-mail, cell phones, and instant messaging more. There are gender differences as well, with boys playing more games (where sexist and violent themes dominate), while girls prefer communication-based experiences. The Internet has also generated its own language including, acronyms like GAFF, "get a life loser" and POS, "parent over shoulder" and icons for shorthand and privacy. There are some interesting cultural differences as well: a smile in English is :), in Spanish it is 8), but in Japanese it's read vertically as (^ ^).

Thanks to advances in nanotechnology, the amount of information stored on a computer chip will double every two years (Moore, 2005). Constant innovations in Internet media will continue to reel us in with ever more engaging ways to be online. The interactivity of text, Web cam, graphics, and audio may increase the potential for harm just by the exponential effect of multitasking with several different media technology at once, each one more life-like than the next. Even now, some feel so in sync with media that it has become a seamless part of culture.

Computer engineers have already mapped out what the next ten years of computer inventions will look like, but they are unsure about the corresponding human effects (F. Labonte, personal communication, February 12, 2006). One way to understand our psychology in cyberspace is to look to the architecture of Internet technology for clues. Communication online was founded on a binary system of 0s and 1s. Every action and keystroke results from different combinations of either 0 or 1. The same model applies to the potential effect of what we do online. For example, radical behaviors like gender tourism or sexual exploration can be viewed from the valence of a binary system: as enriching opportunities for personal growth or an excuse to behave impulsively. If one pretends to be the opposite gender online or explores cyber sexual intimacy are these activities always unhealthy? How about someone who has more friends online than offline? Are they expanding their social repertoire or stunting their development?

What do we make of the possibility that the same behavior or activity online may be healthy *or* harmful depending on who is doing it or how much it occurs? Because the Internet has flattened the world, opposing realities flourish and challenge our worldview. How do we integrate and balance this with our offline lives? One fifteen-year-old was surprised that her father had discovered her MySpace Web site because she had not used her real name. This teen was shocked to realize that Dad had viewed her sexually suggestive photos and postings about herself ("I'm 18"). While the behavior online is of concern, it is also the norm for teenage girls. Her blog may or may not be unhealthy, depending on the degree to which her online behavior leaks into her offline life. So, the problem is not primarily the online activity itself but how these cyber behaviors negatively affect one's offline life.

## Cyber Rules for Cyberspace

How do we determine whether what we do online is healthy or harmful? First, ask yourself how much you really know about cyber culture. Then take the Cyber Quiz 101. Your score becomes the baseline for what you need to find out before you move on to figuring out whether there is a problem. Unhealthy Internet use shares many characteristics with compulsive behaviors offline. These criteria can be modified and applied to what we do online. Look over the "Criteria for Problem Internet Use" and see how many criteria the Internet behavior in question meets. Finally, answer the questionnaire "Do You Have a Problem?" The questions, modeled after the criteria for compulsivity, are reformulated for the Internet and address the following: perceptions of identity, thoughts and feelings about online activities, the ability to control what you do online, the opinions of others, and the difference between online and offline life.

Now you are ready to apply what you know about Internet culture to evaluating whether a problem exists and designing an intervention that goes beyond monitoring, censoring, or abstaining from a certain online activity. Exercise I.3, "Applying It: Online Behaviors and Offline Effects" provides a way to deconstruct online behaviors so that offline problem solving will be more effective.

### Exercise I.1  Cyber Quiz 101

Consider this quiz a pretest and a barometer of your knowledge about the Internet. As you read this book you should come back to the questions you cannot answer. The answers to this quiz are found in Chapter 7 on page 196.

1. How many Americans are online daily?_____

2. People who report more time online feel more _____

3. _____ out of 10 kids are online every day.

4. What is the age when children start to use Internet media?_____

5. List three reasons that people say and do things online that they would not do offline:

   1. _____   2. _____   3. _____

6. List the four components of the Cyber Rules problem-solving model:

   a)                                    c)

   b)                                    d)

7. Explain Friedman's concepts of "the world is flat" and what this has to do with online behaviors and offline effects.

## Exercise I.2  Problem Internet Use

The criteria for determining if there is a problem include:

| | |
|---|---|
| *Use of Time* | How much time is spent pursuing the behavior? |
| *Level of Impairment* | Is the behavior continued despite health, social, or occupational problems? |
| *Dealing with Emotion* | Does the behavior help to numb, alter, or avoid feelings? |
| *Self-regulation* | Are efforts to cut back on the behavior unsuccessful? |
| *Others' Opinions* | Do family or friends believe there is a problem? |
| *Other Problems* | Is the behavior part of another psychological or medical concern? |

### Do You Have A Problem?

Each question has only two possible answers: *yes* or *no*. The more *yes* answers one has the greater the potential for harmful effects offline. For example, a *yes* answer for each question meets one criterion for compulsivity. While each *yes* answer suggests the possibility of developing a harmful pattern of Internet use, *three or more yes answers* meet the criteria for a behavioral compulsion according to the most recent *Diagnostic and Statistical Manual of Mental Disorders* (American Psychiatric Association, 2000)

1. Do you often stay online longer than you intend to?  YES NO

2. Do you argue with others about your behavior online?  YES NO

3. Is your identity online very different from whom you are offline?  YES NO

4. Do you do things online you wouldn't do offline?  YES NO

5. Do you hide anything you do online?  YES NO

6. Are you worried about how much time you spend online?  YES NO

7. Do you often avoid other things you need to do when online?  YES NO

8. Do you become agitated if you cannot get online when you want to?  YES NO

9. Does your online behavior ever cause problems in your offline life?  YES NO

10. Does your online life often feel more satisfying than your offline one?  YES NO

Number of *Yes* Answers _____

## Applying It: Comparing Online Behaviors with Offline Effects

How would a teenager whose parents found out their child was accessing porn sites fill in Exercise 1.3? How would the parents fill it out for their child? How would the parents' and teen's online behaviors and offline effects columns differ? How would you help someone answer the questions in Table 1 who told you they were having a cyber affair? Think about other potential problem behaviors online. What about spending three to six hours per day shopping or playing video games online? Use Exercise 1.3 with a variety of cyber vignettes or cyber habits of your own or someone you know.

## Exercise I.3  Applying It: Online Behaviors and Offline Effects

| Basic Questions | Online Behaviors | Possible Offline Effects |
| --- | --- | --- |
| *Why do I go online?* | | |
| *How much time do I really spend online?* | | |
| *How does media technology affect me?* | | |
| *What are my identities online?* | | |
| *What are the ways that I connect with others online?* | | |
| *What are the feelings I have about my cyber habits?* | | |

After working through these exercises you may ask, how well does this Cyber Rules model actually solve online dilemmas? We can only answer that it has got to be better than what's happening now. While the four components of the problem-solving model in *Cyber Rules* are not the only way to conceptualize harmful Internet use, they are based on sound psychological intervention strategies that work offline. The model is offered here as a concise method to guide your thinking and expand your awareness of the complexities inherent in Internet cultures and human behavior so you are less likely to fall for quick fixes that do not work. Behavioral scientist Keith Beard states that the process of determining whether unhealthy Internet use exists is complex, depending as much on contextual factors, like technology and media literacy, as on psychological ones. He urges us to get on it,

> . . . rather than waiting for a crisis to occur and then picking up the pieces. Introducing new technologies and simultaneously using psychology to counteract negative effects may lessen the onset of

difficulties and the development of crises . . . regardless of whether or not Internet addiction is a true "addiction," there are people developing a harmful dependence on the Internet. (2005, p. 13)

Before we take you to the next chapters where you will be exposed to discussions about how the Internet is expanding our identities and shaping our social connections, remember to keep the Cyber Rules model in mind to inform your opinions about Internet use. The Cyber Rules problem-solving model has four parts:

a) Knowledge.
b) Understanding the criteria that define problem use.
c) Assessing your online use.
d) Comparing online behaviors with offline effects.

# Chapter 1

# Online Identities

$I$s it good for us to *try on* other iden-
tities or *try out* different personalities online? How is the self experienced
online relative to offline? Are they the same? What's the impact of
exploring alternative selves online? Do online alternative selves change
offline personalities? Is one's "true self" more prevalent or powerful
online or offline? And most importantly, can experience online change
who we are? This chapter includes personal stories about how we portray ourselves in cyberspace and also what some of the research says
about who we are online. The data show that we can be more intensely
ourselves online, an entirely new person, or someone in-between. We
invite you to use the Cyber Rules for Cyberspace model (see Introduction) with the exercises at the end of this chapter to understand more
fully who we are online and determine whether this is a problem or not.

Recently, a successful engineer came into therapy confused. Andrew, a
56-year-old father of three, had been joining discussion boards for several
years as a thirty-something woman named Andrea. It wasn't until his
teenage daughter accidentally discovered a recent conversation of her
father's online that he was forced to examine his online behavior. Realiz-
ing how much he had learned undercover as Andrea, Andrew now feels
constrained by the pressures of being a male. He remembered playing
dolls with his sister and always being envious that girls could cry and
show their feelings while boys were ridiculed. As a woman online, Andrew

was able to express vulnerability, and he made many satisfying friendships without his male gender getting in the way and giving the wrong impression. However, his daughter and wife did not understand. They felt it was wrong to do something that was hidden from the family. Andrew is working with his therapist to bring the qualities of the online persona more visibly into his real life. Andrew's story is not unusual. It appears that more heterosexual men than women may want to alter their identity in cyberspace (Suler, 2004) and that 50% of youth reveal that they too lie about who they are online (Valkenburg, Schouten, & Peter, 2005). Whether or not these explorations of self online are healthy depends on many factors.

## Exploring the Self Online

The Internet may add to or deepen our self-awareness, but it also has the potential for adverse consequences. We are just beginning to discover how the experience of self online affects our offline identity. Because the Internet is so interactive, users can project different parts of their personalities and even entirely different identities to others in cyberspace without the same rules that govern face-to-face (f2f) communication. The Internet also feels more private, anonymous, and depersonalized than it really is. Often we do not really know people in cyberspace. As a result it is easy to be someone that we would not be in a f2f interaction. What is said online may or may not be truthful. When communicating online you don't have to see someone's physical or emotional reactions or be accountable for what you say, especially with someone you don't know. Here is another story from a 15-year-old named Tom who called himself Ronald online:

> When I think about it now I can't even remember why I started it. I guess it was because I thought I couldn't have succeeded any other way, but I knew I couldn't win this way either. So I was stuck, and I think I chose the wrong path. Maybe if I had told her what was going on, or maybe if I had stayed as myself, things would be different. But it doesn't matter now. Pretending to be someone else I guess doesn't always help.

My scheme, in all of its stupidity, was to become someone else. Not in person, but in pretense. My friend Alice, with whom I attended school, was one of the people on my e-mail list. I had liked her for a long time but I never acted on my feelings. She was attending a different high school than I, and my timing was screwed. I needed to say something to her. So I did. Not as myself, but as an anonymous friend instead. I e-mailed her with a message asking whether or not she talked to strangers, and if she would talk to me, a supposed stranger.

She responded the next day and she seemed almost eager to talk to me. Isn't it weird how, when you get the chance to be someone else, you become someone else. My irreverent sense of humor disappeared, and I became the sweet loveable Ronald character she would come to know. For the first little while she would just inform me of things I already knew. She would ask me questions, and I wouldn't lie but instead would make details a little different. Ronald is really my first name but in person I go by my middle name Tom. I said I lived in Sherwood Park rather than Edmonton. I had once lived in Sherwood Park, which is located next to Edmonton. I never actually lied but instead I led her on to believe I was someone I wasn't, which was even worse.

Seconds became minutes, turning into hours, then days, as we got increasingly close to each other. She asked if I would call her but I refused, due to the fact that she would recognize my voice. At this point in time I knew my days as Ronald were coming to an end. She tried a few times to set up a meeting with me, and I would always come up with some bullshit excuse to get out of it. Simultaneously I was still e-mailing her as myself (Tom), and I would ask her questions about what she thought of Ronald. Then she would tell me the truth about the other me. It was all falling into place, the only problem being that she didn't know who the hell I was. She would tell the actual me about the fictional me and I would play with her mind. I know now that this is cruel, but when you're having fun it's hard to see the wrong in things. I wanted to tell her who I was but unfortunately I knew she wouldn't talk to me again if I did. (The fact that I knew I was jeopardizing our friendship only made me continue with my plan.)

Eventually though, my day of judgment came (as it always does for people who are doing something wrong). Oddly enough, the person who screwed it up and made my pretense public was my

mother. My mom had answered one of my incoming instant messages and had said that Tom wasn't there. This was a problem
because Alice was trying to get a hold of Ronald. Then she had sent
Ronald an e-mail saying "Hi Tom." This really sucked, because we
were starting to get really close and just then the truth had to emerge.

You see the night before the disaster she told Ronald something
she had never revealed to the real me. She told him about her father,
and how he would hit her. How he would use a giant wooden spoon
he had gotten while in Africa, and he'd beat her. He threw her down
the stairs and threatened her. The only reason she felt safe afterwards
was because one of her teachers noticed the bruises and called the
police. Her father apologized and said he wouldn't do it again. But he
has and still does. Her telling the fake me was like a slap in the face,
showing me that this was wrong. She had put her complete faith in
me, not knowing who I was, and I was trashing it to pieces. The next
day when my mom accidentally told Alice who I was, the relationship was over. The e-mails grew shorter and shorter and eventually
disappeared.

I wish I had done things differently. Maybe if I had, I could have
helped her. Maybe if I had been myself I might have had a chance.
But what good do maybes do? In the end I regret this whole event.
She has lost her trust in me. When you're the one inflicting the pain,
sometimes it can hurt just as much as when it's inflicted upon you.

Tom's readiness to experience a new identity online where "when
you get the chance to be someone else, you become someone else" is
perhaps the most powerful aspect of self online. Tom wanted to be
someone he wasn't able to be in f2f reality because he had a crush on
Alice. Although his pretense ended badly, he learned a valuable lesson
about being true to himself. Tom's story illustrates how projection of a
different identity online, though begun with innocent intentions, can
potentially cause harm. How would Andrew and Tom have thought
about their online behavior after using the Cyber Rules for Cyberspace
problem-solving model? They may have recognized that some of their
activities met the criteria for compulsivity. Also each of them would
have answered yes to at least four questions on the "Do You Have a
Problem?" questionnaire. However, meeting the criteria for problem use

and measuring the severity of the problem are not enough to help most people change harmful patterns of behavior. Table 1.1 below presents both Andrew's and Tom's perspectives.

### Table 1.1: Getting It: Comparing Online Behaviors with Offline Effects

| Basic Questions | Online Behaviors | Possible Offline Effects |
|---|---|---|
| *Why do I go online?* | *A: to experience feeling like a female.*<br>*T: to learn how to be a cool guy that gets the girl. To feel popular.* | *A: tired of the cultural stereotypes of maleness, especially at work.*<br>*T: practice my online moves at school.* |
| *How much time do I really spend online?* | *A: more and more time on more and more blog sites.*<br>*T: trying to reduce the time online.* | *A: my life is too sedentary, I'm online every day.*<br>*T: my school work suffers.* |
| *How does media technology affect me?* | *A: easily able to hide what I am doing.*<br>*T: easily able to hide what I am doing.* | *A: takes up a lot of time keeping my online identity secret on the home computer.*<br>*T: it makes me popular at school because I help others with the latest technology.* |
| *What are my identities online?* | *A: female who has strong opinions but is able to discuss emotions and vulnerability.*<br>*T: someone who knows how to talk to girls.* | *A: sometimes, after being online for a few hours, I look in the mirror and expect to see a woman.*<br>*T: I feel a little braver to talk to a girl I like because I know how they think.* |
| *What are the ways that I connect with others online?* | *A: on blog sites and discussion boards but no personal or sex sites.*<br>*T: via e-mail and IM, also blogs and peer-to-peer networks.* | *A: I think it helps me relate to women offline, especially my daughter.*<br>*T: I feel more confident in a group of girls and also notice how hard it is to have authentic conversations with people you have a crush on.* |
| *What are the feelings I have about my cyber habits?* | *A: no guilt until I got caught but worried that I would be happier as a female.*<br>*T: guilty as soon as I began to receive very personal information.* | *A: guilt, anger that I let myself be caught, curious if I can work through this with a therapist.*<br>*T: worried that I would get in trouble or cause a breakdown in the relationship if she found out I was lying to her for so long.* |

## Internet Identities

The Internet presents a broad range of new definitions that challenge old ways of thinking about identity. Chat lines, discussion boards, and role-playing games give us the opportunity to try on alternate selves. For instance, men can try being women without having to face any social stigma from others, and both males and females can explore a range of affiliations and even entirely new identities. Personality psychologists believe that we have identities comprised of different facets of our personalities. Within this framework we may call upon different aspects of self, depending on our psychological and biological history and our current situation. Although we do not permanently split off parts of our personalities out of our consciousness, as is the case in dissociative identity disorder, we frequently shift who is "on stage" depending on whom we are talking to or the situation. Our capacity to integrate various aspects of our personalities into one functioning identity has long been considered a marker of psychological well-being in adulthood. Recently, more awareness of cultural diversity has added depth to the concept of personality and the way we adapt our identities depending on the context and social cues. For example, an Asian-American female may be the boss at work, the co-parent at home, and the acquiescent daughter with her first-generation parents.

In contemporary society, alternative lifestyles, types of family structures, and cultural models of identity have become increasingly visible, so the various projections of self online, depending on context, may no longer be seen as inherently maladaptive but rather an example of explorations of the self. However, if the person projected online is radically different from one's offline personality, the potential for harm, deceit, and miscommunication increases. It takes energy to manage one's everyday life, much less two (or more) identities that may be radically different in either personality or biology. As Andrew and Tom eventually discovered, pretending to be someone else deeply affects others. Andrew wanted to break the offline constriction of his gender role while Tom called it "playing with Alice's mind," but finally, "his day of judgment came." Ask whether you would say or do the things in person that you do over the Internet. Ask whether you find yourself hiding your online self from friends and family. Is your online self congruent with your offline self? And if not, what is the purpose and meaning behind your experimentation? Are there nuances of your personality that you want to nourish or develop in some way? Or, perhaps you realize that a facet of your identity offline continues to cause problems in the way you relate to others. It may be easier to remediate this character trait by practicing positive social interactions online first.

To the extent that we can integrate different facets of our identities has long been appreciated as contributing to psychological well-being. We see the fluidity between these possible selves initially in adolescence with the uncertainty of establishing one's identity as separate from one's parents. Teens sometimes explore different identities as a way to assert their independence and autonomy, which can annoy their parents or other adults in authority. Young people push limits as a way to be able to leave the comfort of the nest. Blue hair, nose rings, and food fetishes are bodily ways to be unique. The goth, skater, grunge, and stoner cultures allow kids to explore different selves. However, when children try out different personalities in the offline world, they are limited to only a few realistic choices. Some of these are healthy explorations of the self (like vegetarianism or political activism) while others can be harmful (engaging in illegal activities with peers).

Online, opportunities to explore different identities are easy, exponential, and unregulatable and they are also becoming the norm. At the University of Amsterdam, Patti Valkenburg and colleagues surveyed 600 18-year-olds in classroom settings. They asked these students if they had experimented with their identity online using chat rooms or instant messaging. The results showed that "50 percent indicated that they had engaged in Internet-based identity experiments. The most important motive for such experiments was "self-exploration in order to see how others would react, followed by social compensation (to overcome shyness) and social facilitation (to facilitate relationship formation)" (Valkenburg, Schouten, & Peter, 2005 p. 383).

Who did the students in the Valkenburg et al. study pretend to be? Most presented themselves as someone older than they were in real life

(50%) with other variations including pretending they were a real-life acquaintance, an elaborated fantasy person, or a more flirtatious person. A few presented themselves as more beautiful or more macho. These fantasy identities differed as a function of the adolescents' age, gender, and personality, so that extraverts more than introverts presented themselves as older online than they actually were, as did younger adolescents and girls. The real-life-acquaintance alternative self online was more common among boys, as was outright fantasy. These findings are consistent with most theories of adolescent identity development offline, which characterize young people as wanting to be more attractive, older, and belonging to popular groups.

## Online Versus Offline Selves

How do we perceive our identities offline? Not surprisingly, as we try to understand who we are and why we do what we do, we gain an appreciation of our strengths and weaknesses, and hopefully insight. But psychologists know that mood affects how we see ourselves. In a negative mood we are more likely to attend to negative information about the self, while the opposite is true if we are feeling positive. Developmentally, as we move from childhood through adolescence to adulthood, our ability for self-awareness increases our interpersonal skills. Just as mood regulates what shows we choose to watch on TV, it also regulates what we do online. Clinicians know that their depressed patients tend to be less physically active and withdraw from social networks. Now, lonely and isolated individuals can reach out to cyber friends and interact in meaningful ways.

An isolated and depressed young man writes about how online friends helped him change his self-concept:

> I had depression for about 3 or 4 years. My family didn't pay much attention to me because my grades were low. I drank a lot of alcohol, all from our liquor cabinet in the dining room. My friends at school stopped talking to me because they thought that I stole their crushes. Basically, things got from bad to worse. Drinking led to worse marks, which then led to even more drinking. I stopped playing badminton,

and doing everything else that I usually really liked to do except play an Internet war video game called "Starcraft: Brood Wars." At the peak of my depression, I tried to kill myself with the Tylenol 3 I had received from the doctor for my wisdom teeth removal. Life was bleak, meaningless, and meant to be suffering.

The beginning of summer vacation was the beginning of my recovery. One day, I joined a game and my opponents called themselves "Madas" and were in clan "Mada." Surprisingly, I was asked to join. At the beginning, I tried to act like everyone else–cool and happy. They were all in Sydney, Australia, so I changed my sleeping pattern so I could talk to them. But one day, I started yelling at everyone in the channel (which is like a chat room) and the clan leader whom I call Onii chyan, which is "Older brother" in Japanese, asked me for my phone number and called me. I ended up telling him everything. All the horrible things bottled up and he was very supportive. He told the clan what I told him, and they sent me cards, they'd call me sometimes to make sure I was eating because I almost stopped eating altogether. They always tell me to go to Australia and they'll take me around and make sure that I eat a lot of food. Even now, we send each other Christmas cards. They've been most supportive; they told me to find a therapist in Boston, someone I can talk to when they aren't around for me. They showed me a brighter path; they helped me with my homework after summer vacation was over. They edited my essays, tried to teach me math and chemistry, and tried to help me overcome the depression. Whenever I start being sad again, we'd turn on the Web cam and see who could dance weirder. After a while, I caught up in school work and the clouds in my real-world social life started floating away and for the first time since I was about 10, I started to feel happy.

We are seeing how the Internet facilitates important connections, especially for those who are physically or socially isolated. John Beck and Mitchell Wade, authors of *Got Game* (2004), point out that the 15- to 35-year-old generation is comfortable with a variety of electronic media, and especially with video gaming, in ways that the baby boomers find foreign. Psychological research comparing online versus offline identities suggests that some of the processes of developing an online identity follow a similar trajectory of offline development. John Krantz, Jody Ballard, and Jody

Scher of Carnegie Mellon University compared results from identical experiments on men's perception of attractiveness of females conducted on- and offline. They hypothesized that "if the same psychological variables drive the results of both data sets, the trends in data should be similar" (1997, p. 264). This is exactly what they found. In other words, how one rated a female in terms of her physical attractiveness did not differ if done online or in a more traditional f2f laboratory setting. A meta-analysis of Internet-based, psychological research was recently published in *American Psychologist* (Kraut et al., 2004), a premiere journal of the American Psychological Association. The authors found that "not only can the Internet increase the efficiency of studying traditional psychological phenomena; its use is also an important phenomenon in its own right" (p. 105).

Parents, teachers, and clinicians are concerned about the ways we project ourselves into cyber space. Does our sense of self emerge online the way it does offline? What about trying out different personalities altogether? Complete Exercise 1.1 and examine how your online identity compares to your offline one.

### Exercise 1.1. What Do You Know About Online and Offline Identities?

*Goal:*   To compare online and offline personalities in order to understand how the power of Internet communication affects identity in positive and negative ways.

*Age:*   All ages; younger children may need help with the vocabulary.

*Settings:* Any.

Directions: Complete the questions below.

1. Four personality traits below that you think describe you best.

   *shy   outgoing   calm   excitable   a worrier   a loner   curious   loyal*
   *honest   sad   fearful   unattractive   talkative   mean   quiet   a thinker*
   *funny   kind   confrontive   teamplayer   loner   troublemaker   attractive*

2. Now go back and <u>underline</u> four traits that are a part of your online identity.

3. Fill in the chart below, ranking in order of importance to you:

| Offline Personality Traits | Online Personality Traits |
|---|---|
| 1. | 1. _____ |
| 2. | 2. _____ |
| 3. | 3. _____ |
| 4. | 4. _____ |

4. Are the two groups the same or different? Why?

5. Which of your <u>offline</u> personality traits is the most important? Why? _____

6. Which of your <u>online</u> personality traits is the most important? Why? _____

7. Which personality trait(s) do you want to develop more in your <u>online</u> self?

8. Which personality trait(s) do you want to develop more in your <u>offline</u> self?

9. Describe two ways that your personality may change in the future as a function of your online activities.

10. Is there anything that concerns you about your (or another's) online identity? Explain.

## SELF-EXPRESSION OR DISINHIBITION ONLINE?

If our psychological processes are similar online and offline, how come we hear so many stories of people being different, or at least projecting very different parts of themselves into cyberspace? Many individuals find themselves acting in uncharacteristic ways online, due to several unique constructs: easy access, constant availability, and anonymity. The result of these three As is a phenomenon called *disinhibition*. Disinhibition is defined as the inability to control impulsive behaviors, thoughts, or feelings. Online there are few controls for social behavior. When we go to anonymous sites it is easy to communicate in ways that we would not ordinarily do offline. These communication patterns can be positive or negative. A positive example of disinhibition online is the propensity for self-revelation that results in people feeling more intimate and supported. This disclosure can fluctuate, however, from appropriate, allowing for a more authentic connection, to inappropriate, with combative, critical, or angry comments or outright lying online. Adam Joinson (2007) writes about research subjects who were impulsive and combative online but who were entirely different offline:

> Niederhoffer and Pennebaker (2001) report a startling discovery for their experimenter in a study of linguistic synchrony using Internet chat as a methodology. The male experimenter who conducted the sessions debriefed the participants immediately after the interactions without reading the actual transcripts. He noted that the students were always low keyed, unassuming, and moderately interested in the study. No participants appeared embarrassed, shocked, or, in the slightest way, upset or angry. At the conclusion of the project, when he was given the opportunity to read the transcripts, he was astounded–even overwhelmed–to learn what these polite students had been saying to one another (Niederhoffer and Pennebaker, 2001, p. 14). According to their analysis, nearly a fifth (18.8%) of the chat sessions 'involved overt invitations for sex, explicit sexual language, or discussion of graphic sexual escapades. (p. 14)

Professor John Suler, from Rider University in New Jersey, argues that "rather than thinking of disinhibition as revealing an underlying 'true self,' we can conceptualize it as a shift to a constellation within self-structure, involving clusters of affect and cognition that differ from the in-person constellation" (2004, p. 321). In a detailed analysis of this kind of impulsivity online, Suler highlights four reasons that people expand their identities online:

1. *Dissociative Anonymity.* Although not a formal pathology, the sense of self while online becomes compartmentalized into an "online self," which is perceived as alone and anonymous, and an offline self that is different and separate. Because the Internet feels so virtual and boundaryless, it is tempting to perceive "the other" as not real.
2. *Invisibility.* You don't have to worry about how you look when chatting with someone online. One need not worry, Am I smiling enough? Was that sigh of exasperation heard? What you have to write then

takes on deeper meaning. Analyzing the textual clues of communication, without the nonverbal, leans heavily on one's thinking...as thoughts can be the precursor to the written word.

3. *Asynchronicity.* For many online communications, one can respond at one's leisure and the pressure of an immediate response is gone. Here, Suler talks about "emotional hit and run" where a scathing message can be left on a message board and the poster never returns to check on the responses or repercussions of his words.

4. *Solipsistic Introjection.* As absorption in an online exchange increases, some experience the online companion as a "voice within one's head" (Suler, 2004, p. 323). The online friend becomes incorporated into one's intrapsychic world. Like a character in our dreams, our waking thoughts include stories about various people. Some of these people are real and immediate, while others are somewhat less so, such as an imagined comeback to your boss. The boss is real but the exchange is not. The online friend can take on a special status in our imagined internal dialogues, which can result in a felt sense of special closeness existing outside the boundaries of time and space.

A young girl named Penny introjects her online self into her offline consciousness. She describes the intensity and the realness of her identity online: "I remember walking around and feeling like my online friend was somehow inside my head no matter where I went. This felt so special, so close, so intimate." Unfortunately Penny soon discovered that the intimacy of her online experience did not survive reality when she attempted to bring it offline.

Although the disinhibition effect can cause individuals to act in potentially harmful ways it can also transform someone's personality in positive ways. Ernie is a middle-aged civil servant who rarely dated and hardly ever talked about his feelings. A bright man, Ernie enjoyed spirited discussions on various online discussion boards. There he met Brenda, a middle-aged map-maker living on the other side of the continent. Their online friendship eventually evolved into long phone calls and several meetings. Ernie, normally a shy man, experienced an intensity of emotional connection that was so new and frightening that he went to a psychologist asking what was wrong with him. Ernie thought that he was going mad because of all the new feelings he was having while talking to Brenda. Although disconcerting initially, eventually Ernie came to understand that a new identity was emerging. He was emotionally opening up in ways that he had never allowed himself to do in his few f2f relationships. The Internet helped Ernie develope a side of himself that he did not know existed.

New York University researchers John Bargh and colleagues found that "people randomly assigned to interact over the Internet (vs. face-to-face) reported that they were better able to express their true-self qualities to their online partners than their face-to-face ones" (2002, p. 33). Here is another example. Lorraine wrote about observing her shy cousin online:

> Jennifer said she felt more comfortable meeting people online versus in person. For example, she is too 'nervous' to approach a male in a face-to-face encounter. . . . One night I observed Jennifer while she surfed the Internet and communicated in chat rooms and on MSN. At first, I could tell she felt awkward because I was observing her. However, as the conversations got underway it was almost like she forgot I was jotting notes down beside her. Observing Jennifer's online conversations enabled me to understand why and how her personality changed while typing. It gave me the opportunity to ana-lyze her online personality in community-based interactions. . .
>
> Jennifer signed into one chat room as "2 Cool Girl." Her online description of her personality was how she wanted others to see her. Online, Jennifer adopted her new identity. One chat room participant typed, "So do you live up to the name Cool Girl, or what?" Another one typed, "Yeah you must think you're pretty cool or something to call yourself that!" Initially Jennifer responded, "Well . . . yes, I'm a very outgoing, sociable person, that's why everyone refers to me as a cool girl, just because I just am." As I observed this, I was shocked. I never heard Jennifer identify herself like that. Another chat room participant wrote, "You're so conceited and such a loser for calling yourself that!" Immediately Jennifer responded defensively, "You're so immature and being stupid for caring . . . who cares what I call myself anyways?" I wondered what happened to the quiet, reserved Jennifer I knew? She would never confront someone like that in the physical world even if she were provoked. I was surprised to observe

a complete transformation that took place while communicating in the virtual world.

So is Jennifer really outgoing? Is her true self emerging online, or is she really as shy as her offline identity? So, who do you want to be online? What facets of your on ground personality emerge in cyberspace? When it comes to capturing the essence of who we are online and offline, words are never enough. Complete Exercise 1.2 to create your Avatar.

## Exercise 1.2. Avatar: Icon of the Self

*Goal:*     To create a nonverbal identity in terms of how the self is represented online.

*Age:*     All ages.

*Setting:*  Home, school, counseling settings. As part of a classroom art project, each student's map can be "connected" to the others' forming a collage of online/offline selves.

Directions: Draw an Avatar, a pictorial representation of your online personality. What does this representation of your online self look like? What does your avatar say about you? Is this task difficult or easy for you to do? If others view your Avatar will they be able to describe your identity online? Is your Avatar identity integrated with your identity offline? Why or why not?

Sherry Turkle, author of *Life on the Screen* (1995), believes online rehearsals of new facets of our personality can generalize from the virtual world into the real world. Turkle discusses how experiences of multiple user domains (MUDs) can dramatically help or hinder the self. She argues that "[t]he Internet has become a significant social laboratory for experimenting with the constructions and reconstruction's of self that characterize postmodern life" (p. 180). Turkle maintains that by interacting in these mostly text-based virtual communities, some people have found unparalleled opportunities to explore a range of identities hard to come by in real life. Online you can change genders or slay a dragon. Turkle asks the question: Is MUD play psychotherapy or addiction? According to Turkel, MUDs offer a rich place to act out or work through psychological issues, but she notes that when used by someone who has a fragmented self offline, MUDs can be problematic. Today, the Internet and cyberspace constitute one massive multiple user domain.

In interviews with today's players of online role-playing games (RPG), this book's second author has found that nowadays the visual element of the character has become important. When Turkel's initial work was done such games (MUDs) were all text due to the limits of the graphic capabilities of the Internet. But today there is a strong graphical interface that these RPG players consider to be an important component of their alternative online identities. Thus they can choose to be a three-foot dwarf or a bulked-up superhero online, and explore these alternative selves with a powerful visual interface. This does not preclude Turkel's conclusion, but rather adds another dimension to the process of online self-exploration through alternative identities. As in offline interaction, now online role-playing includes how you look and thus if anything it increases the practice element of trying on another identity.

Psychologist Nina Straus suggests that Internet culture is "delivering new kinds of blows to our narcissism or self-absorption because it generates questions we cannot answer without immersing ourselves in a crisis of representation in time and space" (1997, p. 96). The person online is not only sitting on a chair in front of their computer, but is simultaneously in another "space." Urban historian M. Christine Boyer argues that

> ... the computer is to contemporary society what the machine was to modernism, and that this metaphor profoundly affects the way we ultimately grasp reality. But there is ... an inherent danger here: as cyberspace pulls us into its electronic grasp, we withdraw from the world and risk becoming incapable of action in a real city plagued by crime, hatred, disease, unemployment, and under-education. (1996, p. 85)

The ability to get to know people who are on the Internet is deeply reinforcing. We are social beings and we thrive on feeling connected to others who are like us. In Nathalie Yuen and Michael Lavin's (2004) recent study of college students' vulnerability to Internet dependence, the authors found that shy students were more likely to use the Internet compulsively, leading to failing classes and eventually leaving school. Evidently, because shy students preferred online interactions over f2f, their offline social skills suffered. "The Internet provided a safe haven where feelings of social discomfort are alleviated" (p. 382). These shy students cut morning classes because they would surf the Web all night. They preferred to sit at their computers rather than participate in f2f social events to make friends.  The authors admit that colleges and universities have inadvertently laid the groundwork for unhealthy online behaviors; most college dorm rooms are wired with T-3 lines and even have e-mail accounts, home pages, and Ethernet ports among the grass and trees in the quad. Yuen and her colleague propose that "as students enter the collegiate population it is necessary to address the binge drinking, date rape, and the dangers of compulsive Internet use." (p. 382).

## Crafting Personality Online

Children and teenagers are not the only ones who are vulnerable to online/offline identity issues. As we age, we certainly get a clearer sense of self, but that does not mean that our adult identity remains static throughout our lives. Although there are a variety of traits we might use to describe ourselves, researchers have identified some major personality constructs that are relatively enduring for most of us to some degree throughout our lifespan. The primary personality characteristics are outgoing or shy, agreeableness, conscientiousness, emotional stability, and openness to experience (Larsen & Buss, 2005). Few of us think of ourselves only in these ways however; there are other personality characteristics that may emerge as a result of life events and across the various situations. Not surprisingly, given the importance of these constructs, it is the characteristics of introversion and extraversion that appear to determine to some extent one's online habits.

## INTROVERTS AND EXTRAVERTS ONLINE

The most controversial study on the self as a function of life online was done by Robert Kraut and colleagues from Carnegie Mellon University in Pittsburgh (1998). Called the Internet Paradox Study, these researchers found that Internet use increased loneliness and depression in a sample of people who received free computers and Internet access in the early days of the Internet. Their results, which are now considered almost outdated by Internet research standards, seemed paradoxical given other studies pointing to positive social and personal impacts of Internet use. This study is important, however, because it initiated investigation of the psychological effects of Internet use. The new media associated with the Internet also generated a lot of publicity in mainstream and professional journals about the potential for developing or exacerbating our offline psychological problems as a result of our online habits. Some pointed to various methodological flaws in the Internet Paradox Study, while also noting that statistical difference is not always the same as clinical difference. In other words, statistical findings from research about Internet habits often do not explain the subtleties of human behavior or individual differences.

In a three-year follow-up study these same researchers again examined whether Internet use predisposed some toward depression. This time Kraut and colleagues (2002) found positive effects for communication, social involvement, and psychological well-being, depending on personality type. They found that in general extraverts increased their social contacts by being online, but introverts who used the Internet extensively decreased social contact. The same thing was found with loneliness; extraverts became less lonely with extensive Internet use, and introverts became lonelier. Extraverted people may be energized by engaging with a variety of chat, e-mail, and discussion forums online or find that they are spending time juggling too many connections at once. Extraverted people may also be too busy with their offline relationships to have time for much computer mediated communication (CMC). For those who are introverted, forging relationships online may be less threatening than f2f because they can take time to formulate responses carefully and have greater access to like-minded cyber friends. In contrast, people who prefer isolation may become too attached to the online relational mode because CMC is easier to control. If an interpersonal problem arises or one feels discomfort, it is easy to click off.

Internet usage is often suggested as a way to practice social exchanges for shy individuals, but the research just explained would not seem to support that suggestion. However, the findings of the Kraut group are not definitive, as others have obtained different results (Engelberg & Sjoberg, 2004; Wastlund, Norlander, & Archer, 2001). But extraversion is related to being online, as Yang and Lester (2003) discovered. A question in their research was the relationship between extraversion and neuroticism and Internet usage for citizens from 18 industrialized nations. These researchers found that extraversion was positively associated with Internet usage, while neuroticism was negatively associated. That is, extraverts but not neurotics use the Internet across cultures in the industrialized nations. However, in the United States, addiction and trauma psychologist Durand Jacobs believes that, if you correlate neuroses with anxiety or obsessive traits, then people who are more neurotic may be predisposed to developing compulsions online than extroverted people (D. Jacobs, personal communication, February 10, 2006).

## OFFLINE EFFECTS OF ONLINE IDENTITIES

Who you are online affects how you feel offline. Needless to say, some are more predisposed to deceit or impulsiveness online than others, and it may be that your mood offline determines what you do online and how you choose to portray yourself. Charlie Morgan and Shelia Cotton (2003) of the University of Maryland, Baltimore County, found that depressed mood was associated with Internet use but it depended on the *type* of use. Specifically, e-mail, chat, and instant messaging were associated with *decreased* depressive symptoms while shopping, playing games, or information seeking were associated with *increased* depressive symptoms. The basic differences between each set of activities are that chatting involves others, while activities that are solitary appear to increase isolation and thus lower mood.

In personality research it has also become clear that the identity you project into cyberspace is a function of what you are doing (e.g., churches or bars elicit very different aspects of self). Morgan and Cotton's (2003) research also shows that the emotional openness evident in chat rooms can be therapeutic, because we feel able to express ourselves and be understood. In contrast, no such response typically occurs while shopping or gambling online, as these are solo activities.

College professors Janet Morahan-Martin and Phyllis Schumacher (2003) found that lonely college students were more likely to report Internet use for emotional support than non-lonely students. However such research on individual differences in Internet use is not entirely consistent. Peter Hills and Michael Argyle (2003), from Oxford Brookes University, found no association between personality type and overall Internet use while Linda Jackson and colleagues (2003), from Michigan State University found an association between personality and Internet use for the first three months of having access to the Internet but no difference thereafter for extraversion.

In an interesting study on telepresence, researchers hypothesized and found that those high in empathy offline were more able to experience a sense of reality in the virtual world (Nicovich, Boller, & Cornwell, 2005). This differed as a function of gender, with empathic men using the interactions of the virtual world to become increasingly engaged while empathic women simply watched the environment for the same effect. Given that empathy is the ability to identify with another's experience, this is not surprising. It appears that men need more direct engagement to experience telepresence than women. This gender difference is one of many that researchers have found in terms of various electronic media and is taken up in more detail in Chapter 3 in the section "Groups Online."

Personality psychology is often a predicator for problem behaviors on- and offline. Two studies have examined various personality variables as related to problem behaviors online. One study dealt with personal use of the Internet at work (Everton, Mastrangelo, & Jolton, 2005) while the other examined misuse of the Internet by children (Harman, Hansen, Cochran, & Lindsey, 2005). Wendi Everton and colleagues found that "people who use their computers in unproductive ways tend to be men, younger, more impulsive, and less conscientious" (2005, p. 143). Relatedly, sensation seekers were more likely to use their computers/Internet to view sexual material at work.

The personalities of teenagers and their online identities were compared in a recent study at Northwestern State University (Harman et al., 2005). Investigators were particularly interested in deceit online. Children between 11 and 16 who were more likely to lie online about themselves "had poorer social skills, lower levels of self-esteem, higher levels of social anxiety, and higher levels of aggression" (p. 1). When one considers that half of adolescents in the study by Valkenburg and colleagues (2005) faked their identities online, this finding is of concern, if perhaps not surprising. What is also interesting about this finding of Harman and colleagues was that it was not the amount of time children spent online that was associated with these problems in their personalities but rather what they *did* online.

So, if it's what we do online that may cause potential problems, then it's important to understand *identity tourism*, that is, pretending to be someone else online. Parents, spouses, teachers and kids want to know: is experimenting with different cyber identities harmful? The answer depends not only on what you do online, but also on the effects in a person's offline life. Exercise 1.3 gives you some assessment tools and a problem-solving model so you can begin to figure this out for yourself.

## Evaluating Online Identities

The following exercises explore the way perceptions of the self change or remain the same as a function of being online and the effects on one's offline life. Before treatment or interventions can be implemented for potentially harmful Internet behaviors, our online activities need to be deconstructed for meaning, time, and psychological and social purpose.

How you approach these activities depends on your goal. In informal settings they can be read aloud and different perspectives can be compared in a classroom setting, small groups can work together and then present their opinions to the whole class. In a workshop format, the trainer can ask participants to share their written responses to the questions. These exercises are to be used as a springboard for discussion about both healthy and harmful cyber identities.

## Exercise 1.3. Identity Tourism

*Goal:*    To examine whether or not adopting a different identity online is harmful or part of healthy exploration of self.

*Age:*    12 years old and older; younger if monitored by a parent.

*Setting:*    Home, school, counseling settings. Can be explored individually, or with small groups, and as part of classroom discussions or role-playing.

Directions: As you participate in this vignette about Identity Tourism use the three templates from the Cyber Rules in Cyberspace problem-solving model that was discussed in the Introduction (see below). These will help you evaluate whether Dan's exploration online is harmful. Read the following vignette and evaluate whether Dan's behavior meets one or more of the criteria for a potential problem online. Next fill out the questionnaire a) as if you are Dan, then b) as if you are his wife and c) his daughter, after his behavior was accidently discovered. Now compare the responses of all the family members.

*Dan, a 57-year-old married father of a teenager daughter is a computer software engineer who was recently downsized from a high-tech company. Dan regularly explores explicit sex sites, political blogs, and alternative sites. Dan adopts many chat room personas depending on the culture of the site. Some of his favorite online personalities are radical departures from his real life. He explores a range of sexualities, frequently logs on as female, and joins discussion boards espousing both racist and liberal social commentary. He is able to talk to people from all over the world.*

## Exercise 1.4 Cyber Rules for Cyberspace

The Cyber Rules problem-solving model has four parts:

a) Knowledge.
b) Understanding the criteria that defines problem use.
c) Assessing your online use.
d) Comparing online behaviours with offline effects.

After you have read through the Identity Tourism vignette, use the next three components to evaluate Dan's cyber behaviors.

1. Criteria for Problem Internet Use
   Does Dan's behavior meet any of these criteria?

   *Use of Time* How much time is spent pursuing the behavior?
   *Level of Impairment* Is the behavior continued despite health, social, or occupational problems?
   *Dealing with Emotion* Does behavior help to numb, alter, or avoid feelings?
   *Self-regulation* Are efforts to cut back on the behavior unsuccessful?
   *Others' Opinions* Do family or friends believe there is a problem?
   *Comorbidity* Is the behavior part of a mental or medical disorder?

2. Do You Have a problem?

Answer these questions as if you were Dan, his wife, and his daughter. Compare the results and determine if there is a problem that requires an intervention or treatment.

1. Do you often stay online longer than you intend to?   Yes   No

2. Do you argue with others about your behavior online?   Yes   No

3. Is your identity online very different from whom   Yes   No
   you are offline?

4. Do you do things online you wouldn't do offline?   Yes   No

5. Do you hide anything you do online?   Yes   No

6. Are you worried about how much time you spend   Yes   No
   online?

7. Do you often avoid other things you need to do   Yes   No
   when online?

8. Do you become agitated if you cannot get online        Yes   No
   when you want to?

9. Does your online ̣ ̣ehavior ever cause ̣ ̣roblems in      Yes   No
   your offline life?

10. Does your online life often feel more satisfying than   Yes   No
    your offline one?

                              Number of *Yes* Answers_____

3. Fill in Table 1.2 as if you were Dan. Evaluate his responses in terms
   of Dan's
   1. stage of development
   2. psychological needs
   3. relational needs
   4. gender, family, and social roles

**Table 1.2: Comparing online Behaviours with Offline Effects.**

| Basic Questions | Online Behaviors | Possible Offline Effects |
| --- | --- | --- |
| *Why do I go online?* | | |
| *How much time do I really spend online?* | | |
| *How does media technology affect me?* | | |
| *What are my identities online?* | | |
| *What are the ways that I connect with others online?* | | |
| *What are the feelings I have about my cyber habits?* | | |

It appears that our online personalities are sometimes very different
from who we are in person. It is easy to lie online but in cyberspace
we also get to experience parts of ourselves that social convention

makes us hide and also *try on* alternate selves. For adults who have adult-size responsibilities, this disconnect may mask an unmet need or core aspect of self that wants to emerge. With children and teenagers who experiment with new and different identities online, the offline effects may be more intense because they are at very critical stages of development. If, as the research suggests, over half of teenagers regularly lie about themselves online, this propensity may begin to show up offline. However, teenagers who explore facets of their personalities, and the Internet certainly helps in this regard, gain insight and appreciation for their identities. Maybe we can learn something from them.

# Chapter 2

# Children's and Teens' Media Lives

$\mathbf{H}$ow does online media culture affect kids and families? As we search for answers to this question, our full understanding may always remain two steps behind new generations of media technology. For example, by the time we figured out what TV programs youngsters should watch, videos made parental control obsolete. The same pattern is emerging for digital life: text, graphics, and sounds now sync to hybrid systems that can be carried, shared, and accessed almost anywhere. What media leads to which effects is very confusing. It used to be a sign of success for kids to have computers in their rooms, but now front-page stories describe what they are really doing behind closed doors, and it's not just their homework. Child psychologist Ron Taffel finds time-squeezed adults and kids mirroring a parallel process of disconnected selves where "the great roaring hurricane of mass media culture–rushes in to fill the void that family used to fill" (2005, p. 19).

Not only parents are confused; experts are too. Educators and clinicians are products of the time crunch and Morality, Discipline, and Growing Up 101 is a cacophony of contradictory advice over the last 50 years that says: spank, be tough at love, promote self-esteem, let them self-actualize, their impulses are biological, don't/do provide structure and rules, give them power and autonomy, don't have sex until you're married, use a condom, don't drink, don't tell, and let's leave no child behind. Are kids different now than when we were young? Yes. Dr. Taffel believes that adults say they want the best for their children, and they do, but in concert with a lessening of the family's gravitational pull is the collective, grown-up ignorance of most adults. The typical connection in the bosom of an American family in the evening is characterized by multitasking and rush, *after* the shuttle dance of activities and appointments that eats up any down time between breakfast and dinner, which is likely to be consumed standing up or in front of the screen. Taffel knows this sounds harsh but after 25 years of working with kids,

> I am repeatedly stunned when I am told that kids are no different than they were when we were growing up. The underlying  assumption is that we need not do anything differently with our teen clients now than when we were first trained. Yet how can it be that everything in the world has changed so significantly over the past few decades and somehow kids remain the same? This notion has disastrous consequences. Adolescents don't feel understood by adults, even by many professionals. Adults don't know how to break through to kids. Parents feel overwhelmed by ordinary teen life. Teens make decisions that put them in harm's way. (p. 1)

Nevertheless, kids' lives on- and offline are transforming both the self and relationships. One major change is the way we communicate online. Isn't it amazing that the very top of our bodies, engaged by the dance of our fingertips, is responsible for so much? Clearly what we see and do online contributes to *neurogenisis* (the ability of our brains to grow new neural connections) and *neuro-plasticity* (the brain's ability to reorganize its functions based on new information and experiences). Most of us now write using both hands at the same. Youngsters especially can write faster keyboarding than with a pen or pencil. When writing is executed by the left and right hands simultaneously, the information processing areas in both hemispheres of the brain are engaged in making sense of the thoughts that become the written word. Interestingly, the QWERTY keyboard was designed so that our left hand writes more words than the right hand. This design was supposed to

slow down typists who were mostly right-handed. Right-handed people process text primarily on the left side of the brain while images are
interpreted primarily on the right side.

Could the Internet be rewiring our brains? Laporoscopic neurosur-
geon and author Leonard Shlain believes that online activities may be
generating a new way to perceive, think about, and then communicate
with others visual and verbal information. Because of the way youngsters are raised interacting with Internet media at critical stages of brain
development, these Internet media affects may have a greater effect on
kids' lives (L. Shlain, personal communication, October 23, 2004; Shlain,
1998). The hallmarks of Internet communication, keyboarding, and
surfing the Web, foster an ability to retrieve, mediate, process, and out-
put multiple streams of verbal, nonverbal, and auditory information
using both sides of the brain. For young people's growing brains, two-
handed keyboarding is likely to have a significant effect on neurogenisis. Further, the well-known capacity of our fingertips to feel and
transmit minute sensations may also contribute to our sensory experiences online. About a quarter of the motor cortex in the human brain,
the part of the brain that controls all movement in the body, is devoted
to the muscles of the hands. How do we know that the Internet is really
changing our brains? These new synaptic networks appear to be pro-
ducing some measurable effects on cognition. IQ scores appear to be
going up in processing speed and our ability to make sense of spatially
rotated, nonverbal information (Johnson, 2005).

Is there a downside to being online? If we're not careful, our cyber
lives, especially our children's, will mirror the disconnection offline so
aptly described by Taffel. Social scientists believe that our online interactions do change the way we see ourselves and our relationships with
others as a result (Bargh & McKenna, 2004; Warschauer, 2003). What's
happening to the power of in-person communicating online? Is it
absent or transformed in some way? How do the subtleties, nuances,
and reciprocity of our sensing experiences that are so essential offline
manifest in cyberspace? Those who study the physiology of our brains
may have some answers in the discovery of a unique cluster of brain
cells called *mirror neurons* found in the language and sensory areas of the

brain. Mirror neurons are responsible for key relational abilities that insure our survival and well-being because they are partially responsible for essential social intelligences that allow us to imitate, empathize, and resonate with each other. Diane Ackerman writes in *An Alchemy of the Mind* that the brain is "a hall of mirrors, it can contemplate existentialism, the delicate hooves of a goat, and its own birth and death in a matter of seconds" (2004, p. 4). What is happening to this hall of mirrors when we are online?

The American Academy of Pediatrics states that "children, particularly at young ages, should have limited exposure to screen media, including computers" (Calvert et al., 2005, p. 590). Further, research regarding the health risks of media messages targeting youth that glamorize smoking, drinking, adult models of sexuality, and violence are consistent in their results: children's perceptions of relationships, their health risks, sexuality, and violence are altered in ways harmful to their health. California Assemblyman and child psychologist Leland Yee, Ph.D., believes the technological sophistication of media, especially Internet-driven ones, enable "any 12 year old to purchase media that allow him or her to virtually act out violence on lifelike depictions of humans" (2006, p. 23). Yee describes a video game, *Postal 2*, where "the lead character mutters sexist and racist slurs while urinating or pouring gasoline on women and minorities before setting them on fire. In *Grand Theft Auto*, a player can hire a prostitute and then kill her to boost his energy reserves" (p. 23).

According to Yee, the Federal Trade Commission has determined that 70% of 13- to 16-year-olds can purchase M-rated (for Mature) video games. 92% of children play video games and about 40 percent of the 10-billion-dollar video-game industry products are M-rated. The Center for Media Education (1998) and many other child advocacy groups want to guarantee through legislation that adults help young people use media technology to realize their potential and not the other way around. Kids already get the message that the Internet and media are entertaining, good parent substitutes, easier to play with than a friend or sibling, and often more exciting than real life. And they learn this early.

## How Do Children Use Media?

Our kids are wired, consuming media in earnest by the time they are 9 months old. A recent Kaiser Family Foundation study polled parents of children 6 months to 6 years and found that 83% of this age group used any screen media daily (ranging from TV to computer). Only 79% are read to on a typical day or have listened to music and 83% play outside. When screen media is broken down, it is TV and videos and DVDs that constitute 73% of their activities, with computers at 18% and video games at 9%. So although most young children are exposed to interactive media during a typical day, like their older counterparts, it is woven into other media activities (Rideout, Vandewater, & Wartella, 2003).

Two years later Calvert and colleagues (2005) also interviewed parents of 6-month- to 6-year-old children about their media habits. They noted that there were almost no gender differences in early computer patterns. Not surprisingly, as children got older they used computers more. Families with higher incomes and higher education levels were more likely to own computers and to have Internet access from home. In general parents view their children's media consumption and computer use as enhancing their learning. Interestingly, Calvert and his colleagues did not find a positive relationship between playing computer games and reading ability. The progression of preschool children's computer use is illustrated in Figure 2.1.

A young mother's story illustrates how even very young children learn about media:

> I am a mother of three girls, and married to a software developer. We have had computers and children's software in our house since the time my oldest child was about two. Our oldest, Adara, started doing a very good storytelling/drawing game with me called "Orly's Draw-a-Story." She would sit on my lap and point to the pictures and colors she wanted, and I filled them in. Adara was quite delighted with watching a story that she had colored the pictures for. By the time she was between two and a half and three, Adara was using the mouse by herself, because she was impatient about having to wait for me to

Figure 2.1. Age Patterns of Computer Skills and Use Among Children with Any Prior Computer Experience ($n = 518$)

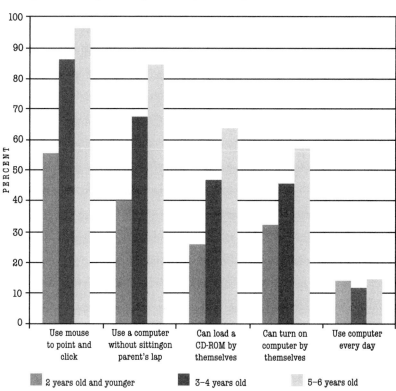

Note: Parents reported that 21% of children 2 and younger (n = 85), 58% of 3- to 4-year-olds (n = 207), and 77% of 5- to 6-year-olds (n = 226) had ever used a computer. Thus, the number of 2-year-olds and younger is relatively small compared to other ages when computing these statistics (Calvert et al., 2005).

find time to do it with her. The next two children, Liesel and Elena, by virtue of being second and third children, didn't get as much one-on-one time with me and the computer, but both of them simply watched their older sister(s) play, and both have been playing and using the computer very competently since they were about two and a half. All my children enjoy a number of drawing and coloring games, as well as various educational games. They learned to use it faster than I did!

The Calvert group pointed out that the more a young child uses the computer, the more likely the parent is to see this as a positive part of their children's development. Media use on the computer among younger children is largely of an educational variety. Discovery School offers a long list of educational software for age groups 1 to 3, with an even longer list for the 3- to 6-year-old age range. Titles range from "Disney's Mickey Mouse Preschool" to "JumpStart Toddlers 2000." The Discovery School site says about this latter title, "Best for older toddlers (or those who have graduated from their baby and other toddler software titles)" and rates it a 4½ out of 5 stars (2005). There is much controversy regarding media-driven educational experiences, however. Critics believe that there is little benefit for kids who consume media at young ages and prefer the old-fashioned models of learning and play. In contrast, listen to what five year-old Rusty says to his mother:

> "What country did Joan of Arc fight?" he asked.
> "France, I think," I said.
> "I know who beat the Iroquois," he said. "Hiawatha."
> He resumed coloring. To think I almost aborted such comments with another one of my assumptions. Joan of Arc and the Indian chief are an outgrowth of Rusty's weekly computer sessions with his Dad. They play a game called Civilization, in which they move famous historical figures through time periods. My husband loves the game, but I objected when he suggested teaching it to Rusty. I have a mandate that my son should not be on the computer. Preschoolers, I think, learn best through what they can see and touch. But, as often happens, I failed to see that there might be an exception to one of my dictums. (Flanagan, 2003)

Children used to learn about the world with the "lap approach." Developmental psychologists know that young children need socialization with adults more than they do solitary- or peer-based interaction. In addition, children grow by engaging all of their senses. A real concern is that computer and media activities are becoming the primary mechanisms for socialization and learning at too many critical periods of growth, rather than real-life experiences. Thus essential sensory, motor, and social development could be delayed or truncated. At the very least, heavy media diets preclude other experiences offline and certainly shape the worldviews of children.

Figure 2.2. Number of Canadian college students who began playing video games at different ages.

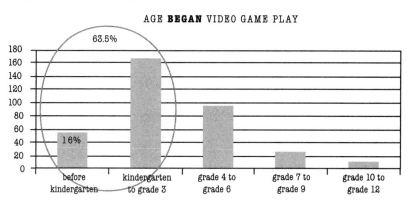

AGE **BEGAN** VIDEO GAME PLAY

In Gackenbach's data 63% of these 18- to 20-year-olds reported beginning to play video games, with use increasing as they moved through middle childhood. These statistics are portrayed in Figure 2.2. Rachel O'Connell, Joanna Price and Charlotte Barrow of the University of Central Lancashire Cyberspace Research Unit reported in 2004 on primary school children's use of the Internet. Most of these 8- to 11-year-olds reported beginning to use the Internet more than two years earlier, and 80% stated that they had a computer at home with Internet access. The most frequent use category was a few days a week, with slightly less than 40% reporting that frequency of use. Although the children surveyed reported feeling comfortable using the Internet, they more often than not said they did not know how to disable filtering software. When asked if they would report to their parents something that they saw online which was upsetting, 80% said they would. Furthermore 80% said they have never accessed an adult site, while only about 17% said they accidentally came across a porn Web site. The picture that emerges is that while middle school children are using the Internet, they are not being exposed to nor seeking information that could potentially harm them. A few are, but most are not.

What about older children? Elisheva Gross (2004) from the Children's Digital Media Center at the University of California, Los Angeles, found no relationship between Internet media use and psychological well-being. This was especially true of music listening and time spent playing video games. However, the Kaiser researchers (2005) disagreed. Their study suggested that heavy use of media increases one's dissatisfaction with life, or that declines in contentedness or satisfaction push one to use media more, or that some other variable(s) drives both dissatisfaction and media use.

## Families Online

Customs, values, and acceptable behaviors used to be shaped by parents and community. That's over now. The Internet has brought the world into living rooms and bedrooms. Parents want to know the effects of so much media time and also how to decide whether what kids do online is healthy or not. They look to the experts in schools and in mental health settings to help them enforce discipline strategies. Many schools and parents want to restrict kids' access to the Internet but this limits legitimate learning. Mental health counselors are not as helpful as they could be because they do not really know youth media culture. Their interventions are likely to be modifications of Parenting Skills 101 uploaded to the Internet.

For example, most adults assume that when kids are media-absorbed, other elements in their life suffer, such as time with friends and family, physical activity, and schoolwork. The Kaiser group examined this question and concluded that the data does not support this assumption. They found that the heavier the media use, the more time was spent with parents, exercising, hanging out with friends, doing chores, working at a job, and engaging in other activities. In other words, active children are active on a variety of fronts. The scientists note "the results raise a red flag against too easily concluding that time spent with media is synonymous with time taken from other activities" (Roberts et al., 2005, p. 51).

A nice example of the interplay between print and electronic media is the Harry Potter book series. Not only have the books gotten children reading more, but the movies have been great draws. A book chain in Canada (Chapters/Indigo) had a contest for 8- to 18-year-olds online connected to the sixth book release. If you won, you got "to join J.K. Rowling at the Edinburgh Castle in Scotland for the release of *Harry Potter and the Half-Blood Prince*. She'll sign your copy and answer burning questions about the latest adventures of Harry Potter" (Chapters. Indigo.ca). In the world of Internet media print, screen, and online worlds have merged, and so have their effects.

A frequently expressed concern about children's and teens' Internet habits is that computer use is socially isolating. In concert with the Kaiser Family Foundation report, Kaveri Subrahmanyam and colleagues discovered that "frequent game players actually meet friends outside school more often than less frequent players" (2001, p. 17). They also point out that 60% of computer time is spent alone, although some of that is online with friends. However, the Kraut group (1998) did find that teenagers seem the most vulnerable to the socially isolating effects of online life but that may be because adolescents are most vulnerable to peer rejection at this stage of their lives.

Sara Kiesler and colleagues from Carnegie Mellon University (2000) found that the teenager in the house tends to become the family expert in regard to the computer and access to the Internet. This has positive cognitive and social consequences for the teen, associated with learning the information needed to master the medium, and having a status position in the family. Although parents are proud of their children for achieving this intellectual skill, they may be disconcerted by the shift in authority for this domain in the family structure. The Folks Online Web site has a relevant story about 15-year-old Ryan, who commandeered the family's new computer while it was still in the box. His mom commented,

> My husband and I knew absolutely nothing about our new pur-
> chase. So Ryan became the main user. He spent hour after hour in
> the blue desk chair typing and working away on the computer. I was
> beginning to become worried about the amount of time he spent on
> it... I asked him later if he taught himself to program the computer
> in a month? He replied, with somewhat of a smirk on his face, "No
> mom. I learned in a week." He and I laughed at his arrogance, but he
> then said, "Mom, I don't think you realize just how much I know

about computers." No I didn't but I was soon to find out. (Benigno, 2001)

With all the concern about the negative effects of media, from violence to social roles, one would think that there would be lots of rules in American households regarding various media use. The Kaiser Family Foundation researchers looked at rules for four types of media: TV, music, video games, and computer. With all four major media types the minority of these children reported parental rules. Most rules are in regard to TV viewing, with the fewest rules regarding music listening. Although that is not always the case, according to Ceira, aged 13, who writes on the children's Web site "It's My Life" (2005b) about how strict her parents are: "I can't even talk to my friends on the Internet!!! They are really strict!!" or 13 year-old Colin, who says, "Whoa! My mom won't let me get any contacts, cellphones, or spend the night at my friend's house or go off our home alone. I got grounded for the computer until I get my grade up to a B in math!" But perhaps the relative lack of parental rules is better demonstrated by the following:

> "What I like about staying home is that I get to play on the computer with you guys! Well, got to go, bye," says Ticheyla, who is eight years old.
>
> "You get free access to the TV, computer, and the pantry. The thing I like the least is that our house's floors make noise and it's spooky," says Kelsey, who is nine (It's My Life, 2005c)

The Kaiser group did not investigate the use of blogs by Internet-savvy kids and teens. Bob Sullivan (2005) of MSNBC writes about one mother's discovery regarding her eighth-grade daughter's blog. "Marcy's 13-year-old daughter has a knack for switching computer screens or shutting the laptop when mom walks in the room." Eventually Marcy found out that her daughter had a blog where she was posting various pieces of personal information. When Marcy checked further, she discovered that one-third of her daughter's classmates had blogs, but that only 5% of the parents knew about them. In some of them, not only was their personal information posted, but also pictures of a suggestive nature. Sullivan reported that about half of all blogs are by teens. About

70% of these child bloggers gave their first name and age and 61% gave contact information.

It appears that, among many families, there is no effective discipline in the home regarding media use. Not surprisingly, rules were easier to implement with younger children. The Kaiser data reveal that when there are rules that are consistently enforced by parents, there is less media exposure. However, they note that the more media-rich a household is, the *less likely there are to be consistently enforced rules regulating its use.* In addition, parents are stymied when it comes to older kids when total control or constant supervision of Internet and media access is not possible. Many experts propose that parents protect their children while online with filters or Nannyware. The Parents Information Network (2003) suggests that, while most products do offer some level of protection, none can be relied upon by parents as a complete solution.

Strategies for protecting children might involve the use of a filtering software product and checking the "history" of Web activity but should also include clear guidelines about online times, unsuitable content, and unsafe online contacts. However, what is appropriate activity online for an eight-year-old is different from what 14- or 16-year-olds can do. It's clear that parents have a hard time explaining to adolescents why some media and Internet activities may be harmful especially when media effects are often subtle and/or confusing, giving kids ample opportunities to disagree with, either covertly or overtly, their parents' opinions about digital experiences.

Internet journalist Jim Hopper (1996) notes that there are two major problems with placing the responsibility solely with the care-giving adults. Advocates of the filtering solution have not acknowledged the importance of corporate responsibility. This includes responsibility for the nature of advertisements displayed on services (e.g., search engines) that children need to navigate the Web. Advocates of the filtering solution have not addressed the predicament of children whose parents do not effectively use these technologies, nor the reality that most children have little enforced constraints on their Internet behaviors.

In terms of family life and community networks, Robert Hughes and Jason Hans of the University of Missouri–Columbia reported on a survey of neighbors who all had free access to the Internet as a way to examine the various social relationships in the neighborhood. They reported that the wired neighbors "recognized almost three times as many neighbors, talked with nearly twice as many, and had been invited or had invited one and a half times as many neighbors into their homes" (2001, p. 783) as the nonwired. The Internet fosters many opportunities for deepening one's connections with family and friends around the world. Online, anyone can be in your "backyard," even those you may never have the chance to meet in person. Tenzin, a Tibetan student at Dominican University in California, shares her experience online:

> Emailing has made my life so much easier. My friends are so many miles away. Getting calls from them is like once in a blue moon. I am able to talk about things that happen everyday here in California so they know what's up with me. I know that with mail and telephone it would be too expensive and I would just lose touch with them.

Not only is Tenzin able to maintain important relationships online but she is able to maintain her ethnic identity in the face of challenges of living in a totally different culture.

However, Norman Nie and colleagues from the Stanford Center for the Quantitative Study of Society used a method that relied only on use of the computer from the day before. They found that "for the average respondent, an hour on the Internet reduces face-to-face time with family by 23.5 minutes" (2004, p. 4). Of course such Internet use could be contacting family at a distance, but Nie reports that this is a small percentage of use. Further, in contrast to the Kaiser Family Foundation study, the Nie group reported that "time spent using the Internet is negatively associated with time spent with family, with TV watching, and with sleep among other things. The relationship held even after statistically controlling for a number of possible confounding variables" (p. 12). While the research on whether the Internet positively or negatively affects young people's development and family connections is inconclusive, the Internet does enable us to experience moments of connection unfathermable before:

> One evening, I asked my Dad, age 84, to take a look at the on-screen excitement I had been buzzing about all summer. He graciously sat

besides me as I accessed the Net. Dad was suitably impressed by the magnitude of the information available. . . But he really perked up when I suggested we search for our surname to see just what was available. He was staggered to see that there were over 3,000 references online. We searched through the first ten and spotted his cousin, R.O. Blechman, a major cartoonist. We went to this site and I printed out a photo of his cousin. After it dropped out of the ink-jet printer, I placed it in his hands, he said, with a big smile on his face, "I haven't seen this man in 30 years. He looks just like his father!" I knew I had scored. (Blechman, 1997)

The value of electronic media as it contributes to family forms of entertainment is illustrated by the recent announcement of the new X-Box by Microsoft. With a softer, almost feminine look, the purpose of this new gaming center is to capture all the family members' media needs. Lev Grossman (2005) writes in a cover story for *Time* magazine that Microsoft sees the X-Box as a "D.E.L" (digital entertainment lifestyle) unit. He points out that Microsoft will be putting out high-risk gaming genres like romantic comedies. New media may actually unify the family's media use within the home and with each other.

## Interactive Media Effects

Although there is much we do not know about the effects of interactive media on children and teens, there is a lot we do know. The American Psychological Association, National Communication Association, and major universities in this country and around the world are leading the research. Most notable are some of the cognitive effects emerging as a result of interactive-media activities. The requirements for analyzing rotating spatial information rapidly appears to increase kids' nonverbal-information processing speed and reaction time. Thus visuo-spatial acuity is enhanced, scientific problem-solving skills are honed, and general intelligence as measured by standard tests are going up in these areas of cognition (*Digital Childhood: A Research Agenda on Human Development & Technology*, 2000; Greenfield, Brannon, & Lohr, 1996).

Because of the amount of time most kids spend online, there is no research to date supporting the belief that kids' attention spans are reduced as a result of video-game and Internet activities. To the contrary, there is evidence that these interactive media increase parallel processing abilities and a corresponding ability of youngsters to multi-task effectively. Digital children are better at doing a variety of media at once, but this may have a negative consequence of losing depth of information processing while gaining breadth (Greenfield, 2000). At this point, however, the reality of switching models of media online, from cell phone to IM to Web cam to texting, may increase the cognitive flexibility in children. Cognitive flexibility has been associated with increased self-awareness, creativity (Langer, 1996, 1989), and psychological adjustment (Gillispie, 2006).

One element of cognitive ability and complexity is the creative use of the imagination. Online fantasy and creative forms of self-expression are everywhere. Does this creativity enhance or harm kids' psychological make up? Not only are we concerned that kids tell the truth online about who they are or where they live, which may cause problems in their offline lives, but we are also afraid that their imaginations are running wild in cyberspace. Young children cannot tell the difference between virtual and media content and reality. For example, kids under age five or six view advertisements as part of the storyline or game. Marketers know this and capitalize on their naiveté. Educational psychologist Sandra Okita examined this question in older versus younger children. She discovered that "younger children are more likely to assume a similarity across media than older children, and that the specific media did not change this pattern. Thus, to prevent young children from confusing media and reality, it will be necessary to find explicit ways to help them mark the differences" (2004, p. 471).

Confusing media effects and lack of clarity about what's real or virtual in cyberspace concern all of us. Online advertisers and spammers have become so adept at subterfuge that you often think you are reading or responding to something you initiated. Hyperlinks or bogus headers are inserted in the same color and font as the page you accessed and seamlessly redirect you to a different page. In addition, personalized text messages fool you into clicking on a message or link so that spyware is able to attach to your system and track your Internet use without your knowledge. In a recent data search for a book on "Cognitive Liberty and Ethics," the authors were directed to a conference at Stanford University in May of 2006 on Technology and Human Rights. On the left sidebar, however, was a link for "Freedom of Thought at the Crossroads" in the exact same font as the Stanford article. This link led to an e-mail address that advertised "free sex pics in over 84 categories: kids, dogs, sex with shit, brutal sex...."

We know that older children and teenagers go online and practice new social skills that are then transferred offline, but they also engage in radical identity exploration and push the limits of curiosity, assisted by Google sidebar ads. While research shows that half of adolescents surveyed reported lying online, Gross and colleagues from the Digital Media Center at UCLA discovered that "Online pretending was reported to be motivated by a desire to play a joke on friends more often than to explore a radical identity, but participants reported a range of pretending content, contexts, and motives" (2004, p. 633).

## DOES THE INTERNET HELP OR HINDER LEARNING?

If confused parents and puzzled clinicians wonder how to guide children's media use and Internet habits, educators probably head the list of concerned adults. Cyberspace is in the classroom. Teachers regularly assign online projects and communicate with students and parents via e-mail. Kids do homework and learn in groups online and now bring scholarly research to their projects. There are online schools where smart screens automatically adjust software pedagogy and pace to the facial expression of the user (e.g., puzzled, anxious, lost, excited, bored, engaged). Students have been known to crack the passcodes to their school's database and alter grades and other "secure" information. Even worse, there is probably no school or university that does not encounter student plagarism and outright cheating as a result of Internet use.

While teachers are often the first to notice when their students are engaging in potentially problematic online behaviors, very few educators know what to do about it. In California, which has the largest public school district in this country (and indeed the world), no professional training or curriculum for teaching healthy habits online exists (J. Wright, personal communication, February 2, 2005). At best, school districts around the country respond to crises like harassment, cheating, and cyber crimes online as they occur rather than from an informed, preventative perspective. Should teachers and administrators intervene if Internet problem behaviors occur off school grounds but involve other students? What about student's who behave in ways contrary to the school's mission statement and guidelines? Is it an educator's responsibility to dictate to parents how young people should conduct themselves online both at school and at home? Consider what teachers like these face everyday:

Ellen, a middle school teacher from a small town, learns that one of her students is being harassed online for being gay.

Fr. Andrews is deleting cookies on the computer after a student accidently leaves her blog site address in the history and sexually suggestive photos of her appear on the screen.

Ms. Smith, a high school English teacher, suspects a student of plagiarizing in a recent assignment. The teacher types in a few sentences of the essay into Google and the original source appears.

When looking at school grades, the Kaiser group found that there was no difference in grades regarding which kind of media was used: TV, videos/DVDs/movies, audio, or computers. However, there was a difference in grades associated with video-game play. Lower grades were associated with longer play. Computer applications for education have been developing for many years, certainly before the era of the Internet, and today there is a large and fairly consistent body of research reporting that proper computer implementation enhances the educational experience. Enhancements range from the most fundamental (e.g., learning to do mathematics), to the more applied, like developing a Powerpoint presentation.

The now long-standing use of computers in education has revitalized but also revamped how we are educated. In any educational organization there are early and late adopters of technology innovations. For instance, while e-mail is now widely used by instructors at all levels of education, this is a relatively new widespread adoption. In addition to the very real problem of the inexperience of educators, there are a number of problems and issues surrounding the use of computers and the Internet in the classroom. Issues include both problems of pedagogy–how to incorporate new technology into class-room teaching methods–and problems of logistics–reconciling the increasing need for continuing tech education with the cost of computer use.

Many of the concerns expressed by Bernard Poole (1997) in his review of technology in the classroom have been addressed with the rapid expansion of the Internet. For instance, in her dissertation, Robin Chiero (1998) found that the teachers generally perceived computers as having a positive impact on their work. For example, WritingFix is a typical site that guides teachers in helping their students to create better essays:

> When we do centers [in kindergarten], I use my computer as a literacy center. The 3 or 4 students at that literacy center that day have to create an oral story based on one of the *WritingFix for Kids* word games and practice telling it together so they can tell the rest of the class. Each student has to tell one sentence in the story out loud. My kindergartners really like the Crazy Animal Game.
>
> –Jodie Black, kindergarten teacher

> Before our writing workshop begins, I log the classroom computer in to WritingFix. I choose a prompt that I believe will interest most of my students. My current favorite is the *Title-Making Prompt*, but I also really like the *Great Sentence Creators*, like the *Need for Speed Stories*. If I notice a student during writing time not writing, I send him/her up to my computer to click on the buttons, and within 2 minutes he/she always comes back to the desk with an idea to begin drafting. It works every time!
>
> –Dena Robinso, middle school teacher

Problems of pedagogy are also addressed by Trish Stoddart and Dale Niederhauser (1993), who pointed out that in the nineties, we again faced a call from some of the major educational institutions and organizations to change our educational system. Although such calls for reform happen regularly, they generally meet with resistance from a system that is extremely conservative. These authors went on to say that, despite the large body of research into the advantages of computer-mediated education, there is not as much integration of computers into the classroom or teaching environment as might have been expected. There are clearly many advantages to online learning, but Paul Kirschner and Jan van Bruggen explained that "current technologies meant for learning and working in teams are often designed for functional collaboration, but fail to support learning, understanding and team forming..." (2004, p. 135). Dan Hobbs (2002) pointed out that a major pedagogical problem can be solved by the continued active involvement by the professor. John Santrock and his colleages (2004) noted in their *Educational Psychology* text that:

> Attempts to promote the use of information and communication technologies in the classroom over the past two decades have not been as successful as anticipated. Computers are still used too often for drill-and-practice activities rather than for active constructive learning.... More positively, teacher candidates in faculties of education throughout the country are learning to work with information and communication technologies and are expected to use these tools in their teaching practice. We believe that these teachers will be the agents of change who will develop the tools and practices that will map and redefine the landscape of how technology is used in education. (p. 338)

This is not to say that teachers are not using computers and the Internet. In a report on a nationally representative sample of teachers, Susan Chipman (2003) said that half have used word-processing software, while a third have used CD-ROM references, the Web, and games/drills. Twenty five percent of teachers have used simulations and graphics, and around 10% have used spreadsheet software, multimedia authoring, and e-mail. Liqing Tao and Beverly Boulware (2002) reported on a study they did with second-grade students and their teacher, in which the researchers, teacher, and students interacted using e-mail. These researchers noted that:

E-mail communication provided the teacher with teachable moments for teaching her students technology skills, communication conventions and literacy skills, and social skills. Her second graders had a weekly opportunity to learn some of the basic functions of computers, such as how to turn a computer on and off, how to save, and how to use the keyboard in technology classes. Students learned to use word processors for composing messages and then send them via the teacher's e-mail account. By the end of the semester, almost all the students felt comfortable using computers. (p. 286)

These educators reported that the young children were excited about receiving an e-mail from the researchers and shared it among themselves, as well as with their families. Many even continued the e-mail correspondence with the researchers when they went on to third grade. The students were motivated on their own to revise and edit their messages without prompting from the teacher. Tao and Boulware illustrated: "Students would sit down as a pair to check each other's messages before they were sent. The buddy could say, 'Well, I see some capitalization errors' or 'I see some spelling errors'" (2002, p. 287).

Obviously the integration of the computer into the classroom has come a long way since its introduction in the early 1990s. Roberts and his colleagues offered a look at how children/teens use electronic media for schooling. Computer use for schoolwork has increased since 1999, but the relative percentage of computer/Internet use for school versus recreation has decreased. In other words, kids are using computers and the Internet quite a bit more for entertainment than for schoolwork, even though they are also online longer.

Computers and the Internet offer the opportunity for students to be more active in their learning experiences, but computers can also reinforce, depending on the design of the material for which they are used, the repetition and drill routines that characterize most public school education. Where computers are used, they are still often made to fit the paradigm of traditional pedagogy: teacher-directed transmission of information to passive learners. Secondary educators are calling for more emphasis on active-participant learners. Technology analyst Poole (1997) summarized the ways that computers and Internet technology affect learning:

- Students felt more positive about the writing instruction and their own writing skills.
- The quality and fluency of their writing improved.
- Students were more self-motivated about their writing.
- Lieracy was improved as a result of the computer's visual, auditory, and physical support.
- Students editied, reread and revised their compositions more frequently and more easily than a control group using pen and paper.
- Students were able to correct more errors than when using pen and paper.
- Students made fewer grammar, punctuation and capitalization errors. (pp. 18–20).

Furthermore, Poole noted that when students were encouraged to work together on writing assignments using computers, they produced, compared with individualized learning, a higher level of mastery and achievement in the application of factual information. However, Poole also warns that there are research findings in the field of computer-assisted reading and writing that remind us that no tool is suited to all situations, and that sometimes the tool can create or reveal unanticipated problems:

- Children of seven years of age or younger may lack the cognitive skills necessary to socialize and collaborate effectively, in writing or otherwise; the writer's age, level of cognitive development, and composing style is critical to how the computer tool is used.
- Collaboration is not effective for all writing tasks.
- Computer writing needs to be integrated with the use of other traditional writing and drawing tools.
- Some students neglected planning when using the word processor.
- There need to be an adequate number of computers for students to work simultaneously and individually. (p. 22)

Finally, an interesting study examined the characteristics of students who elect for online education, relative to those who elect face-to-face (on-campus) education Mattes and colleagues found that "Students taking online classes scored higher than on-campus students on scales of abstract reasoning and apprehension, and lower on the scale for social boldness. Online students were also more comfortable with computers than on-campus students, and were more likely to be nontraditional students (26 and older)" (2003, p. 89).

## CELL PHONE SELVES

Cell phones were introduced more than 20 years ago, and were designed primarily for the white business man in North America. Today most teenagers have cell phones. Even 10 years ago, parents appreciated that cell phones could increase safety for their children, and the richer parents were also getting them for their kids. Today, parents cite safety as the most common reason for purchasing cell phones for their children. One could argue, in fact, that cell phones are now perceived as a necessity. According to an article from CNET News (CNET News.com Staff, 2005) cell phone subscribers were expected to reach 1.7 billion by the end of 2005. Although cell phones are often initially purchased by parents for their children so they can keep track of them, the reality is that cell phones increase the contact between the child and his or her peer group. Of course, a child accidentally hitting the speed dial number for a parent, who then overhears her child's conversation with friends, offers the parent an audible view into her child's life! In this age of mobility, parents appreciate being able to call their child at any time, no matter where the child is, to be sure they are OK and doing what they said they would be doing. And from the child's perspective they are handy when needing a ride home or help in case of trouble. Despite these advantages, a recent warning in the United Kingdom cautioned parents that children may be especially vulnerable to radiation from cell phone use due to their rapidly developing nervous systems (Rohde, 2005). A report from Health Canada (2002) disagreed about the issue of health risks in using cell phones:

So far, there is currently no convincing evidence, from animal or human studies, that the energy from cell phones is enough to cause serious health effects, such as cancer, epileptic seizures or sleep disorders. Some scientists have reported that cell phone use may cause changes in brain activity, reaction times, or the time it takes to fall asleep. But these findings have not yet been confirmed.

Surprisingly, or perhaps not, the mobile phone has become a status symbol among teens, as well as a fashion accessory. Lara Srivastava (2005) of the International Telecommunication Union points out that owning a mobile phone has become an important milestone in the process of a child achieving independence from her parents. Thus they are personalized with different covers, colors, ring tones, wallpapers, and functions. In Europe, the text messaging ability of cell phones has become the preference for communication over a call, and in fact young people will often text first to be sure that it's an OK time to call. Lights out at bedtime no longer means lack of communication with friends, as the built-in lighting on the phone means kids can text message well into the wee hours of the morning without their parents being any wiser.

## Avatars and Cell Phones

Relationships online are not limited to the Internet. Other media like video games and cell phones also offer opportunities to communicate electronically beyond the obvious talking and competing. When creating one's virtual body for various online role-playing games or chat rooms, one can chose nonrealistic elements like wings and tails or ideal male or female body parts. These visual online selves are called Avatars. In contrast to the text-based communications of instant messaging, e-mail, and discussion boards, which have been the focus of our discussion in this chapter, Avatars live in the virtual worlds of gaming. Now, for the first time, many if not all of the limits of communicating online with others have strong visual elements beyond emoticons or limited-range Web cams. In one such recent addition to the online role-playing game genre, you can not only build yourself a new body and clothes, you can fly around an increasingly complex and beautiful virtual world. When you land you can play games, build devices, chat with strangers, or shop. You use your arrow or mouse keys to maneuver your virtual body around walls and towers as well as trees and other bodies. It's amazing how fast the "rules" of normal offline communication come into play. So when Isabel Draper was chatting with a store clerk in the computer game Second Life she found she was uncomfortable until she positioned her Avatar self facing the clerk and thus duplicated nonverbal spatial use that she would have done in an offline interaction.

University of California researcher Jeremy Bailenson and colleagues pointed out that virtual worlds offer behavioral scientists the opportunity "to conduct ecologically realistic experiments with near-perfect experimental control" (2003, p. 819). As in offline interactions, these scientists found, just like Isabel in *Second Life*, that "participants maintained greater distance from virtual humans when approaching their fronts compared to their backs. In addition, participants gave more personal space to virtual agents who engaged them in mutual gaze. Moreover, when virtual humans invaded their personal space, participants moved farthest from virtual human agents" (p. 819).

Not only are spatial behaviors duplicated but social responses can also be manipulated and reacted to. English researcher Laura James and colleagues (2003) inquired if social anxiety would be greater in a virtual bar than in a virtual train station. They found that indeed social anxiety was higher at the virtual bar. In other research with Avatars as online interactive partners, contrary to expectation viewing low-anthropomorphic (cartoon-like) virtual avatars resulted in higher social attraction and credibility than viewing either no avatars or those that looked like humans. The researcher explained, "this could be evidence that anthropomorphic images set up higher expectations and in this case these expectations were not met, which resulted in less positive attributions" (Nowak, 2004).

Avatars are now being used outside the gaming and research environments in online education to help students understand Freud's theories with a talking webbot at Athabasca University's department of psychology (Heller, 2005). Avatars have also been suggested as useful in clinical interventions by a group of Italian scientists (Gaggioli, 2003).

How much more compelling will games be when the three-dimensional element and the ease of use become seamless? Why watch a movie when you can be part of it in these online virtual worlds? How might this increasing temptation to live vicariously online with improved graphical interfaces and Mature-rated virtual lands affect life offline? These are questions that the public is now facing.

Another electronic realm of communication is revamping the mediated communication landscape: cell phones. In an earlier chapter we explored the use of cell phones among children and teens. Here we will examine their social implications. As noted earlier, mobile-phone subscribers now outnumber land line subscribes in the U.S. This turnabout happened in 2002 and will likely be replicated throughout most of the world soon. The cell phone is no longer merely a phone so much as alarm clock, calculator, gaming device, video camera, instant text-messaging device, and MP3 player; it has replaced the personal digital assistant and perhaps even the laptop computer for ease and convenience. Cell phones have become fashion accessories and status symbols (Srivastava, 2005). The public world has been overlaid with a simultaneous private one as people take calls during dinner, on the bus, at work, or while jogging or cooking. The text-messaging capacity allows passing "notes" during a board meeting or classroom lecture and in some places is preferred over a call. Rules for cell phone use are now being made, with regular reminders to "turn off your cell phone" now flashed at the beginning of movies.

But are cell phones increasing our sociablity or decreasing it? Srivastava added "while admitting to an overall increase in spontaneous and widespread social interaction, some argue that mobile phones may be reducing the quality of face-to-face social interaction" (2005, p. 123). An interesting social phenomenon has emerged with the widespread use of cell phones. Now meetings are set for approximate time or place with the idea in mind that one can cancel at the last minute or change the venue because the person you are meeting is easily contacted on their mobile phone.

Bluejacking is another spontaneous social interaction mentioned by Srivastava in his excellent review of cell phones and the evolution of social behavior. This involves sending spontenous text messages to others in your physical surround based on being able to determine that they are Bluetooth enabled (Bluetooth is a new form of short-range radio technology). The Swiss researcher wrote, "a lanky young woman with long brown hair was waiting to take a train at London's Waterloo Station, when she got a surprising message on her mobile phone from a complete stranger. 'I like your pink stripy top.' The woman, who looked around in confusion, had just been 'bluejacked' by a 13-year-old British girl" who was nearby (2005, p. 125).

Despite all these interesting variations on cell phone use, problem-use patterns are emerging as well. In some states cell phone use is illegal in some circumstances, such as while driving, or considered impolite in others, such as during a movie. Nonetheless, some users continue to use them under questionable circumstances. Adriana Bianchi and James Phillips (2005) from Monash University in Australia found that such problem use was more likely to occur among extraverted young people with low self-esteem.

## DIGITAL TOYS

What could be better than a child *imagining* his or her dolly is crying and fussing or a truck is zooming along the floor? Dolls that cry, eat, laugh, and wet themselves and vehicles that are remote controlled are part of a new wave of digital toys. A real pet too much trouble? Try the virtual pet. One Japanese researcher believes that digital pets embody (virtually) traditional Japanese culture, which "allows treating animals on an equal basis with human beings" (Kusahara, 2001, p. 299). This tradition, in combination with Japan's industry lead (at the time) in anything electronic, resulted in these electronic pets. Frederic Kaplan, from Sony France, argues that the pets are popular because they are free and useless. Kaplan points out that they make you feel responsible. If you don't clean, play with, and nurse this virtual pet, it will die or run away from home, or just not want to interact no matter how much you cajole it. There are also special blog sites for your virtual pet where you can communicate with other pet owners. Many of these sites are actually advertising  products for sale under the guise of pet care.

Kaveri Subrahmanyam and colleagues explained that these sorts of toys, among others, have effects on children's perceptions of reality. Although it is well known that young children have difficulty distinguishing between what is real and what is virtual, they note that anecdotally, at least, there is some suggestion that even older children can get confused. They cited the case of a 15-year-old who believes that with computer games "you could 'get things that are alive in the computer,' and that just as 'we get energy from the sun, the organisms in the computer get energy from the plug in the wall'" (2002, p. 21). Virtual pets are especially popular among girls because of their appeal to their socially reinforced gender roles as nurturers. Parents buy them for their children because they believe that it helps them understand what is involved in taking care of real pets.

Recent generations of virtual pets include ones that talk back to you. First introduced by Hasbro with its Furby in 1998, the newest generation is twice as big and has voice recognition software. Not only will this toy learn and speak back to the child what it hears, but it also has eyes and a face that will pattern emotions. If young children were confused about the "reality" of *Sesame Street* characters on TV, how confusing for them will these toys potentially be, especially as these virtual pets engender real feelings of love, acceptance, and empathy in their owners?

## ONLINE MARKETING

One of the more heated concerns regarding the effects of Internet media is the idea of marketing to children online in ways that are unethical and developmentally seductive. Virtual pets are now also online, especially at the well-known neopets.com. Reporter Nick Wingfield illustrated their attraction in a *Wall Street Journal* article with the story of a fourth grader who is not supposed to be online during the week but who sneaks online to feed his virtual menagerie at the neopets Web site. The child notes that "I feed them until they're bloated so they'll be full for a couple of days" (2005, p. B1). As compelling as this site is for children, however, it has also become a bastion of selling to children.

The speed at which the toy manufacturers are rolling these electronically wired toys out, though, means that the research to ascertain their effects on child development has just not been done.

The well-received Canadian documentary film "The Corporation" (Achbar, 2003) offers interviews with various experts explaining that one of the fastest-growing selling markets is targeted toward children. A common belief among marketers is that if you don't achieve brand loyalty before age six, it's too late. Another expert spoke of the "drool factor," that is, marketing to infants!

There are four major ethical and legal issues around advertising online.

- the inability of children to differentiate ads from programs
- the use of ineffective and inaccurate disclaimers
- advertising for drugs, tobacco, and sex to minors
- covert marketing embedded into children's programs

Research has shown, however, that as children get older and more experienced with media hype, they become skeptical about the advertising messages but probably inured to their more subtle effects. Media researchers (Gunter & McAleer, 1997) state,

> Increasingly, research has revealed that children exhibit a growing sophistication about advertising during their formative years. Although early on in life they may have no proper understanding of the dishonest character of advertisements and their purposes compared with programs, this soon changes. Research has shown that advertising does not directly influence its audience. It may, nonetheless, play an important role in children's consumer socialization, teaching them consumer values and ways of expressing them. (p. 134–135)

But children, and especially teens, are not only receivers of web advertising. They soon will be agents of change in corporate media. One of the most famous examples is how Napster changed the music industry's manner of offering their product, from CDs to downloads. Shawn Fanning, the founder of Napster, was a 19-year-old

college freshman when he created it. After three years of court bat-
tles, Napster was officially closed down. He is now running Snocap,
which is a shareware site that allows people to buy songs off the
Internet (Borland, 2004). Here is a story that illustrates what happens
when a child has the same name as a movie star who advertises
online:

> My first name happens to be the same as that of a television actress.
> Normally, this sort of coincidence wouldn't be remarkable, except
> that when you type "Email Raven" into an internet search engine, it
> is my email address that comes up. This means I get a lot of mail
> from girls who think they are contacting their favorite TV star. Much
> of it is innocent, along the line of "I'm your biggest fan" or "I love
> how you do your hair" but some of it makes me very worried about
> what these young girls are doing on the Internet. I've had them email
> me with their complete addresses and phone numbers, tell me which
> school they go to and when they get out of class. I've had girls ask
> if they could ever meet me, and offer to come and visit. Some have
> even emailed me their photos. Most of them are between the ages of
> 10 and 14, and don't realize that they have emailed personal info to
> a complete stranger.

Safety concerns do not address Web site content alone, but also
exposure to advertising that is often embedded into noncommercial
Web sites (Greenfield, 2004). For instance, the Center for Media Education (1997) conducted research examining alcohol and tobacco marketing on the Web. The study found that alcohol and tobacco companies
are using the online media to advertise and promote their products
through a variety of marketing techniques that capitalize on the
medium's strong and unique attraction for young people. These cam-
paigns are being launched at a time when drinking and smoking among
youth are already at alarmingly high levels and a major public health
problem in the U.S. Alcohol is a factor in all leading causes of death for
young people, ages 15 to 24, and while smoking among adults is declin-
ing, smoking among youth is on the rise. Advertising and marketing
play a major role in influencing the offine drinking and smoking habits
of young people.

In another study from the Center for Media Education (n.d.), investigators found the following disturbing marketing practices aimed at children online:

1. invasion of children's privacy through solicitation of personal information and tracking of online computer use; and
2. exploitation of vulnerable, young computer users through deceptive forms of advertising.

Legislators and child advocacy groups are taking these concerns very seriously. In 1998 the Children's Internet Protection Act was passed. According the Federal Communications Commission the "(CIPA) is a federal law enacted by Congress in December 2000 to address concerns about access in schools and libraries to the Internet and other information. For any school or library that receives discounts for Internet access or for internal connections, CIPA imposes certain requirements. In early 2001, the Federal Communications Commission (FCC) issued rules to ensure that CIPA is carried out" (2003). However in 2004 the United States Supreme Court reversed this ruling stating that the language of this law was too restrictive and trampled First Amendment Rights ("A law too far," 2004).

## Kids' Media Lives: What's a Parent to Do?

As we have seen in this chapter, media and the Internet accelerate and multiply change in our children's and teenagers' lives, while too many are disconnected from adults and caring communities. Few grown-ups know how to be effective and real with kids. Parents cast about, not knowing whether to unplug their children from media, spy on them, or try to find an expert that will tell them what to do. Clinicians must maintain confidentiality but parents want to know if their kids are having sex online or off, drinking, smoking pot, or contemplating other risky behaviors, all in 45 minutes per week. Most of us know that, on any given day, the young people we interact with are somewhere between life-threatening crises and ordinary life, but now ordinary life can have some very dangerous potholes. The next exercise will help you apply some of the information in this chapter to an intervention with a young teenager.

## Exercise 2.1. What Would You Do?

*Directions:*   Read through the scenario below and then work through the
              exercises using the Cyber Rules Problem-Solving Model for
              Families outlined below.

*Goal:*       To examine effective discipline strategies for parents about
              the amount of time kids spend online and what they are
              doing.

*Age:*        10 years old and older.

*Setting:*    Home, school, and counseling settings. Can be explored indi-
              vidually, or as a family activity. Julia's story can be used to
              generate the following discussion questions:

              1. How many hours online is OK for Julia?
              2. What online activities are OK for Julia and for kids at
                 younger or older stages and ages of development?
              3. What kinds of parenting discipline styles are effective
                 for Julia's media and Internet use and for kids at other
                 stages of development?

Julia is in ninth grade and spends 2 to 4 hours after school and 20
or more hours per weekend online (e.g., cell phone, instant messaging,
e-mailing, and file-sharing music). Her parents are concerned that she
is spending too much time on the computer. Julia has never been very
outgoing and prefers to be alone in her room rather than hanging out
with her parents. Her parents are worried about what she could be
doing online. They don't want her to connect with people that they
do not know. Julia and her parents now fight continuously about the
amount of time she spends online. They have installed Nannyware,
and have placed the computer in the living room. Occasionally they
have unplugged her completely. So far, nothing has worked very well
and the parents realize that, as Julia gets older, they will have less control over what she does. Julia, on the other hand, is exasperated and
angry because she believes that her parents don't understand. She has
tried to explain to them that "all my friends are online" and for the
first time she feels connected to other kids who "know and like me."
What should the parents do? Is Julia's behavior online healthy? How

should the parents monitor their daughter's media use now and in the future?

# Cyber Rules for Families

Refer back to the Cyber Rules Problem-Solving Model discussed in Chapter 1 before applying this method to helping these parents with their daughter's Internet use. The metaphor of crossing the street is a way to clarify both safety issues online and children's developmental needs for choice, mastery, accountability, and independence. The four components that undergird the Model are 1) to measure what you know about cyber culture, 2) to provide criteria for potential problem use, 3) to assess the severity of the problem, and 4) to compare online use with offline behaviors. The "Effective Discipline and Kids' Media Use" charts illustrate effective discipline strategies at different ages.

The Cyber Rules Problem-Solving Model:

a) Knowledge.
b) Understanding the criteria that defines problem use.
c) Assessing your online use.
d) Comparing online behaviours with offline effects.

### Criteria for Problem Internet Use

Does Julia's behavior meet any of these criteria?

| | |
|---|---|
| *Use of Time* | How much time is spent pursuing the behavior? |
| *Level of Impairment* | Is the behavior continued despite health, social, or occupational problems? |
| *Dealing with Emotion* | Does behavior help to numb, alter, or avoid feelings? |
| *Self-regulation* | Are efforts to cut back on the behavior unsuccessful? |
| *Others' Opinions* | Do family and friends believe there is a problem? |
| *Comorbidity* | Is the behavior part of another mental or medical disorder? |

### Does Julia Have A Problem?

Directions: Answer these questions from the perspectives of *both* Julia and her parents. Compare their answers and determine if there is a discrepancy in how the problem is assessed within the family.

1. Do you often stay online longer than you intend to?     Yes   No

2. Do you argue with others about your behavior online? Yes   No

3. Is your identity online very different from whom you
   are offline?                                                                    Yes   No

4. Do you do things online you wouldn't do offline?          Yes   No

5. Do you hide anything you do online?                          Yes   No

6. Are you worried about how much time you
   spend online?                                                              Yes   No

7. Do you often avoid other things you need to do
   when online?                                                               Yes   No

8. Do you become agitated if you cannot get online
   when you want to?                                                         Yes   No

9. Does your online behavior ever cause problems in
   your offline life?                                                            Yes   No

10. Does your online life often feel more satisfying than
    in your offline one?                                                      Yes   No

Number of Yes Answers_____

What do the scores mean? An important place to begin with parents who want to guide their child's behavior is to explore the way "the problem" is perceived by all involved. If Julia's and her parents' answers to the questions above agree, then guidelines can be negotiated about the behavior from the same point of view. But many times parents and kids see the issues in question from a very different light. Before guidelines can be developed in these cases, more information (e.g., research data and age norms) must be generated to make families and kids more knowledgeable. However, even then kids and parents may not agree on some of their responses to the questionnaire "Do You Have a Problem?"

but at least the areas of disagreement can be clearly addressed rather than provide fuel for covert behaviors on the part of youngsters and exasperation on the part of parents.

## Exercise 2.2. Getting It: Comparing Julia's Online Behaviors with Offline Effects

Directions: Fill in the Getting It table as if you were helping Julia and her parents understand what is a developmentally appropriate way to guide her media life. Evaluate and discuss Julia's responses in terms of her:

1. stage of development
2. psychological needs
3. relational needs
4. family and cultural norms

| Basic Questions | Online Behaviors | Possible Offline Effects |
| --- | --- | --- |
| *Why do I go online?* | | |
| *How much time do I really spend online?* | | |
| *How does media technology affect me?* | | |
| *What are my identities online?* | | |
| *What are the ways that I connect with others online?* | | |
| *What are the feelings I have about my cyber habits?* | | |

# Effective Discipline and Kids' Media Use

So far media affect our children in ways that remain elusive but also in ways that shock and confuse us. Using the metaphor of crossing the street, something that we teach kids how to do for their own safety, Julia's story can be deconstructed by using the Cyber Rules model and the accompanying activities as a way to understand the relationship between effective parenting at different ages, safe and developmentally healthy media and Internet use, and the duty of parents and adults to protect kids from harm when they are young and give them good advice that they can buy into at any age.

There is an appropriate, but brief, stage when we *hold on* to our children at all times. Would you let a toddler or a three- or four-year-old cross the street alone? This is the *no-discussion-control* discipline strategy. Parents and caregivers must control all the media activities encountered by children. However, as they mature and become more independent, ages 5 to 14 depending on the environment, there are some well-planned choices that can be included to begin to give kids some independence and responsibility. This is the *control-choice* discipline strategy. Some children can learn how to navigate the street, cars, traffic, and pedestrians with supervision ("I will watch you as you cross this street") and then eventually a few years later ("You may walk home from school or go to the mall"). However, this stage of development depends on the maturity of the child as well as the awareness of the parents and the particular environment. It may be that a child can cross the street to school in the morning with a crossing guard but not in the afternoon, when many buses enter the school grounds. As kids mature, the most effective discipline strategy becomes *choices-supervise-discuss.* Translated beyond crossing the street to media use, parents are not always going to be able to watch their children but they can still be in charge. This is the stage when parents must supervise their children's Internet and access to media but begin to give them well-thought-out choices to prepare them for the reality of being accountable for their actions. The next level of effective discipline is *discuss-monitor-discuss.* While parents should know what goes on in their homes, they cannot protect and restrict kids from the life outside the door. During this stage young people are in the world, at school many hours every day, often behind the wheel, or at their friends' houses. At 18, remember, we send them to war. Neither laissez-faire nor autocratic parenting works at this age. Adolescents want a life in connection with others. They get it online and with media. Parents on the other hand need to really know and connect with their kids and be in control of their own reactions so that their children will want to talk to them… which leads to the last, and most effective discipline style, and one that will hopefully last: *discuss-discuss*. Here kids, even grown ones, and adults can have differences of opinions but these differences do not lead to shame, secrecy, or disconnection from family and community.

Figure 2.3 provides a model for kids and parents to negotiate effective discipline strategies together.

Finally, during childhood and adolescence it is important that parents realize they can better prepare their children for a media–saturated life by first modeling positive communication and health themselves, and then by listening to what their children have to say. Adults also need to give advice sometimes but this advice needs to be 1) informed–listen and ask for details first without freaking out, 2) short–3 minutes tops or you'll lose them, and 3) real–don't minimize what you're doing. Teenagers are curious and they need some privacy and autonomy but they also need to be accountable for their behaviors. What rules guide your 10- or 12-year-old as he or she crosses the street? How about a 14- or 16–year-old? It cannot be stressed enough that parents' discipline methods with teenagers cannot be the

**Figure 2.3. Effective Discipline and Kids' Media Use**

Helping Kids to Cross the Street Safely with Media

| Parent Discipline Style | Most Effective at what Ages? | | | |
|---|---|---|---|---|
| FROM CONTROL TO CHOICE TO DIALOGUE | AGE 1 | 5-8 | 10-15 | 16-18+ |
| No discussion-control | ⟶ | | | |
| Control-choice | ⟶ | | | |
| Choices-supervise-discuss | | ⟶ | | |
| Choices-monitor-discuss | | | ⟶ | |
| Discuss-discuss | | | | ⟶ |

same model used when they were young or they will simply hide what they are doing or go elsewhere to do it. Parents realize that they are often not there to hold their teenager's hand when they use media but that young people still want good information and guidance about this important area of their lives. The next three chapters explore the ways we interact with others online and how these contribute or detract from healthy development.

# Chapter 3

# Net Relationships:
# From Fake to Falling in Love

$C$yberspace is a great way to be with people. It's easy, fast, and mostly free. All sorts of meaningful (or not so meaningful) interpersonal relationships evolve via e-mail, instant messaging (IM), game playing, discussion boards, Listservs, and blogs. Additionally, cell phones, palm pilots, digital cameras, and portable computers are in sync with daily life. We now have multi-user systems, voice-activated everything, graphics, streaming action, 3-D environments, and neural implants to add to our digital repertoire. Are these connections for real? Are they as meaningful as face-to-face encounters? Eighty-nine percent of Americans use e-mail or instant messaging, according to *The UCLA Internet Report* (Cole, Suman, Schramm, Lunn, Jedrix-Sean, Fortier, et al., 2003), but the idea that deep and meaningful relationships can form at a distance is not new to the Internet.

The cultural history of human relationships has always been represented through ancient media, with artifacts depicting both everyday and imagined life. Now media culture uses the Internet and broadband connections to propagate computer-mediated versions of life. Most of us know couples who have met online and then married. We can IM our kids in the next room or e-mail business colleagues around the world. The Internet allows us to manage a social life instantly that does not depend on someone else really being there when we are. The technology of the telegraph, telephone, and film warmed us up to connecting via broadband. Now we are exponentially creating social networks in multiple ways that seamlessly merge our online lives with our offline ones. Between 35 and 55% of all online contacts eventually meet offline (Gackenbach, 2007; Gerchener, 2003; Greenfield, 2004a; Gross, 2004; Hu et al., 2004; Jones, 2000). With communication technologies we can always find someone willing to be with us. We love to connect.

## Close Encounters

All relationships are grounded in the universal human need to belong. This, in part, can be traced to biological underpinnings insuring our very survival. Affiliation and emotional support are essential components in human relationships but they differ both from situation to situation and from person to person. Some people have a relatively low need to be around others, while other people are very outgoing. Needless to say, friendships and intimate connections online mirror this reality.

In the early days of the Internet a few e-mails (in asynchronous time) were all most of us could handle. Yet, at the time, it appeared revolutionary. Now, just a few years later, Internet communications are interactive, multiple, and simultaneous. Juggling all this technology can be stressful even for computer science (CS) and tech experts. A CS university professor was embarrassed because he could not do what most sixth graders could do with ease: field 16 instant message windows at the same time while checking his e-mail and answering his cell phone. When we wonder what effect the digital age has on our ability to form meaningful social connections online we must also consider that most adults are not as skilled as young people in this arena. Not only are kids online from infancy but they use digital media and the Web as a vehicle for continually creating self and relationships online. Young people are more adept at cyber discourse, and take up new technologies that make sense without worrying about the effect of online communication.

Why do we like to connect with others online? Because it's there and does what we tell it to, especially things we can't do offline. Is Internet relating a time saver or a time sink? For youngsters, and most of the rest of us who want to be heard, the Internet has become a way to harness "collective intelligence" and still be yourself. Users in MySpace, with its attendant porous boundaries, connective tissue (cheap geeky software), and live Web action will soon pass Yahoo as the traffic leader on the Web (Levy & Stone, 2006):

> …people, especially younger people who grew up with mouse in hand, would get more out of [the web] if they could express themselves by putting all their information where friends could see it … MySpace is in the 2000's what the malt shop was in the 1950's, if the malt shop could hold 65 million adolescents, many of who had no qualms about showing pictures of themselves half drunk in their underwear. (pp. 50, 52)

It's interesting that so much of what kids write about in their blogs *sock it to* grown-ups (parents, teachers, political figures). YouthNoise blogs and many other online youth forums give kids and young adults a public arena from a private place where discontent abounds for those in charge of the world they will inherit. Child Psychologist Ron Taffel puts it succinctly. Media culture has become "the second family" for kids today (2005, p. 135). Taffel believes there is a wall of silence offline about what kids are really doing but online it's all there. Taffel tries to help his young patients and their parents learn meaningful ways to relate but he acknowledges the amorphous pull of pop culture and cyber life. Taffel thinks parents are almost totally disconnected from what their kids are really doing (even if they are in the same room). Media-glamorized relationships, sexuality, and drugs model a new normal for adolescence. Taffel is concerned:

> Kids are challenged to create portable relationships: to develop superficial connections with professional grown-ups, coaches, after school leaders, tutors,… kids move along a virtual conveyor belt from one child wrangler to the next. (p. 75)

Is this why kids are living online? To wrangle more real connections than they have offline? Seventh-grade student Maria accidentally began instant messaging a girl in her class that she had seen as her enemy. Over time, comparing notes about each other's lives, the girls came to realize that in fact they had a lot in common and gradually became good friends. This online communication led to a positive change in their offline relationship.

Shawn's story is different. Shawn hid his IM experience from his parents until he ended up in the hospital after a suicide attempt. The parents were shocked and could not think of any clues that they had missed about their son's emotional state. The emergency physician told the parents to check their son's computer, especially the Web history, IM, and e-mail. The stunned parents found evidence of brutal sexual harassment and terrorist threats written to their son from classmates over a period of several months. This text history helped the parents understand some of what led to Shawn's suicide attempt. Two of the youths, the masterminds behind the intensity of the cyber harassment, ended up in Juvenile Hall, charged with sexual battery and false imprisonment as a result of their on- and offline behavior toward Shawn.

How do we help kids and each other navigate relationships and networks online when we are not sure what offline social rules apply in cyberspace? There have been news stories and much talk-show discussions warning us about the dangers of online relationships, cyber predators, and cyber crimes. Recently, however, a *New York Times* article questioned the hysteria and urgency of fear-based messages to kids and parents, calling them overblown (Bahney, 2006). Parents and schools are curtailing kid's access to the Internet, taking away Web cams, and imposing strict rules largely as a result of these messages, rather than as the result of careful study. These tactics already do not work offline so why should they be effective in cyberspace?

Mike Males (2006), sociology professor at the University of California, Santa Cruz, is more concerned about a phenomenon he calls "adult brain atrophy" than pornography, pedophiles, and cruelty online. Males defines adult brain atrophy as a lack of self-awareness and an inability to rationally assess the unfamiliar, coupled with reflexive fear of youth and anything new:

Teens and the Internet are newness squared ... with predators and the worst cruelties lurking in our largest institutions, families and churches, where can teens safely interact? Why on the Internet, preferably alone and unmonitored. Statistically adults who supervise teens are more likely to abuse them than anyone they met online. Consider the sterling record of personalized websites such as MySpace.com, whose 46 million registered users (the vast majority young) share billions of unsupervised interactions daily, with no deaths and few dangers. (n.p.)

## Comparing Online and Offline Interactions

What do healthy relationships look like online? Probably like face-to-face ones, but more intense and less constrained by time and place. One advantage of online communication is that it offers a way to practice social skills with many different people. But, as a result, there is greater potential of generalizing this expanded repertoire of social behaviors to offline connections. Remember Ronald from Chapter 1 who pretended to be someone else online with a girl he had a crush on? Over time this somewhat socially awkward young teen was able to transfer his online social skills into more socially adept f2f interactions. Cyber communication strategies can also have negative effects offline. We can share too much too soon. We can also misunderstand text especially without the essential nuances of nonverbal cues. Research also demonstrates that we can rapidly lower our inhibitions and communicate more impulsively, probably in ways we could not get away with f2f. The Internet may teach us to be impatient with long explanations. We may become adept at reducing complex information to simple sound bytes, and we may develop limited tolerance for frustration and ambiguity (Suler, 2004).

Usually, when we first meet someone, what we see and sense creates part of the connection and our ability to understand each other. Physical attributes and nonverbal signals are important ways we learn to gauge our responses and respond to others. In the realm of offline social relationships, how we look is especially relevant. If this isn't enough, media reinforces this message. When we don't measure up to external criteria of attractiveness we suffer from negative self-talk of one sort or another. How do facial expression, eye contact, and body language manifest in online relationships? First, online relationships do not depend as much on the observable characteristics that are so important offline. The earliest studies about online communication and relationships from the 1980s found that text-based computer-mediated communication was often perceived as cold and unfriendly. Even today, opinions about the meaning and efficacy of online relationships are based on this previous research even though new technology now makes the data obsolete (Bargh & McKenna, 2004).

We have learned how to continually adjust to text-based and more rapid interactive online communications, probably like our grandparents learned how to assimilate the telephone into their communication repertoire. More technological changes are on the horizon that will continue to modify online behaviors and offline reactions with the increasing availability of mobile and wraparound communications.

With the lack of so many f2f cues online we are learning how to relate online more effectively and accurately but we still have a tendency to interpret Internet connections within the parameters of offline social constructs, prejudices, and assumptions. Margaret had such an experience with a friend:

> I have a friend who tends to have a low opinion of herself. She takes any implied criticism very personally. When I talk to her in person, especially face to face, rather than over the phone, she generally takes my questions and comments as I mean them–as innocent inquiries, or as comments that are meant to be either helpful or joking. When I talk to her by email, however, there have been several incidents when she interprets what I said in the worst possible way–in ways that didn't even occur to me. I have recently been much more careful about what I write by email.

Conversely, there are some very positive things about online relationships. If we are insecure about our looks or are shy f2f, we can be empowered by technology that allows us to communicate at a distance without the anxiety of managing in-person dynamics. New technology also affects people who have been accustomed to being in charge. Online the power dynamic is not controlled from the top down. It is rotated from a hierarchical position to a horizontal one. Status online is more equalized as offline entitlement or authority does not upload effectively to the Internet. While there may be loafers, lurkers, monopolizers, or flamers in cyberspace, these personalities can be shunned, disconnected, or ignored and back channel conversations (e.g., those that occur out of the view of some participants) can circumvent this dynamic. As a result of this emerging dynamic of cyber groups and in contrast to early Internet data, research suggests that forming personal relationships online is more positive than initially thought. Katelyn McKenna and her colleagues (2002) at New York University found that the degree of liking for their partner among those who met first on the Internet versus f2f was greater than offline meeting. The same team of researchers (Bargh et al., 2002) found that people randomly assigned to interact over the Internet verses f2f were better able to express their personalities to their partners online first. In contrast, Mallen, Day, and Green (2003) discovered that students reported that they were more satisfied with face-to-face interactions than with those online. These opposing viewpoints illustrate the difficulty of generating useful hypotheses about the value of Internet relationships. It appears that some online meetings progress to very satisfying offline relationships, while others do not.

## Relationships Online

We're all looking for love and the online relationship phenomenon capitalizes on this powerful human need. How easy is it to like or love online? We know from the divorce rate (50% give or take) that sustaining love is not easy. We know that friends are good online, but can we initiate meaningful friendships in cyberspace? Can we fall in love online? Can wired attraction endure when unplugged? Chatting with strangers, meeting people online, extending one's offline friendships to online and vice versa are all part of the new millennium of cyber relationships. The phenomenon of Internet relationships transferring to real life raises many questions and concerns. Ten years ago psychiatrist Avodah Offit (1995) noted:

> I think these attempts at sensible affiliation are brave and adventurous. The new connections encourage a life of the spirit to become a life of

the heart. Before monogamy and commitment, however, perhaps E-mail most obviously invites people to flirt–and to do it in the safety of the home. Which is why E-mail has been said to be the most fun people can have with their pants on. Email companionship can be a new kind of spectral friendship, even a spiritual companionship, unlike any in the accustomed world. It should be approached with sacredness and caution, a sense of wonder, and an acknowledgment that you are dealing with major emotional forces–the power of people's minds to reach directly to each other. (n.p.)

Some researchers propose that it is not who we meet online that dictates meaningful connections but how we feel about the Internet and its associated media technology. Our attitudes about online communication appear to affect the nature of our experience. David Leon and colleagues (2003) at the University of West Florida and personality psychologists Steven Rouse and Heather Haas (2003) examined the way we project our personalities online in comparison to our offline ones. These researchers concluded that we change our perceptions of our online relationships over time: they become more like our offline ones.

John Bargh and Katelyn McKenna (2004) surveyed nearly 600 usenet group members in order to find out how authentic online relationships are compared to offline ones:

> A substantial proportion of respondents reported having formed a close relationship with someone they had met originally on the Internet; in addition, more than 50% of these participants had moved an Internet relationship to the 'real-life' or face-to-face realm. Many of these online relationships had become quite close–22% of respondents reported that they had either married, become engaged to, or were living with someone they initially met on the Internet. (p. 581)

## LOOKING FOR LOVE ONLINE

Falling in love online has become a major area of study for behavioral scientists. Sustaining fulfilling and loving relationships offline is hard to do. Similarly, it looks like we need help learning cyber rules for online intimacies too. Online dating services are taking notice. Sites like eHarmony and Match.com are some of the fastest-growing online businesses.

According to recent research, slightly more men than women between 35 and 55 are looking for love online using Internet dating services (Daily Market and Media Intelligence, 2004). Gerchener (2003) notes,

> There are about 40 million visits to online dating sites each month. Whatever their motives, singles and not-so-singles are paying record dollars to try online dating. Consumers spent $214 million on online personals in the first half of 2003, up 76 percent from $121 million last year . . . Internet dating became the largest source of paid content sales in 2002, overtaking the business/investment and entertainment/lifestyles categories.

Just how do we go about looking for love in cyberspace? Through personal advertisements. Systematic examinations of personal ads online have been conducted by Phua, Hopper, and Vazquez (2002) of City University of New York. Twenty-four hundred personal online ads were analyzed. These investigators concluded that models of sexual behavior as portrayed online did not address the realities of safer sex negotiation and thus were likely to lead to unprotected sex offline. In another online personal ad study, Donald Strassberg and Stephen Holty (2003) of the University of Utah found that the most popular ad of the four types of ads the researchers created was one in which a woman described herself as financially independent, successful, and ambitious. Surprisingly, these personal advertisements received 50% more responses than those with the more typical solicitation of attractiveness and slimness. Darin Matthews from the department of psychology at the Citadel studied the preference of the personal ad *writer* instead of the ad *respondents.* Matthews discovered that "heterosexual men seek younger women and heterosexual women seek older men" (1999, p. 227).

When we consider the extended period of adolescent development (8–15 years), older age of marriage (ages 27–28 years), a 50% or more divorce rate, and reduction in the numbers of people getting married at all, how long can we expect cyber connections to last when offline relationships have a 50% failure rate? And remember that this is not to say that the 50% who remain married enjoy fulfilling and loving connections or that marriages are the only meaningful way to experience intimacy. Katelyn

McKenna and colleagues (2002) looked at how long online relationships lasted after moving offline. They discovered that Internet relationships were still intact two years later; a much higher rate than relationships initially built upon face-to-face meetings. Tom Tyler (2002), in a special issue of the *Journal of Social Issues* devoted to Internet life, concluded that:

> Relationships that develop through the Internet are close, meaningful, and long lasting, suggesting that many of the concerns expressed about the quality and meaningfulness of Internet interactions are unfounded . . . people bring relationships formed on the Internet into the real world. (p. 197)

There are many successful stories about people who have met online and taken the relationship to the next level and even gotten married. Peter, a successful business entrepreneur, had struggled with his weight since childhood. He was ashamed of his looks. At the urging of friends, he began an online romance. After many months of developing an Internet relationship, he and his long-distance partner met each other for the first time. All his life, Peter was used to being rejected for the way he looked. However, his new love accepted him largely because their relationship had developed without the negative constraints that face-to-face meetings would have created.

## CYBER RULES FOR A CYBER AFFAIR

Unfortunately, happy stories like Peter's are right next to harmful ones. Janice Wolak and fellow researchers (2003) from the Crimes Against Children Research Center at the University of New Hampshire note that preteen and teen Internet users who formed a close relationship with someone they met online were more likely to have problems with parents or be troubled themselves. Furthermore, the success of bringing an online relationship into one's face-to-face reality depends, not surprisingly, on the reception of significant others in one's life (Wildermuth, 2004). Cyber affairs and cyber hookups are common. When these experiences interfere with offline life, no one is quite sure how to solve the problem. Is it an online or an offline one? Is it both? Because it is so easy to initiate and conceal a cyber relationship, we do not have a lot of good data that helps us deal with the issue. However, recent research by two Israeli psychologists, Aviram and Amichai-Hamburger (2005), found several personality and environmental predictors of online infidelity. Their results suggested that those who engaged in Internet relationships had higher tendencies toward manipulation and control of others, exhibitionistic traits, lower self-disclosure, and lower cohesion in offline relationships. Interestingly, and in contrast to offline relationships, lack of sexual satisfaction did not appear to predict a higher likelihood of experiencing a cyber affair.

The phenomenon of cyber affairs may have something to teach us about offline intimacy because it pushes our thinking in ways that aren't constrained by psychology offline. Consider the case of a 42-year-old married Latina woman. Elena has been in therapy for nine months because she feels emotionally disconnected in her marriage and unable to control her teenage sons who have recently gotten in trouble with the law. Her treatment goals include learning ways to recharge her relationship with her husband and also to become a more effective parent. After eight months of therapy, Elena disclosed that she had developed a lesbian relationship in an online chat room. She and her cyber lover are planning to meet offline. Elena asks her therapist if this is healthy and wants help in understanding why she has engaged in this online behavior. As with all of the material that patients bring to the couch, the therapist in this case wants to help Elena process the meaning of this affair. But what should the therapist say about the *online aspect* of Elena's behavior?

Offline cultural rules and psychological theories are not adequate to understand Elena's Internet behaviors. Is her cyber affair a healthy, sexual fantasy? Does the lack of intimacy this woman experiences offline push her into cyberspace? Is she "really a lesbian," or is she avoiding working on her real issues? Perhaps this is not a problem at all. In order to help this woman understand her cyber affair, the therapist and Elena need to expand their thinking to include cyber psychology. Is Elena more vulnerable to the negative effects of her Internet behavior because she does not realize that the cyber psychological constructs of disinhibition and annonymity facilitate (at least initially) intimate connections? In addition, if the therapist and Elena do not understand how identity is projected online they may misinterpret a crucial piece of information.

Perhaps the lesbian with whom Elena is becoming emotionally and sexually intimate with is really a man! Finally, is Elena susceptible to behavioral addiction? Are her Internet activities becoming compulsive?

On the most basic level, it may be more important to examine the meaning of Elena's behavior. The expression of healthy sexuality, especially sexual identity, encounters many barriers offline. Stereotypical and inaccurate labeling of sexual orientation as discrete categories, homophobia, ignorance, and hate crimes prevent us from acknowledging sexual differences, sexual needs, and sexual affiliations. However, online access and anonymity allow parts of ourselves to emerge that may not be able to offline. Is this Internet affair essential to Elena's exploration of the self? Initiating an online lesbian relationship can be viewed as a healthy and adaptive way to engage in sexual fantasy and/or explore a disowned part of her identity.

What's a therapist to do? Is Elena at risk of derailing recent therapeutic gains and rupturing the trust in her marriage if she continues with this relationship, or is she at risk of shutting down a crucial aspect of her development at this stage of her life? Research about cyber affairs suggests that online intimacy becomes more and more difficult to contain in cyberspace and there is an increasing chance that the relationship will move offline and begin to affect other areas of every day life. The therapist can help Elena understand her denial and avoidance of offline issues by engaging in fantasy projections rather than continuing to work through her *real* problems. The fact that it is a lesbian relationship may make it easier for Elena to deny that this is a "real affair" or to see this as a threat to her marriage and avoid taking responsibility in the here and now to improve her life.

An opposing conceptualization of Elena's cyber affair is to view her Internet behavior as a healthy exploration of her identity. Adaptations of social identity theory to Internet behaviors (Bargh & McKenna, 2004) suggest that some intimate relationships online serve an important function in identity development, especially when certain identities offline are marginalized or stigmatized. It may not have been safe or possible for Elena, as a mother, a Latina, or a married woman, to acknowledge that she wants to explore her sexuality within a lesbian relationship. However, this desire may be central to her dissatisfaction and emotional disconnection in her marriage. An essential ingredient for personal growth in therapy is to acknowledge and bring into consciousness one's unmet needs. The support, intimacy, and pleasure Elena experiences in this cyber affair may be a safe way for her to gain this awareness and decide how to transfer this to her offline life.

Use Exercise 3.1 below to expand your thinking about Elena's online and offline experiences. Be open to at least two conceptualizations. The purpose of this exercise is to deconstruct Elena's Internet behaviors using constructs of cyber psychology (Bargh & McKenna, 2004; Gackenbach, 1998; Plant, 2001; Suler, 2004), in order to compare how Access, Time, Technology, Identity, Relationship, Emotion, and Power manifest in cyberspace. These constructs provide data for several possible clinical interpretations that will contribute to an eventual problem-solving plan. This exercise illustrates how clinicians and their patients can design very different treatment interventions based on combining cyber psychology with offline theories of psychotherapy and psychology. Mental health clinicians are not known for embracing opposing clinical viewpoints in their offline work but this is essential online. Applying psychological understanding of our patients' online selves and relationships provides a much needed opportunity to expand our efficacy in the digital age.

## Exercise 3.1. An Online Relationship and Its Possible Offline Effects

| Basic Questions | Online Behaviors | Possible Offline Effects |
| --- | --- | --- |
| *Access (place)* | | |
| *Time* | | |
| *Technology* | | |
| *Identity(ies)* | | |
| *Relationship* | | |
| *Emotion* | | |
| *Power* | | |

After filling in the table, Elena can explore the meaning of her online relationship and its effects on her offline life. She is now ready to assess her online behaviors by completing the Cyber Rules "Criteria for Problem Use" and the questionnaire "Do You Have A Problem?" Hopefully, as Elena evaluates her cyber behavior, a plan for what to do about her cyber affair will emerge, in the context of her offline therapy.

### Criteria for Problem Internet Use

|  |  |
|---|---|
| *Use of Time* | How much time is spent pursuing the behavior? |
| *Level of Impairment* | Is the behavior continued despite health, social, or occupational problems? |
| *Dealing with Emotion* | Does the behavior help to numb, alter, or avoid feelings? |
| *Self-regulation* | Are efforts to cut back on the behavior unsuccessful? |
| *Others' Opinions* | Do family and friends believe there is a problem? |
| *Comorbidity* | Is the behavior part of a mental or medical disorder? |

### Do You Have a Problem?

1. Do you often stay online longer than you intend to?     Yes     No
2. Do you argue with others about your behavior online?   Yes     No
3. Is your identity online very different from who you
   are offline?                                           Yes     No
4. Do you do things online you wouldn't do offline?       Yes     No
5. Do you hide anything you do online?                    Yes     No
6. Are you worried about how much time you spend
   online?                                                Yes     No
7. Do you often avoid other things you need to do
   when online?                                           Yes     No
8. Do you become agitated if you cannot get online
   when you want to?                                      Yes     No

9. Does your online behavior ever cause problems in
   your offline life?                                          Yes   No
10. Does your online life often feel more satisfying than
   your offline one?                                           Yes   No

Number of Yes Answers_____

## Groups Online

Like Elena, we are learning about relationships online: friends, lovers, and sexual partners but we are also becoming involved with groups of people in cyber meeting places. Group psychology tells us how groups function offline but do online groups function differently than f2f ones? It appears that theories of cyber psychology have expanded to include cyber groups. However, group theory does not translate easily to cyberspace. The effects of what we do online are compounded by 1) a global community, 2) human diversity, 3) exponential interaction effects, and 4) rapidly changing technology that alters communication modalities.

Social psychologists Robert Baron and Donn Byrne (1994) acknowledged that online groups can provide information, support, and opportunities for learning. Establishing social identities is a major reason that people may seek out the company of others online. Here's what communications researchers Catherine Ridings and David Gefen (2004) have to say about why we meet each other online:

> Across 27 communities in 5 different broad types, 569 different reasons from 399 people indicated that most sought either friendship or exchange of information, and a markedly lower percent sought social support or recreation. The reasons were significantly dependent on the grouping of the communities into types. In all the community types information exchange was the most popular reason for joining. Thereafter, however, the reason varied depending on community type. Social support was the second most popular reason for members in communities with health/wellness and professional/occupational topics, but friendship was the second most popular reason among members in communities dealing with personal interests/hobbies, pets, or recreation. (n.p.)

One of the most talked about and most visible cyber group phenomena concerns young people. The Internet is the place to meet from
middle school through college and beyond. There are daily news stories, teacher meetings, and dinner-table conversations about young
people's blogs, FaceBook and MySpace postings, cyber bulling, cyber
sex, online assignations to meet pedophiles at the mall, and countless
other dire warnings about risky behaviors in cyberspace. Despite news
stories to the contrary, U.C. Santa Cruz sociology professor Mike Males
(2006) found the hysteria about risk to be unsubstantiated. In Los
Angeles, for example, the Southern California High Tech Task Force
reported no cases of criminal behavior connected to MySpace.com.
Males labeled adults uncreative and ignorant when it came to really
understanding young people. He found the paranoia about the dangers
of the Internet dishearteningly emblematic of the disregard for the real
menaces youth face offline.

When asked, parents and educators admit that they are in over their
heads when it comes to youngsters meeting in cyberspace. While parents of younger teens still orchestrate where their kids go and with
whom, the influence of the second family is pervasively maintained by
the seduction of media and the disenfranchisement of youth from
adults. Media messages whizzing digitally into the eyes and ears of our
kids are the primary teachers of sexuality, social discourse, and relationships. Adults have not figured out how to counterbalance this
equation. Net nannies and unrealistic rules are some of the uncreative
and uninformed ways that adults try to keep kids from doing what they
are doing online and off. It doesn't work.

Just what are young people doing in cyberspace that is so disturbing to adults? It appears that younger teens, middle and high school
students primarily, regularly post journal entries with pictures of themselves to blog sites where other teenagers can view and comment on
their entries. Many of these blogs are sexually suggestive by default. The
latest fashion, especially for females, requires less and less material.
Youth culture, especially online, encourages self-disclosure, shares
advice about how to party, including which drugs are the "safest," and
of course, tips on hooking up. Even school administrators are trying to

curtail some of their students' online behaviors after school and in homes if they violate their codes of conduct for students. Most schools now block or restrict certain sites from classroom computers but most tech experts acknowledge that smart students can still break into a district's mainframe.

## FORM AND FUNCTION ONLINE

All groups have the dynamic constructs of form and function but online these constructs are transformed by cyberspace. For example, the forms of online groups drive the function. But function online owes everything to the increasing interactivity and pervasiveness of the Web. Put more simply, the Web is *live*. It's everything we do offline plus everything we do online, with power, time, place, and cohesion potentiated by broadband. Parents, clinicians, and educators who want to understand what kids are doing meeting each other in MySpace or in other Web-based activities better learn about how and why online groups are different.

Like Elena's exploration of her cyber affair, there are ways to compare online and offline group dynamics that help us get it about online groups. The "us" here refers to adults, because young people are already developing their own norms and group netiquette. It is frightening and confusing to many that adults are not in control of kids' online lives. Offline models of discipline–censorship, restriction, authority, and social or moral value-driven, top–down decisions about what kids' can or cannot do–are ineffective online. Most kids learn from what adults do, although kids view adult power as ignorant, or worse corrupt and self-serving, especially when it comes to their culture and the Internet. While becoming aware of the difference between online and offline group constructs is not a panacea for unhealthy Internet behaviors, it is a place to learn how to participate in an online group more effectively. We need to know more than just how our identities or relationships manifest in cyberspace, we need to learn about how to interact successfully in groups of people so that we can teach youngsters better netiquette. Yes, bullying, lying, emotional abuse, and harmful models of sexuality are online, *but they have always been present offline,* and we have not done a great job in the past of addressing these real threats to children's and adolescents' development. Table 3.1 below compares several online and offline group constructs.

As you can see from Table 3.1, there are some interesting ways that cyberspace changes the group process. Cyberspace encourages fluidity and creative uses of power, perceptions of time, place, and boundaries of social roles. Online group process is facilitated by offline theories and online dynamic. Even when there are disruptions and roadblocks, the online environment has unique ways of managing problems. Anonymity online contributes to both confrontation and lurkers. Lurking, or spying

### Table 3.1 Comparing offline and online group psychology.

| Constructs | Offline | Online |
|---|---|---|
| *Power* | *Hierarchical, leaderless, or shared power, perceived verbally and nonverbally.* | *Horizontal, diffuse power structure, shifting, perceived through text.* |
| *Time* | *Monochronic, linear, finite, measurable, fleeting.* | *Polychronic, extended and stretched, delayed or now.* |
| *Place* | *Here, illustrates the dynamic of concrete, contained, power and social roles.* | *Here, there, anywhere, formless, multiple, flat.* |
| *Productivity* | *Task oriented, usually within a predetermined schedule. Setbacks are perceived as disruptive. End-product is the goal.* | *Multitasking, simultenaity increased. Can be chaotic but accomplish more. Setbacks are perceived as ways to be more collaborative and creative. Process is the goal.* |
| *Roles* | *Clearly defined, visible, difficult to alter, relies on stereotypes and status.* | *Boundaries are permeable, roles are flexible, changeable, and do not rely on nonverbal characteristics or hierarchy.* |
| *Cohesion* | *Groupthink, scape-goating, polarizing, loafing, consensus.* | *"virtual Jihad," less accountability for individual behavior, lurking, flaming, disconnecting, and connecting.* |

online without making one's presence known, may be an online version of social loafing. Alecia, a college student from Texas, talks about her experience:

> I recall a situation where somebody in a chat room setting claimed to be suicidal. . . . It was interesting to see the reaction of the group members. Myself, I just sat back and watched because I had been exposed to all kinds of online behavior, and I just quit reacting to things.

Besides lurking online and being invisible, social behaviors adopted by group members online can be more impulsive, more personal, and more authentic. Individuals can be more outgoing in a positive way or combative in a negative one. Another interesting construct of groups is the concept of power. Often, in-person groups are hierarchical in nature, e.g., someone is in charge or, in the case of leaderless groups, some have more perceived power than others. In cyberspace, power is more likely to be shared (horizontal). Even if there is a designated person in charge, the power is largely unregulateable. Because cyberspace encourages expression, many shy individuals speak up more in group settings online, becoming more leader-like and willing to share their opinions. And conversely, if someone wants to misuse or monopolize power in cyberspace, harassment or flaming often become contagious, hard to contain, and an unofficial group norm. But unlike offline, negativity can be much more effectively silenced in cyberspace.

Offline, the form and function of groups lean heavily on negotiating and interpreting social cues to build cohesion so that work or communication are team oriented. In cyberspace, virtual group participants are not constrained by time and place. Interpreting and responding at a distance to social cues of people who are culturally and/or temporally diverse require knowledge of cyber psychology. For example, how we manage time in online communications is central to successful group process online (Yum & Hara, 2005). Most Western-oriented societies view time as monochronic: linear and finite. Western work and social groups have deadlines, delineated social roles, implicit or explicit agendas for speaking and listening, and clear ground rules. However, in many non-Western countries, both online and offline, perceptions of time and the resulting social discourse are characterized by a poly-chronic or extended-time philosophy. Polychronic cultures are often synonymous with collectivist rather than individualistic philosophies and investigators have discovered that these cultures are very effective when they meet in cyberspace, perhaps more than their Western coun-terparts (Lee, Tan, & Hameed, 2005).

Cyberspace meetings are now influencing our offline lives. Lee and col-leagues (2005) found Western cultures' offline group dynamic often con-strained by linear and fairly rigid, task-oriented social rules. In global communications, individualistic group process is often a liability and at times insulting to those who operate with a polychronic and pluralistic mindset. While Western societies abhor disruptions and divergence from schedules and agendas, collectivist societies embrace interactivity and may get more done. Non-Western cultures "appear able to squeeze more time out of every meeting by doing several things at once, restructuring when necessary, and not getting bogged down by regimentation or frustrated by pressure or uncertainty" (p. 2). Interestingly, polychronic cultures tend to maximize their group effectiveness even more online than offline despite the fact that many of these countries lack the technological infrastructure of Western countries. Perhaps the Internet will enable Western and non-Western group dynamics to cross pollinate and enrich the other.

Psychologists Jonathan Lazar and Jennifer Preece offered a basic defini-tion of online groups: "a set of users who communicate using computer-mediated communications and have common interests, shared goals, and shared resources" (2003, p. 128). Being together in cyberspace takes learning a special set of netiquette in addition to knowing how the Internet transforms identities. Christina Underhill and Murray Olmsted (2003) from the U.S. Department of the Navy compared focus groups conducted online versus those conducted face-to-face. Several advan-tages of online groups were identified: cost savings, data capture, and ability to reach remote populations. The authors found that online group types were comparable to offline ones in terms of both quantity and quality of information gathered.

In contrast, Marisa Salanova and colleagues (2003) examined how time pressure and competence effect group performance of face-to-face versus online groups. These investigators found that a group's sense of competence at the task (collective efficacy) was more important than "where" the groups met (online or face-to-face) in determining group performance. In other words, a group could be online or face-to-face but the important component in predicting their performance is not that factor, but their level of cohesion. Under some circumstances online groups appear to perform the same as f2f while under other circumstances they do not. Perhaps technologies like PalTalk, an online audio chat program that allows participants to talk to each other with microphones and to see each other with video cameras, will give us new data about how online social interactions compare to offline ones. Betsy Page and colleagues (2003) found that students reported feeling connected and that groups facilitated learning when an online audio component was included. Just the idea that chat participants are online at the same time seems to increase inclusion, involvement, and effectiveness compared with talking at different times (Nowak, Watt, & Walther, 2005).

## HAVE GROUPS WILL TRAVEL

Sherry Turkle (1997) argued that the community-building opportunities online are increasingly local despite globalization. That is, the initial interest people had in going online and talking to others was partly a result of the thrill of having a friend halfway across the world; but, like the evolution of land lines to cell phones, Internet use is now portable and becoming an essential part of daily communications. People want to talk online to others who are physically within reach, and the dialogue moves seamlessly from online to offline and back. One increasingly popular online group form is the blogging community. The sense of community that can evolve with regular blogging is nicely illustrated by Adam's reflections:

> I am involved in blogging. My particular type of blog is a livejournal [LJ]. As a result of its structure, LJ has taken on a very distinct "community" feel. In this way, LJ is a way of broadcast as well as two-way interactive communication. Journals on LJ are highly networked (partly due to the fact that up until a year ago, you had to be invited to join by an existing member) so there is a very strong feel of community and

things get around quickly . . . one author wrote something unfavorable towards American president George W. Bush in her personal journal. A reader read her opinions, interpreted them as a threat and reported her to the FBI. A couple of weeks later, the secret service visited her home and investigated her for threats against the President. . . . [These] online activities bled over into her real life in a surprising and disturbing way. Within only 7 hours of posting there were already 30 pages worth of comments. Reactions from the cyber community were emblematic of other forums. Frustration expressed easily and bloggers feel that the Internet domain should be a "safe haven" and "free" from governmental control.

Telecommuting is becoming a viable alternative to being at work. Even at work more meetings, communication, and just plain chatting occur online. Research from the area of computer-mediated communication suggests that there are both positive and negative aspects to groups that perform decision making online. In the early days of the Internet, making decisions through e-mail tended to take longer than face-to-face (Zigurs, Poole, & DeSanctis, 1988). However, now we realize that more people contribute to the group discussion process than in face-to-face meetings, which may temporarily derail problem solving but is more likely to increase productivity over the long-term. Wayne Eckerson (1992) explains about electronic meetings where participants use a LAN-attached personal computer to record comments, cast votes, or evaluate alternatives in response to a question or problem posed by the meeting facilitator. In addition to enhanced worker productivity, the group support software improves the dynamics of group meetings because it allows users to contribute ideas anonymously and in a less-inhibited manner.

Mathew, an employee who rarely contributed to face-to-face group meetings, describes how he became more productive via an e-mail work group:

What was interesting to me was how less inhibited I became using the e-mail. I opened up a lot more. I found that in my work situation I didn't think twice about e-mailing my boss with a question or to raise a concern and I did this on a regular basis. The same was true the first time I was involved with a company meeting that took place via e-mail. I found myself contributing a lot to the discussion whereas in the face-to-face meetings I contributed almost nothing.

## GROUP THINK ONLINE

Susan Zickmund (1997) argues that the Internet has transformed the nature of community and identity within the U.S. Her concern is that the Internet has also affected the cohesiveness of subversive organizations by allowing marginalized voices access to a much wider audience. Zickmund notes that individuals propagating Nazi ideologies have previously operated in relative isolation, but with the emergence of the Internet, such subversives have discovered a means of propagating their message beyond the narrow confines imposed by previous avenues. John Deirmenjian (2000) of the Department of Psychiatry, University of California, Los Angeles, offers the following example of hate groups online.

> Ernest Zundel, a Holocaust revisionist, operated a World Wide Web site in Canada dispersing hate propaganda and information denying the holocaust of millions of Jews by the Nazis. His estranged ex-wife testified that he supplied material from his Toronto office to the operator of the web site in the United States. Since hate speech is illegal in Canada, he used an American Internet service provider to operate his web site. (p. 1021)

Joseph Schafer (2002) of Southern Illinois University at Carbondale examined Web-based hate propaganda sites and found that less than 10% provided any warning statement on their sites about its potentially offensive nature. Of the information provided on these sites, the most common form was links to other sites with a smaller percentage offering online libraries of images and/or text. Interestingly, only half of the sites he studied offered some form of communication ranging from subscription to mailing lists and chat rooms to guest books and personal ads. Finally this researcher found that both women and youth were targeted. He noted that:

> Web sites operated by various white supremacist organizations allow users to sample and purchase "white power music." The violent, hateful, and profane lyrics found in such music are set to a heavy metal tune;

Figure 3.1. Hate group distribution according to hatewatch.org.

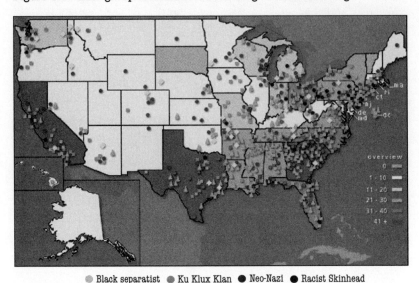

● Black separatist  ● Ku Klux Klan  ● Neo-Nazi  ● Racist Skinhead

● Christian Identity  ● Neo-Confederate  ● Other

Retrieved January 13, 2005 from http://www.splcenter.org/intel/map/hate.jsp.

the music may be a powerful inroad for extremist groups in their quest to attract younger members. (p. 78)

Researchers from Stanford University (Lee & Leets, 2002) examined what youth found persuasive about hate sites. They found a complex relationship between the predisposition of the adolescents toward hate ideas as well as the narrative quality and explicitness of the messages. The highest immediate impact was found with those sites that had a lot of text but an implicit message. As exposure continued and increased, this pattern changed. Less text was associated with an explicit message and was found to be the most influential.

In an online discussion board for a psychology of the Internet course at an Alberta university one student with extensive online group experience reflected:

It is my experience that online communities frequently have a core group of users and a larger number of "peripheral members." . . .

There are a few main producers of content within most online communities and the rest may lurk or come and go without affecting much of the dynamic of the group. In this way, an online community can grow and develop so long as the principle players remain active in maintaining the group.

The problem with this form of community is that it always has the potential to change . . . With so many users drifting in and out of the community, the group occasionally reverts back to the forming or storming stage as new dominant members appear, old members leave, or casual members do not adhere to the codes of conduct. Many groups have FAQs that outline these codes and rules in an attempt to eliminate some of these potential threats to the flow of the group. However it is often my experience that every online group experiences an "identity crisis" due to its instability in its developmental stages. . . . Rules and codes that defined the group were broken and the group reverted back to an earlier stage of development as users re-negotiated rules and related netiquette. . . .

It is also my experience, however, that online groups have the memory of a goldfish. That is a group could be really disrupted by a user but as soon as that threat leaves, the incident is quickly forgotten. This is not always true, but given the length of time Internet fads last . . . it is hardly a surprise. Of course the irony is that in cyberspace almost everything is recorded somewhere, which in theory would make cyber memory more enduring. It could be this dynamic that allows groups to survive despite their constant re-building of themselves. Online groups may be so flexible that they can adjust to anything. Although the stages and 'types' of groups defined in the book may serve as a good model, it seems that online communities are constantly moving within the model which may be the secret to their survival.

There are ample examples of deeply meaningful online groups and examples of the worst kind of group think, ones that promulgating ignorance and hate. The trick is to know how online relationships and groups function, especially the ways that are very different from our experiences when we meet offline. The following exercise helps you measure what you have learned from this chapter so that you can then apply this to your understanding of online relationships and groups.

## Exercise 3.2. Net Relationship Quiz

1. Connecting with others in cyberspace facilitates (circle all that apply):

   *impulsiveness   intimacy   self-revelation   flaming   inclusion   lying honesty   confusion   clarity   insight   belonging   conflict   agreement stigma   meeting offline   discord   productivity   participation   lurking loafing   (other)* _____    _____

2. People in online groups behave in ways they would not in a face-to-face meeting because_____and

   _____.

3. Identify online and offline group constructs.

| Group Constructs | Offline | Online |
|---|---|---|
| *Power* | | |
| *Time* | | |
| *Place* | | |
| *Productivity* | | |
| *Roles* | | |
| *Cohesion* | | |

4. Good Group Netiquette is_____and

   _____.

5. In the future online meetings will

   include_____

   and _____.

# Chapter 4

# Video Games:
# The Dark and Light Sides of the Force

$H$ere's a familiar story: I used to worry about the amount of time my son was on the computer. At first, it seemed as if he played games virtually all the time. He would stay up late and then get up and repeat the process all over again the next day. This went on for six months. It was hard for him to get out of the house because he was afraid of what he was missing online. It was almost as if he were addicted to video-game play. Everything was set up by his computer desk, food, drink, music. I could not believe that someone could be so addicted to a computer game. Once a particular game was conquered, he would then buy a new game and start all over again.

Now he is in his twenties and a graphic designer. He's on his computer all the time, but this time to make a living. I don't think that he would have ever realized his abilities to be a graphic designer if had never been so engrossed in playing games on the computer. He is really great at his job and he loves it. He still spends a lot of extra time on the computer for fun but I think his early years gaming may actually have rewired his brain in three-dimensional abilities.

This story illustrates the apparent contradictions of video-game play. If this mother had prevented her son from so much access to online game playing, would he still have chosen to be a graphic designer? We are concerned today about the extent to which children, friends, and students play video games. While there are some potentially negative effects, there are certainly positives as well. As with most entertainment, the Internet and electronically mediated video-game play have both good and bad aspects. While research suggests that violent game playing increases the likelihood that players will transfer this aggression to real-world interactions in some form, gaming also increases problem-solving abilities. Gaming may become compulsive to some players but it also provides a way to socialize with others. Video gaming has a mixed bag of effects.

As early as nine months of age, young people are viewing shows and playing games (Ridout, Vandewater, & Wartella, 2003). Parents applaud video games that educate because they prepare children for school, but these learning experiences soon morph into what appears primarily to be entertainment gaming, many with themes of violence and social aggression prominent (Brown & Hamilton-Giachritsis, 2005). Some investigators claimed that a strong contributing factor to the horrible incident at Columbine High School, if not the cause itself, was that the two students who fired the weapons were avid players of the popular video game called *Doom*. Explicit sexual themes are another concern that we have about video gaming. These games depict females in subversive stereotypical roles and also include social aggression and sexually predatory themes. For example, video-game creators were caught having inserted a sexually explicit scene into the game *Grand Theft Auto* that could be retrieved through access codes (Wingfield, 2005). Finally, the amount of time people of all ages spend playing games is also worrisome. In lengthy interviews with high-end gamers (those who play several times a week, several hours at a time, have played since the third grade or earlier, or who have played more than 50 games) many expressed concerns about being addicted, or noted that others claimed they were addicted. On the one hand it was refreshing that these serious gamers worried about their own use, while on the other hand their sense of personal stigma due to their video-game play was equally palatable and more often than not misplaced. These were all college students who were pursuing their education as well as often working and in other ways leading rather normal and healthy lives.

Just what effect does all this game playing have on our offline behavior and social skills? And how does all this effect children's development? Much to the surprise of most adults, research on video-game playing shows that it appears to enhance cognitive skills. In fact, Janet Murray (2005) argued during a keynote address at a recent meeting of the Digital Games Research Association that video-game playing enhances cognitive development, especially visuospacial information processing. Jeffrey Goldstein of the University of Utrecht, The Netherlands, in a review of the video-game literature, acknowledged that "those who are least familiar with video games are most likely to believe that they pose a threat" (2003, p. 26). What follows is a tour through the fundamentals of game play and the gaming industry. When you have finished this chapter, whether you are a clinician, parent, or educator, you will know how to choose games with pro-social themes. More importantly you will have some basic knowledge of the research that will help you evaluate the appropriateness of video games for kids at different ages and stages of development as well as determine how much playing time is too much. You'll find that rather than the stereo-typical scene of the child alone in his or her room glued to the computer/TV playing a game, an image of parents and children in the living room sharing the thrills of a game will come to mind. Ralph, a young college student, explained that his dad introduced him to video games and for years they played together. Although his dad continues to play, Ralph rarely plays with him anymore. "He's too slow," the 20-year-old explains! But the shared passion brought father and son together for years and continues to be a main topic of conversation when his dad finishes his regular Friday night game with players his age.

## Online Gaming 101

The chair of the department of popular culture at Bowling Green University said:

> I don't believe anyone ever expected videogames to have such a fundamental impact on our society in so many areas. [They] have become an integral part of the fabric of American life, changing the

way we think, the way we learn, and the way we see the future. (Geist, 1997)

The very nature of video games is different than push media. Video games are an example of push/pull media because they allow a dynamic interaction between the player and the media rather than a passive acceptance of what is delivered. Media like TV are pushed at the observer and the only choice the viewer has is the remote-control button. This offers some control, certainly, but not the sort of creative interactivity characteristic of video games. One young man named George explains that playing a video game is "like being in a movie or a novel where you get to be a character in the unfolding drama and you get to pick what will happen. It's much better than just reading or watching."

Additionally, the realism of video games has increased tremendously over the years since their introduction several decades ago, due to rapid and significant improvements in technology. Thus we have moved from the single dot bouncing back and forth across a screen in *Pong* to being able to pull SuperMario's nose longer and longer as we fly around his three dimensional body from a third-person point of view. Due to this dynamic realism, playing video games allows the player to experience a blurring between fiction and reality. This was no more powerfully illustrated than during the Columbine shootings when one of the shooters commented on the blood spatter patterns to his friend, a variable that the player can control in the video game *Doom*, which they were known to play.

The power of this realism is also illustrated by the military. After World War II too few of the soldiers actually fired their weapons during combat. Soldiers needed to be taught to make killing a conditioned response, thus the military introduced one of the first interactive video games: the silhouetted man as a target. Eventually shooting skills became more fully embraced with the use of video games. Now the military offers a realistic video game as a free download, not only a recruitment device, but also a training vehicle (http://www.goarmy.com/aarmy/index.jsp). This suggests that those that play frequently have already acquired this conditioned reflex; the only difference is that in video games you can always get *un*dead, and you shoot faceless strangers, not friends and neighbors. In police and military training devices that use gaming technology, however, these unlimited conditions do not exist. When a character dies, they stay dead unless you entirely restart the game.

## WHAT'S IN AN ELECTRONIC GAME?

On the simplest level a video game is just a game that is electronically mediated–a pinball game on the computer, or an electronic chess game. As video games cross not only a variety of platforms designed specifically for them, with X-box, Nintendo, and Playstation being the big three, but also across electronic media, they have become much more than an electronic board game. There are handheld devices devoted to play, such as the Sony's PSP or Nintendo's Gameboy, and they are part of the attraction of personal digital devices. Games are now standard on cell phones. Video games can also be played on computers either through the Internet or on CD. Another venue for the gaming industry that are still going strong are the arcades. Just about all the machines in arcades are a form of computer game. Although different physical presentation forms of video games may affect the player, our approach will be to generalize across the physical devices unless there is some need to separate one out.

What are the qualities of video games that are the most popular? A recent survey by Global Market Insite (2005) sheds some light on this question. You can see in Figure 4.1 what players identify as the most attractive components of video games. Respondents identified that the actual playing experience and improved graphics and realism accounted for most of the qualities that gamers liked in games across cultures. Furthermore, the amount of uncensored violent or adult content was not an important reason that gamers liked to play games.

In a more conceptual analysis, educator James Paul Gee (2005) pointed out that the qualities of successful video games include:

1. Projective Identity (part game character, part self)
2. Trajectory (gaming space and history)

Figure 4.1  Results of a survey by Global Market Insite: from the GMI Web
site: Used by permission.

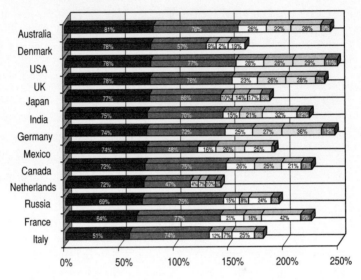

3. Thematic Abstraction (the basics of the game are given and you elaborate upon it)
4. Affordances (various features in the game world that elaborate upon
   our brain's built-in tendency to react to the world in terms of actions
   it can take)

A simple way we can also answer the question about what makes a
video game playable is to look at the types of games. Here is a list of
types of games:

1. *Action.* Action games tend to have a large amount of violence due to
   their fast-paced nature. Action games may pit person against person
   or person against animal/alien. Some examples are *Halo, Star Wars: Jedi
   Knight,* and *Enter the Matrix.*
2. *Adventure.* Adventure games are usually less graphic than action games
   and typically have an element of surrealism and/or fantasy. Puzzle-
   solving skills are needed in abundance. Often these games are combined with a role-playing element and allow the character to initiate
   dialogue. Examples of this genre are *Starfox Adventures, Billy Hatcher,* and
   *Metal Arms: Glitch in the System.*

3. *Arcade.* Arcade games can be almost anything from the violent *Street Fighter* to the classic *Pacman.*

4. *Role Playing.* Role-playing games make the player feel as if he is in the game as a main character with a large amount of freedom. These games tend to be more puzzle-oriented, with some amount of violence. Many feature a lot of myth and fantasy creatures. These games include *Final Fantasy* (any version), *Morrowwind,* and *Legend of Mana.*

5. *Strategy.* Strategy games most often involve tactical movement of troops and/or players. These games may be warfare-based or may be as simple as chess. Combat is often slower paced and allows time for strategic thinking. Some examples are *Advanced Wars I & II* and *Chessmaster 2000.*

6. *Simulation.* Simulation games can involve flying aircraft, such as a jet or helicopter, and may include some plot, tactics, or strategy, or may focus solely on the destruction of enemies. Other types simulate cities, businesses, or families, sometimes even political and economic systems. Some games in this category include *Secret Weapons Over Normandy* and the *Sim* series.

7. *Driving.* Driving games are most often focused on racing, but some are also crash derby or mission-based. Players usually get a choice of car and get better and better cars over time. Some of these games are *Project Gotham Racing, Grand Theft Auto,* and *ATV Offroad Fury.*

8. *Puzzle.* Puzzle games require thinking and logic skills but don't involve a plot or role playing of any sort. A common puzzle game is *Tetris.* Many others are Tetris-like or involve color- or pattern-matching skills.

9. *Sports.* These games put you right in the action of your favorite sports, sometimes in the shoes of your favorite athletes. Games can be simulation or arcade style. Some games are *Tony Hawk's Underground, NBA Live, Madden NFL,* and *Tiger Woods PGA Tour.*

10. *Traditional.* This category includes card games, such as solitaire, free cell, or mah jong as well as electronic versions of traditional board games like *Monopoly.*

In a questionnaire posted online at John Krantz's *Psychological Research on the Net* (http://psych.hanover.edu/Research/exponnet.html) from November 2004 through May 2005, this book's second author, Jayne

Gackenbach (2005), solicited information from players about these types of games. About 350 gamers responded to the questionnaire.[1] In a statistical analysis looking at what is associated with each type of game she found that frequent play, as defined in a variety of ways, was associated with action and adventure game types. This finding was primarily for younger, less-educated males. Younger females did not play overall as often, but when they did play, it was more likely to be arcade and role-playing games. Perhaps, as video-game player Graham Dickie noted, women play to be with their boyfriends. He explained that his girlfriend plays with him and "that's kind of why she is my girlfriend!"

Arcade and role-playing games were also associated with a second group of players who were older and more educated. Strategy, simulation, puzzle, sports, and violent games were associated with each other, but not with age, gender, education or any of the play frequency variables. This data suggests we don't really know much about who is playing these games. It appears that the same people are playing all types of games.

Another question parents often ask is, which types of video games are the most popular? In 2002 the Electronic Software Alliance reported that action games were the best-selling among all console games, followed by sports and racing games. Strategy games were number one for computer gaming, followed by children's and shooter games (Beck & Wade, 2004). The market popularity of these shooter games suggests that, while violent themes are not identified as a feature that players intentionally choose in their game purchases, sadly it has become a predominant selling theme for the gaming industry.

---

[1]This questionnaire asked for various pieces of demographic information, such as sex, age, and education. The next section covered video-game habits and experiences: frequency of playing games in terms of number of days, length of typical session, length of last session, number of different video-game formats played, age when played first game, age when peak playing occurred, who played with. This was then followed by a list of video-game types and the respondent was asked to indicate the frequency with which he/she played each: action, adventure, arcade, role playing, strategy, simulation, driving, puzzle, sport, and violent. The section closed with several questions regarding symptoms of apparent motion during video-game play: nausea, stomach awareness, increased salivation, eyestrain, difficulty focusing, blurred vision, headache, dizziness, and vertigo.

Robinett (2003) offers a structural perspective from *The Video Game Theory Reader* that suggests why people play. The story, the controls, the technical enablers, and the game world, including display, playability, and secrets all add to playability. For instance, if the controls are intuitive, the user interface is easy to learn. Robinett felt the game world size was important, with lots of rooms or levels being preferred. As with the video gamers' self-reports noted earlier, the display features were important, such as bat wings looking like they were indeed flapping. These are all qualities of a game that increase the sense of presence in the virtual reality of the game world. So when teenager Tori explained to his mom why he loved his new game *Halo 2*, he pointed out that he was especially struck by the way the shadows moved exactly as they should along the walls as his character snuck up on another player. He explained that you could identify someone coming with much subtler cues than an earlier version of *Halo*, which did not have player shadows, would allow.

This structural approach to the nature of video games is more formally investigated by Richard Wood and colleagues (2004) from Nottingham Trent University. They asked players about a wide range of game qualities. Their respondents reported preferring realistic sound and graphics, as well as character development over time with the ability to customize a character. Additionally, the researchers identified who preferred relatively longer versus shorter games, and games that a player got absorbed in rapidly. Here an interesting gender difference emerged, as males preferred long-duration games more so than females. In general, rapid absorption was an important quality of a good game for all players. Other characteristics of preferred games identified by players were that they wanted various control options, and liked exploring new areas, being surprised, and fulfilling a quest. Finally and most important was the ability to regularly save the game.

Perhaps the simplest way to understand the appeal of video games is from gamer Steve Reiter, who points out that playing a video game is like reading a good book, but better, because you get to interact with it.

## WHO'S PLAYING?

Video-game play has been around for more than 20 years, but need-less to say, there have been changes and growth in the market. Gack-enbach (2005) examined video-game players from 1998 and compared them to those from 2005. Not surprisingly, today's video-game players are starting younger, play more, and have fewer negative side effects (e.g., less motion sickness while playing) than those surveyed in 1998.

So how many kids play video games today? Preschool children's use of video games was examined by a group of researchers at the Kaiser Family Foundation (Rideout et al., 2003). They found that children from 0 to 6 play video games less than their use of any other media (i.e., watch TV, use computer, listen to music). Only 3% of this group had played a video game compared to 11% who had used a computer and 74% who had watched TV. This, however, does not count the educa-tional games on computer that are really games. The data was based on interviews with 1,000 parents of children, but it may not jive exactly with the memories of some college students, 16% of whom claimed they began playing video games before kindergarten (Gackenbach, 2005). Given that Gackenbach's Canadian college students were 25 years of age or younger, that would make their early years occurring before the Rideout data. Further, given that video-game play continues to dramat-ically increase, there seems to be some discrepancy. Such discrepancies in the data between parents' perceptions of children's media use and reports from the kids themselves, though, is quite common in media effects research.

Not surprisingly, as children get older, their video game use increases dramatically. Another Kaiser Family Foundation Study by Roberts and colleagues (2005) examined media use in 8- to 18-year-olds. Their sub-jects were classified into three age groups; 8- to 10-year-olds, 11- to 14-year-olds, and 15- to 18-year-olds, with peak play in the younger two categories. They found that 60+% played more than an hour a day in these age ranges. More boys played than girls, and for more than twice as long, across age ranges. Black children played significantly longer than white or Hispanic children. Surprisingly, there was no difference in rates of play as a function of parents' income. Perhaps the digital divide is not so clear among video-game-playing children.

As young adolescents move into young adulthood, game-playing strategies continue to evolve. Jones and colleagues (2003) from the Pew Internet and American Life Project revealed that 70% of college students reported playing video games at least once in a while. Of these, 69% said they started in elementary school. Interestingly, Steve Jones of the Pew Internet Organization (personal communication, July 12, 2005) explained that they did not ask about experiences earlier than elementary school. In Gackenbach's (2005) study, about the same percentage (63.5%) reported having started by third grade. This is an important point because children may begin playing video games at considerably younger ages than much of the data suggests. This can have serious implications for the development of the brain, if frequent game play is occurring during those very formative early years.

But game playing is not just for kids anymore. A large percentage of players are adults. One study reported that 60% of online players of *Everquest*, a popular role-playing game, were older than 19 years of age (Griffiths, Davies, & Chappell, 2003). This group of researchers went on to compare adolescent to adult players and found that

> adolescent gamers were significantly more likely to be male, significantly less likely to gender swap their characters, and significantly more likely to sacrifice their education or work. In relation to favorite aspects of game play, the biggest difference between the groups was that significantly more adolescents than adults claimed their favorite aspect of playing was violence. (Griffiths et al., 2004a, p. 87)

This, however, is at odds with the Global Market Insite (GMI, 2005) results noted earlier when collapsed across age (see Figure 4). Although the GMI results likely include more than just adolescents, the largest playing group is mid-teens to mid-twenties. In a personal communication from Brian Noyes of GMI (August 16, 2005), he pointed out that young men 18 to 29 years of age reported that uncensored violence was one reason for choosing a game but not the top reason. As respondents got older, this reason for a game purchase dropped out as an important one. Additionally, the GMI data was generated from 13,000 responses. The Griffiths et al. data was based on 540 *Everquest* gamers. Given the size and the narrowness of the Griffiths data, the findings of the GMI group are likely more accurate, placing violence as one aspect of attractiveness of games, but not the first or second most important quality.

## WHY PLAY VIDEO GAMES?

The baby boomers are concerned about this most basic question. Parents and educators do not seem to understand why their children are so engrossed in this form of entertainment (Beck & Wade, 2004). A father and high school teacher from Ohio explains that he recognizes and appreciates game-playing skill but that he still has concerns about how much time his own teenager and his students are online playing games. However, when he asks them why they are so into video games, they report that it gives them an exciting way to connect with other youth all over the world. One gamer poignantly remarked, "I wish my dad knew what it's like." His friend and fellow gamer Steve Reiter remembers his dad coming into his room while he was playing and asking why he was playing alone in his room. Reiter turned up the volume so his dad could hear the voices of the 15 other people he was playing with online. Both friends recognize but regret that their folks don't really get why they are so passionate about gaming. Here is another example of the generation gap in gaming viewed by Maria during a recent trip. Two well-dressed businessmen are sitting in an airport waiting for their flight. One is in his fifties, the other in his twenties. They are both playing video games on their laptops. One game is solitaire the other is a "shooter" game. Guess which game belongs to each player? If you guessed solitaire with the older person and the shooter game with the younger, you'd be right.

A similar example is offered by John Beck and Mitchell Wade (2004), authors of *Got Game*. During the E3 (Electronic Entertainment Expo) in Los Angeles, they watched the older vice presidents of companies approaching the gaming booths and almost never reach for the controller. Their younger colleagues, however, tried the game first before talking to anyone about possibly ordering it for their customers. Even though the younger businessmen were in public playing an unknown game, it was a natural and comfortable activity central to their business choices, while for the VPs it was a chore. This is a gaming generation gap that these authors argue is occurring across Western society, and around the world according to the Global Market Insite (GMI, 2005) research report.

No one who has ever booted up one of the more popular games can deny the reality that games deliver truly interactive entertainment. The baby boomers and those who are not familiar with gaming don't get this. In fact they are the loudest critics of video-game play. Thus the summer of 2005 saw Hilary Clinton blaming video games for "stealing the innocence of our children" (Leaders, 2005, p. 5) but can you picture sitting down with gamers and appreciating what these kids actually are doing online? Most adults, even teachers, don't appreciate why kids are attracted to gaming. We do not allow kids to have much control in their offline lives. In schools especially, there is not much more freedom for high school students than we give kindergarteners. Like 5-year-olds, 17-year-olds are still told what to do and where to go for most of the school day. With video games you are a star, an expert, a tough survivor. In the game world there are always answers and everything is possible. You learn by trial and error. Problems can be figured out and solved, and there is always a neat and tidy solution to be found. Relationships in the gamer world can vary, but in most games "it's all about competition" (Beck & Wade, 2004, p. 13). Other relationship realities of this world are that they are structured, with single dimensional characters, and you are ultimately alone even if playing with others. Finally, in the world of gaming, young people are in charge. They don't have to pay attention to parents or teachers or other controlling adults. With games, young people have a stake in making the rules. Beck and Wade suggest that this skill allows young people to enter the business world with a very different set of expectations. Some of these are the same ones that have been around for generations, like "if you get there first you win." Others have their own unique implications for how gamers will interact in the world, such as "not succeeding is no big deal"–you can always try again (p. 43).

Gamers Steve and Graham, explain that they have learned from games that if there is anything that can be exploited, it will be, and point to the case of Chinese Gold Farming. This is the practice where Chinese peasants are set up with a computer and Internet connection by entrepreneurial Americans. They are paid to play all day in order to get characters to high levels in a game. Then their employer sells the character online for a substantial profit. Steve and Graham are quick to point out that character selling is quite illegal and was banned from E-bay but continues on private Web sites. But, not to miss a potential market and make a profit, Sony recently announced that it is devoting separate servers to such online dealing of game elements. Online blogger "fire-belly" (2005) elaborates on this new form of sweatshop:

> [What] I will focus on tonight is World of Warcraft by Blizzard Entertainment. In games like this, there are places to buy and sell virtual items. But people have found ways to sell items outside of the game for real money. One way is to sell your password to your account to someone so they take over your character. I personally made 500 U.S. dollars doing this. Companies now are buying up maxed out characters and using them to populate the game with farmers. Characters whose entire purpose is to avoid other contact from players and kill beasts and minions for in game gold, to be sold online for real money. You will know when you see them, they never talk or respond to you and run away if engaged in combat. They kill the same creatures for hours and hours. . . . I witnessed one farmer kill lizards for 4 hours.

This blogger then points out that just because it's high tech does not make it any less a sweatshop. "It's not like they are actually playing the video game either, they have to go to a spot, and kill the same thing for hours . . . 8 or more hours, and they can't talk to anyone" (fire-belly, 2005). It seems, as Steve and Graham pointed out, that they are learning about the realities of the business world in ways they never would have imagined.

Let's return to our question of why people play video games. Goldstein (2003) also answered this question by pointing to a range of psychological and social reasons that kids continue to play video games, from experiencing vicarious excitement and impressing friends, to the lure of facing a challenge. The social element of some gaming, like multiuser domain games (MUDs) attracts females to the gamer's world.

## GENDER AND GAME PLAY

Although females are less likely to play most forms of electronic games there are some that they play more often. Jones and colleagues (2003) reported that women are more likely to play computer (32%) and Internet (15%) games than males (19% and 12% respectively) but less likely to play video games (17% of females versus 53% of males). Their reasons for playing also differed as a function of gender. Jones et al. noted that women were more likely to report playing because they were bored while men played for fun. Also women were "much less likely to believe that gaming improved their relationship with friends than men believed" (Jones et al., 2003, p. 11).

This is illustrated by a recent Nielsen/NetRatings (2004) study that found that for online gamers 35 or older it was women and not men who dominated. Overall this research study reported a slight lead by men (51% versus 49%) in online gaming. However, some online games still show the male preference. For instance, prolific video-game researcher Mark Griffiths and colleagues (2003) reported on two very large surveys from online role-playing games (*Everquest* and *Allakhazam*). With almost 18,000 respondents on a question about gender about 85% were male. Thus, one can conclude that players in general tend to be male more so than female with a few exceptions.

Goldstein (2003), in a review of the gaming literature, noted that this confounding of gender with playing frequency has misled researchers in some of their conclusions about the results of gaming. Results may have more to do with gender differences than game playing frequency differences. This is illustrated in another study about online role-playing games. "Boys in same-sex pairs interacted with one another through action, rapid changes, and playful exchanges. Girls in same-sex pairs interacted primarily through written dialogue. In mixed pairs, boys wrote more and engaged in less playful exchanges, and girls wrote fewer and increased their actions" (Calvert et al., 2003, p. 627). These are play behaviors that are typical of gender and not necessarily of online play per se.

What about females? It has been suggested that "female gaming is the last frontier; 2006 is going to be a milestone year" (Dickey & Summers, 2005). A recent *Newsweek* story suggested that, although 50% of game purchases are done by women, no one really knows the exact percentage of women playing games. It is widely thought that most of the purchases are for males in their lives. The overlooked potential of women as gamers was discovered by the surprising popularity of *Sims* among women. Fully half of players online and off are women who enjoy the relationship and creative aspects. In *Sims*, the player can make her own home and engage in various social interactions. But also to the surprise of the industry, "girls and women started flocking to the fantasy landscapes of sword-and-sorcery universes like World of Warcraft" (Dickey and Summers, 2005). These, as well as other newer online role-playing games like *Fascade* and *Second Life*, are bringing in female gamers.

## VIRTUAL IMMERSION

Two decades of research about the effects of television viewing on young children showing that they cannot tell the difference between advertisements and programming has also shown that younger children who first play video games report feeling "stuck" in the game world (Funk, Pasold, & Baumgardner, 2003). It feels like real life. This immersive experience may in part be due to enhanced telepresence (e.g., felt sense of reality) in video games. Witmer and Singer (1998) found that high telepresence in VR occurred with increases in involvement, control, selective attention, perceptual fidelity, and mimicking real-world experiences. All are aspects present in the VR of video games. A parallel construct for the sense of presence in waking reality is psychological absorption, that is, the degree to which an individual becomes entranced by a book or a movie or simply someone's conversation.

A model of the relationship between the potential variables that affect a person's sense of immersion in video games is offered by Finnish researchers from the Hypermedia Laboratory (Ermi & Mayra, 2005). It is shown in Figure 4.2. Three types of immersion were delineated: sensory, challenge-based, and imaginative. In this flow chart, investigators suggest that these forms of immersion are affected by and affect various elements of the gamers' played and real worlds. They explain that

> **sensory immersion** [is] related to the audiovisual execution of game . . . **challenge-based immersion** . . . is the feeling of immersion that is at its most powerful when one is able to achieve a satisfying balance of challenges and abilities . . . **imaginative immersion** . . . is the area in which the game offers the player a

Figure 4.2 This model by Ermi & Mayra (2005) illustrates how three features of immersion are affected by and affect a variety of other media. Reprinted with author's permission.

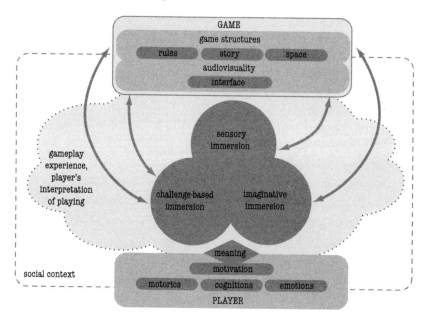

chance to use her imagination, empathise with the characters, or just enjoy the fantasy of the game. (p. 8)

When the concepts of immersion were applied to games based on children's ratings of the games from a questionnaire developed to illustrate each immersive dimension, the researchers found that this is how some games are rated in the dimensions:

1. Sensory immersion

   high: *Half-Life 2*

   low: *Nethack*
2. Challenge-based immersion

   high: *Nethack, Civilization III, Rome: Total War, Pro Evolution Soccer 4*

   low: *The Sims 2*
3. Imaginative immersion

   high: *Star Wars: Knights of the Old Republic 2, Half-Life 2*

According to the research, immersion, the sense that you are really there, is the key factor in describing what video games are and why people play them. The more realistic and complex the immersive experience, the better the game. As far as who plays these games, clearly it starts very young for most people today and continues well into adulthood, but it remains, at least in childhood and early adulthood, still largely a male domain. Now with some understanding of the what, who, and why of video-game play, let's consider its dark and light sides.

## Negative Aspects of Video-Game Play

Immersive video games are part of a new generation of training tools for soldiers. David Grossman, a retired U.S. Army Officer and the author of *On Killing* (1995), explained that soldiers are naturally reluctant to kill another human being. The army calculated that during World War II only 15% of soldiers who had a clear shot fired their weapons. Through the use of various learning methods the shooting response was up to 50% by the Korean War and 90% in Vietnam. An important difference from commercial video games is that soldiers and police, who use similar training techniques, are also taught when not to shoot. In the documentary film *Game Over: Gender, Race and Violence in Video Games,* the filmmakers interviewed army recruiters who freely admit that they look for young men who play video games and offer them the excitement of the game in real life. *Time* magazine reporter Lev Grossman (2005) talked about the popularity of the army's recruitment game as having more than 4.6 million registered players. The game *America's Army* is so true to life because the game designers are familiar with boot camp. They "ride in Black Hawks . . . and wander around a frozen meadow in the dark wearing night-vision goggles" (p. 43). The difference between this violent video game and others, is that it's free (www.americasarmy.com). There is an extreme emphasis on making it authentic. Another important element of the reality of the game beyond ejecting bullets on the correct side of the gun is that if you kill a civilian you are sent to virtual jail.

One of the most widely known experts on the effects of media violence is Craig Anderson from Iowa State University. Anderson and his colleagues reviewed the research on violence in television, films, video games, and music. They concluded that "there is unequivocal evidence that media violence increases the likelihood of aggressive and violent behavior in both immediate and long-term contexts" (2003, p. 81). The negative effects are the greatest for milder forms of violence but negative effects with severe forms of violence are also substantial. They further noted that concern about the effects of violence in video games has recently become a major worry. Parents note the sheer number of hours their children are actively participating in games with violent themes and interactive experiences and worry about the long-term effects. Unfortunately, the Kaiser Foundation study revealed that while 40% of parents have rules about how many hours their children can use the Internet, fewer than 12% of them actually enforce these rules and even know what kinds of games the kids are playing online (Roberts et al., 2005).

Anderson et al. (2003) report that 89% of games had some violent content. These investigators noted a discrepancy in what kids and parents have to say, in "surveys of children and their parents, about two thirds of children named violent games as their favorites; only about one third of parents were able to correctly name their child's favorite game, and most of the time parents were unable to identify their children's favorite game." (p. 101). A word of caution here, the children did not say that it was actually the violence that was their favorite element of the game, but rather their favorite games contained a high degree of violence.

In reviewing the research specifically on the effects of video-game violence on aggression, Anderson and colleagues concluded that the aggressive outcome effect was independent of physiological arousal. Various forms of real-life aggression have been studied, including aggressive behavior, cognition, and affect, as well as helping behavior and level of physiological arousal. The results of meta-analysis on research examining video-game-play effects on social aggression can be seen in Figure 4.3.

It is interesting to note that offline social aggression was not influenced by increased physiological arousal. Further, in longitudinal surveys these reviewers noted that aggressiveness as a personality trait does not predict violent video-game play either, but violent video-game play does predict aggressiveness at a later point in time. The causative relationship has been found across all media (2003).

More recent research also suggests that violent themes in video games have negative offline consequences. In an article in *Communication Monographs*, Williams and Skoric (2005) reported that subjects were randomly assigned to one of two conditions. One group played an aggressive game for about two hours a day while the other played a nonaggressive game; neither group had played that particular game before. Players were asked over the month to report on their aggressive feelings. There were no group differences, therefore playing an aggressive versus a nonaggressive game made no difference in subsequent aggressive feelings. So although some argue that engaging in simulated aggression in video games carries over to real life, there is still some doubt. Let's turn our attention now to what some of the moderating variables for aggressive outcomes from video-game play might be.

Figure 4.3 Effects of violent video games on aggressive behavior, aggressive cognition, aggressive affect, helping behavior, and physiological arousal. Results are shown separately for studies without any of the potential methodological problems (best-practices studies) and those that had at least one problem. Helping behavior in the opposite direction means there was a significant lack of that behavior after playing violent video games. Reprinted with author's permission.

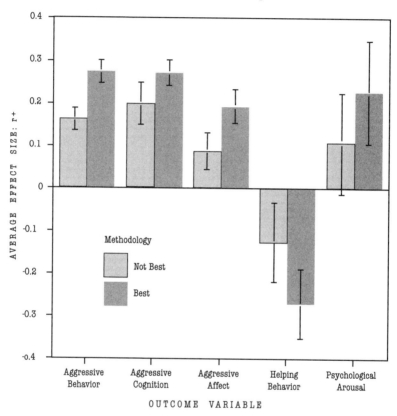

## MODERATING VARIABLES OF GAME PLAY

Most of the research on the effect of violent content in media has focused on older media, like television, music lyrics, and film. However, it's reasonable to assume that this research will be extended to video-game play. Furthermore, an analysis of video-game content, although not as extensive as that on film and TV because interactive media via the Internet is a relatively new phenomenon, has shown that themes of interpersonal violence and themes of aggression are a large part of the industry.

Some of the variables that appear to influence the negative effects of playing video games include age, gender, previous aggressive behavior, intelligence of player, media content aspects, and social environmental elements. Younger children appear to be the most susceptible to the negative effects of media violence, although that does not mean that older teens and adults are not affected. Indeed, most game players concede that they become better "shooters" and "attackers" the more they learn how to play the game. And in fact one gamer commented that he is a better paintball player due to his playing first-person shooter games. In a more serious vein, he also remarked that if he ever had to participate in a war, he would be very glad that he had played video games.

Contrary to common assumptions, Anderson et al. (2003) found little gender effects on how violent media affects aggression. Previous research revealed strong gender differences, with boys more affected by violent content in games than girls. Boys were found to enjoy violent video games more than girls. However, we know that game designers cater to male characters and interests, with the heroes and action characters always being male. Research now shows an interesting gender difference: girls generally prefer fantasy violence, while boys prefer human violence. These are of course in line with traditional sex role-play preferences and consistent with the gender differences in online role-playing games noted earlier in this chapter. One interesting gender difference came up when high-end gamers were asked if they were ever sad during playing a video game. Although the male informants said perhaps they had been when a key character died unexpectedly in *Final Fantasy 7* but only one interviewee admitted to tears at this unexpected turn of events: Sara, age 19, an enthusiastic gamer.

Not surprisingly, highly aggressive individuals show greater effects of playing video games on subsequent social aggression. When video-game violence is combined with high exposure to violence in other media, the risk is especially high. However, intelligence can lead to opposite predictions regarding violent media effects. Anderson et al. report that "statistically controlling for intelligence has frequently lowered observed media–violence correlations in cross-sectional and longitudinal studies" (2003, p. 98). In other words, those with higher scores on tests of intelligence are less likely to be affected by viewing violence in media. Arnold, an avid car-racing gamer, admits that when he drives after having an especially long video–game racing session, he does have the impulse to floor the accelerator and take chances in traffic. But this college student recognizes that such behavior on city streets is stupid and he controls the impulse.

Consistent with our earlier discussion of the importance of the immersive quality of VR in gaming, the more realistic the portrayals in games, the more influence the game has on the player when not playing the game. Identification with the game character is an especially important construct of realism. "When people are asked to imagine themselves as the protagonist in a violent film, the effects of viewing the film are enhanced, perhaps because of the viewers' relatively greater psychological involvement" (Anderson et al., 2003, p. 98). It doesn't take a great leap in logic to translate this to the video–game environment where the player becomes the main character!

However, several personality variables were found to mediate gamer playing style. According to Bolton and Fouts (2005):

> Higher levels of empathy were significantly correlated with the avoidance of killing innocents, i.e., a non-aggressive style of play. Higher levels of novelty sensation seeking were positively correlated to different aspects of aggressive play style; intensity sensation seeking was negatively associated. Contrary to expectation, higher levels of aggression were not consistently related to aggressive play.

The ability for self-reflection is another character trait that may also influence how much violent themes in games move to a player's real-life interactions (Bittanti, 2005). In his presentation at the annual meeting of the Digital Game Researcher Association meeting in Vancouver, BC, Bittanti discussed the extremely violent game *Manhunt*. He captured the inner dialogue of a player who is both witnessing and participating in the extreme violence during the game while at the same time appalled by his very own play. Part of this inner dialogue was the player's awareness that this is something he would never do in real life. Yet the player became curious about himself and why he was engaging in this sort of highly violent virtual life.

Other elements of the media itself can have effects on any resulting aggression. Staldt (2005) argues that investigating the effects of violent video-game play is complex: "the individual player's fascination [with] death and violence is formed by a combination of cultural and social experiences, media biography, gaming experiences, psychological distinctions, and biological/genetic dispositions. Even though how much a player can relate to the character is one element contributing to modeling affects, the overall attractiveness, power and charisma of the perpetrator can be more important" (Anderson et al., 2003, p. 98). Also, if the violence is justified and rewarded in the game, then research shows that there may be an increase in offline aggressive behaviors. There has been little research on why viewing the negative consequences of violence in a video game would not act as more of a deterrent. Researchers point to reasons such as desensitization and normalization of the real consequences of violence as potential explanatory mechanisms. What research there is seems to find an increase in aggression.

Another mediating variable that appears to protect against social aggression for video-game players is the social environment of the players. A culture of learned nonviolence appears to at least partially mitigate against outcomes of increased social aggression from gaming. Anderson and colleagues (2003) reported on an Israeli study where kibbutz and suburban children were compared, with no violent media effects on the former but the usual effects on the latter. The researchers explained that kibbutz children who played violent games were much less likely to be aggressive offline due to the strong cultural injunctions on the kibbutz against violence. However, one has to observe that there is so much violence in their communities against the Palestinians.

Low socio-economic status, another mediating variable, appears to be associated with higher media viewing. It may be that many parents who live in poor neighborhoods are more concerned about the real violence in their communities and prefer that their children stay inside and watch television rather than hang out on the streets. However, children in poorer households did not show more social aggression when compared to children of higher socio-economic status. Anderson et al. warned that "high doses of media violence given to low-SES children is yet another risk factor for adulthood violence in this population" (2003, p. 99). However, we know that kids who are poor, live in unsafe neighborhoods surrounded by drugs, crime, and lack of opportunity, a much more realistic risk to healthy development than playing video games.

The behavior of parents is another mediating variable on the game-playing habits of their children. If parents monitor and thus restrict what children play as well as discuss with children what they have played, then parents can have a positive influence. Additionally, researchers note that there is "little evidence that factors such as *parents'* [emphasis added] aggressiveness, coldness, personality, or viewing habits increase or decrease the effects of exposure to violence" (Anderson et al., 2003, p. 100).

Several types of explanations have been offered regarding how violent video games influence real-life behaviors. Imitation, priming, automatic aggressive cognitive scripts, the kindling effects of arousal, and emotional desensitization are all ways that players internalize violent messages in video games and normalize aggression toward others. Children learn from what is modeled around them. Emotion networks in the brain are primed, as players get aroused and become insensitive to the consequences of violence when playing violent video games.

Goldstein (2003) cautions us not to conclude that playing games leads to more aggression. Goldstein believes that kids' aggressive play, pretending aggressive behavior, and real aggression are different. "In the rare studies that measure both aggressive play and aggressive behavior violent games affect the former and not the latter. The strongest effects of video games are found with the weakest, most ambiguous measures of aggression, those most removed from real violence" (2003, p. 33).

Children's play allows youngsters to model social relationships, learn power dynamics, practice gender roles, and gain a sense of their identity. The distinction between game play and behavior suggested by Goldstein as a criticism of the literature on violent media effects must be received with some caution in the light of the other mediating variables discussed earlier.

Furthermore, some have argued that one cannot simply generalize research on TV viewing and aggression to include video-game playing and aggression. One study concluded that "measures typical of the 'television world' are not related to playing video games" (Van Mierlo & Van den Bulck, 2004) because, among other things, one activity is passive and the other is interactive. In other words, the subtle, long-term effects of television viewing may not translate accurately to the same effects of video-game playing.

## COMPULSIVE GAME PLAYING

Video gaming is rapidly becoming a world-wide phenomenon. Global Market Insite (2005) has done extensive surveys on video games, and had respondents from all but two of the 13 nations surveyed (including some third world countries) reporting that they play video games. Patients at China's first officially licensed clinic for Internet addiction are often addicted to video games (Ang, 2005). For example:

> "I wasn't normal," said a 20-year-old man from Beijing who used to spend at least 10 hours a day in front of the screen playing hack-and-slash games like Diablo.
>
> "In school I didn't pay attention when teachers were talking," he said. "All I could do was think about playing the next game. Playing made me happy, I forgot my problems."

In addition to concerns about violent video-game play, especially real-time effects on subsequent social interactions, another concern is whether video games can be addictive (see Chapter 1 for additional discussion on the phenomenon of Internet addiction). Young (1999) classifies computer-game playing as one form of computer addiction. Indeed, some video-game players express concern about younger family members who couldn't leave the house without their Gameboys in hand. It is important to remember that the number of hours spent using an electronic instrument does not in and of itself equal addiction. Rather, it's the degree to which such use disrupts other elements of life that more directly indicates addiction. Many of the same variables that appear to influence compulsive Internet use are present in video-game play. When does absorption and dedication to playing become mal-adaptive? Several authors have suggested that a moderating variable of compulsive video-game playing may be flow (Chou & Ting, 2003; Kubey & Csikszentmihalyi, 2004), that is, the experience of deep absorption in an activity which is so rewarding that some players are so captivated and continue to play beyond what is healthy.

Goldstein (2003) and Griffiths et al. (2004) report that it is a small percentage of players, mostly boys and men, who are excessive users of video games. Goldstein considers the same variables that contribute to compulsive Internet use may apply to video-game players. That is, the player's passion for the game may vary across time and thus labeling high levels of game playing problematic may not be accurate. He speaks of one Canadian survey where even the highest users preferred to go out with friends and engage in other activities. This is consistent with our video-game informant who tells the story of traveling to British Columbia to meet several people he had been playing *Counterstrike* with online. He explained that he was surprised that they didn't play many video games when they met, but instead went out to the bar and did other activities. This is not to say that problem video-game play does not exist, but only that its prevalence may be overstated.

## OTHER PROBLEMS ASSOCIATED WITH VIDEO-GAME PLAY

While seizures have been reported with some video gaming (Gold-stein, 2003), this seems to be a problem only for those who have pho-tosensitive epilepsy. Under certain conditions, like the hertz level of the screen (higher is less dangerous), and distance from the screen (further is less dangerous), individuals with this condition can be more likely to experience a seizure.

Probably of more immediate concern about video games in general is the fact that women and ethnic groups do not fare well in them Women and ethnic minorities are characterized as weak, sexualized, oppressed, and in need of domination. With a few notable exceptions, such as Lara Croft in *Tomb Raider*, female heroines are rare. More often, women are depicted as sexual objects in games, scantily dressed, existing for the pleasure or domination of the main character . . . a man of course. Female characters often act as an advertising come-on, an enticement for selling the game. Women and young girls are more likely to be seen as damsels in distress with unrealistic body proportions. Men's bodies are also exaggerated in video games, with prominent muscles and powerful physique stressed. However, the potential market of female players has game designers reconsidering how to design and market games to women, as pointed out earlier in this chapter.

Race is also presented in both stereotypical and distorted ways in video games. Most shooters are white, with blacks seen as exotic or dangerous. In either case, gender or race, there is little if any challenging of sexist and racist stereotypes in today's video games (Huntemann, 2000).

## The Light Side of the Force

Most of what we hear from parents, teachers, clinicians, and researchers about video gaming is doom and gloom. It cannot be denied that an entire generation of our youth has become gamers to one degree or another (Beck & Wade, 2004). Could it be that there are advantages to this form of play? Without denying the problems we have just delineated, there are benefits to video-game play that we will now explore.

## Playing Games Makes You Smarter

Anyone who has ever played an interactive electronic game realizes that it improves one's reaction time. You might be surprised, however, to learn that it also improves the ability to process information. For instance, playing Tetris, a puzzle-type game where you have to put falling pieces into appropriate slots resulted in improvements in various cognitive skills in the elderly (Drew & Waters, 1986; Goldstein et al., 1997). Scientists Jackson, Vernon, and Jackson (1993) explored the performance of computer-game-like measures of dynamic spatial ability that are linked to measures of reaction time and speed of mental processing, thought to be linked to general measures of intellectual ability. When a player is seeking out the enemy as the first-person shooter and suddenly five aliens come around a corner, a very fast choice about which to kill first has to be made. Practicing reaction times improves one's ability to process information quickly. When gamers take cognitive tests that measure processing speed, their scores improve.

The major work in the area is being done by Greenfield and Cocking (1996) from the Digital Media Center, who have studied the effects of gaming on a generation of kids. These researchers conclude that game playing increases choice reaction time performance, spatial skills, scientific problem-solving skills, and intelligence. If you think about what kids do in these games, this really isn't very surprising. They are not only shooting aliens but in many games they also have to get their armies geared up for a battle. The *Warcraft* games require mining minerals to make guns, getting food for soldiers, and cutting forests to build ships. This is problem solving involving real-life logistical scenarios.

In fact there is some evidence that the increase in IQ scores and cognitive flexibility that has been occurring over the last half century may be due in part to imagery and electronic technologies like video gaming (Johnson, 2005; Maynard, Subrahmanyam, & Greenfield, 2005). Maynard and colleagues elaborate by pointing out that compared to the introduction of print media, the computer, and in this case video games, has shifted the emphasis from verbal to visual skills.

Kaveri Subrahmanyam and colleagues from California State University at Los Angeles summarized research into the cognitive results of video-game play. While these investigators note that most of the published work is on older generations of arcade-type games, they assert that the fundamental nature of the game has not changed. In fact, it has gotten increasingly better at functionality and representation. "The current generation of games continue to include features that emphasize spatial and dynamic imagery, iconic representation, and the need for dividing attention across different locations on the screen" (2001, p. 13).

In addition, the specific cognitive skills that appear to be improved by players' interaction with games are "mental rotation, spatial visualization, and the ability to deal with two-dimensional images of a hypothetical two- or three-dimensional space" (Subrahmanyam et al., 2001, pp. 13–14). Although not every video-game will be associated with the development of these skills, overall video-game play does improve them. Iconic skill is the ability to read images. In video games, images communicate more information than words, so not surprisingly, playing such games increases this skill. These two types of skills, spatial and iconic, are "crucial to scientific and technical thinking" (Subrahmanyam et al., 2001, p. 14).

Researcher Lyn Henderson (2005) from James Cook University maintains that:

> advocates . . . repeatedly proclaim the educational worth of playing video games. Their contention is that students . . . are switched-off at school but not when playing a video game that demanded thoughtful involvement. (n.p.)

In fact, the educational worth of video games is the focus of the well-received book *What Video Games Have to Teach Us about Learning and Literacy* (Gee, 2003).

## VIDEO-GAME PLAY AND CONSCIOUSNESS

On perhaps the most profound level, there is evidence that video-game play may affect our consciousness. Let's begin with an elemental aspect of consciousness: attention. Green and Baveller (2003) found that habitual electronic game players experience improved visual attention. Visual attention needs to be divided in order to play video games and Subrahmanyam et al. reported that skilled video-game players had "better developed attentional skills than less skilled players" (2001, p. 15). Basically, in order to navigate through the VR of a video-game landscape, you have to divide your attention across the landscape in order to anticipate rapid changes in the situation. Maynard and colleagues (2005) reviewed the attention and video-game-play literature. They found that experimental manipulations with attention as the dependent variable resulted in improved attention among those assigned to the video-game-playing condition. But the type of game can affect the outcome. One study finding was that a battle game was better at improving attention than *Tetris*, a puzzle game. "Video games make it possible for the first time to actively navigate through representational space" comments prominent developmental and media effects researcher Patricia Greenfield (1996, p. 91).

Psychological absorption is another, broader measure of attention. Capacity for absorption can be thought of as a capacity for total attentional involvement. Jeanne Funk and colleagues (2003) at the University of Toledo point out that although absorption in computer-game play is often reported, it is seldom studied. Psychological absorption in gaming has been examined by Glicksohn and Avnon (1997), but they found no relationship between video-game play and psychological absorption. These authors noted that when the game was violent, it "tended to 'turn off' the focus" for their subjects' subjective experiences. In contrast, Woods et al. (2004) found that rapid absorption into games was rated as highly important by gamers. Preston (in press) reviewed the research on absorption and VR immersion, which is most often experienced in video-game play. She concludes that those that score high on psychological absorption:

> evaluate information in a distinct way that links it to self. This strongly implies that, regarding vision, audition, touch and balance, information to more modalities increases absorption. Multimodal stimulation creates a greater sense of presence in immersive VR. Immersive VR has the potential to offer low absorbers access to altered states of consciousness like those which high absorbers experience and also has the potential to offer to us all access to a higher level of consciousness. (n.p.)

Consciousness has also been conceptualized as a type of metacognition, a higher form of thinking. Often called "thinking about thinking,"

In the developmental literature, metacognition is considered a normative, emergent characteristic of cognition, even for preschoolers (Karmiloff-Smith, 1992; Kuhn, 1999) and not unique to gifted children. Elements of consciousness, which may be viewed as a form of metacognition, have been reported as a result of video-game play. For instance, Voiskounsky et al. (2004), Chou and Ting (2003), and Choi and Kim (2004) note a relationship between video-game play and the experience of "flow" as conceptualized by Csikszentmihalyi (1990), which in turn can be conceptualized as another form of psychological absorption.

In a startling series of studies, Gackenbach and colleagues (1998) suggested that video-game play may not only affect the ordinary forms of consciousness discussed thus far, but also affect the development of what contemporary developmental psychologists have called higher states of consciousness. Psychologists have theorized that qualitative changes in cognition do not stop at the abstract verbal level, but development continues to what has been called higher, more complex stages of consciousness (Hunt, 1995). These nonverbal or nonlinear levels are thought to be characterized by spatial thinking, multimodal speeding of processing, and the integration of self and affect with cognition. Theorists suggest that exposure to appropriate amplifiers is necessary to move to the next higher level of consciousness (Alexander et al., 1990). These amplifiers have traditionally included meditation and prayer, recall of dreams and self-reflection among others. Recent research by Gackenbach and colleagues (Gackenbach, 2005; Gackenbach & Preston, 1998; Preston & Nery, 2004) suggests that video-game play may be another such amplifier.

In previous research, Gackenbach (1991) argued that a naturally occurring "virtual" reality (i.e., lucid dreaming) is a bridge to the experience of higher states of consciousness. Lucid dreaming, that is, awareness of dreaming while still in the dream state, is one of various preliminary indicators of the development of higher states of consciousness. The importance of the state of lucid dreaming as essential for self-awareness and cognitive growth, undergirds various inspirational, philosophical, and spiritual traditions including Tibetan Buddhism (Varela, 1997).

From a cognitive science perspective, it has been pointed out (Blackmore, 2003) that our understanding of our sense of self in the world, or our perception of ourselves and the world around us, is a mental construction of reality. Lucid dreaming is another such mental construction, with a different set of input variables than those experienced while awake. During dreams, "reality" is self-generated from memory, rather than from sensory reception as when awake. Gaming provides much the same thing; the input data is technologically generated, rather from our minds, and we can become equally immersed in that electronic "reality." The specific hypothesis of the Canadian researcher Gackenbach is that extensive video-game play would translate into more accurate state recognition in dreams (i.e., an increase in lucid dreams).

Game players are quite aware that they dream about their games. Frequent players report that they often dream that about playing a certain game on the computer. Research has also shown that players of the puzzle-type game called *Tetris* reported intrusive, stereotypical visual images of the game at sleep onset (Stickgold, Malia, Maguire, Roddenberry, & O'Connor, 2000). Among psychology and sociology students, Gackenbach (2005) found that three dream variables showed video-game player group differences; that is, there were more lucid dreams, more dream control, and more observing dreams for the frequent video-game players than for those who play less frequently. These dreams among gamers are illustrated with quotes from video-game players at the same college (McLean, 2005):

> "I don't always remember my dreams when I wake up . . . When I do, though, they're extremely lucid."
> "I've had lots of dreams where I've seen it in first and third person, . . . It's like, 'Oh, wow, now I'm a player in Halo.'"

A student explains how in a dream he became lucid. During a break from school he was playing *Diablo 2* all day and into the night. When he finally fell asleep, not surprisingly he found himself playing that video game. Initially, his point of view in the dream was the same as playing the real-life game, but then it shifted, and he was in the first-person perspective. It suddenly dawned on him in the dream, that there is no such perspective in *Diablo 2*, thus he concluded this must be a dream. This sort of inconsistency between what is recalled and what is viewed is often a trigger for dream lucidity (Gackenbach, 1988).

In another sample taken from an Internet questionnaire with more detail about dreams, Gackenbach (2005) found video-game group differences on two negative dream experiences (nightmares and night terrors) such that the high video-game-playing group reported fewer of these scary types of dreams. This is not surprising if one can assume that nightmares and night terrors are related to waking stressors, like watching a scary movie (Barrett, 2001). One of the oft-cited results of frequent video-game play is an increased insensitivity to violence (Anderson & Dill, 2000), which reasonably might generalize to a lack of concern in the face of violence or threat in a dream. Or alternatively, it could be because avid video-game players are used to having some control over their "reality," so that in the middle of a scary dream, they take control rather than waking in helpless terror. This is supported by Gackenbach's finding of higher-control dreams among avid video-game players.

Although still requiring more research, the thesis of Gackenbach and colleagues that video-game play may be shaping and expanding the growth of consciousness, especially in the area of an enhanced ability for lucid dreaming states, is certainly provocative.

## PLAYING GAMES AT SCHOOL AND IN THERAPY

Video games are not only in homes under the fingers of children, they are also being adapted for a variety of uses in school, clinics, and elsewhere. We've seen earlier how the military is using games as both recruitment and training devices, but schools not only allow the use of games as a reward for good performance, they are now designed to teach. This is most apparent in the preschool-age genre, but as noted earlier, the electronic game is after all a learning device. James Paul Gee, educator and author of *What Video Games Have to Teach Us about Learning and Literacy* (2003), lists 36 learning principles that computer games can offer educators. He explains in an interview how he got interested and how video games can help schools:

> I started only two years ago and, when I did, my fellow academics thought I was crazy. Now there is a gold rush to study games and gaming. What got me into it was trying to play adult games to better understand how and why my then six-year-old played games. I was 53 when I began and was blown away by how long, challenging, and complex games like *Deus Ex* were. Yet millions of people pay a lot of money to buy them and they learn them very well, including kids who wouldn't spend twelve concentrated minutes really learning algebra in school. It dawned on me that good games were learning machines. Built into their very designs were good learning principles, principles supported, in fact, by cutting-edge research in cognitive science, the science that studies human thinking and learning. Many of these principles could be used in schools to get kids to learn things like science, but, too often today schools are returning to skill-and-drill and multiple-choice tests that kill deep learning (Bedigian, 2005)

Goldstein (2003) also mentions that video games are increasingly being used in therapy, either as a remediation tool or as a diagnostic tool. Video games have been used as a therapeutic tool with children who have problems with attention and concentration (Goldstein, 2003; Shaffer, Jocokes, Cassily, Greenspan, Tuchman, & Stemmer, 2001). Psychiatrists Bertolini and Nissim (2002) recognize fragments or characters from the video games in the material of children's dreams. They conclude that due to this radical change in children's play patterns, they must now incorporate video games into their child therapy practice.

Pain management with children has been another important clinical use of electronic games. Reporter Sheryl Ubelacker (2005) reported in Canada's *Globe and Mail* national newspaper on research with children with burns. Pain levels dropped by 75% when they were absorbed in video-game play during therapy for their burns. Although necessarily coupled with analgesics, it was significantly more effective than analgesics alone.

Goldstein (2003) reports on the use of video games for the elderly to help them with various cognitive skills maintenance. In a bit of a turnabout, James Malec and colleagues at the Mayo Clinic examined video-game play as a potential treatment for brain injury. They reported no treatment affects in attention training, which was their goal, associated with video-game play, but noted in their discussion that "subjects in the study appeared to enjoy and to be engaged by the video games. The subjects actively participated in video game sessions even though many were highly uncooperative and distractible in other rehabilitation activities. These observations recommend the diversional use of video games with brain injured patients" (1984, p. 22). Needless to say, the immersive and realistic qualities of games have substantially improved since 1984.

Suzuki and Kato (in press) reported on the development of video games to help children monitor childhood diabetes. They point out that "in this game, players were required to help their characters monitor their blood glucose, take their insulin, eat balanced foods, etc. In a study with 59 patients with juvenile diabetes aged 8 to 16, researchers found that compared to a control group that played a non-medical video game, those who used the *Packy & Marlon* game showed improved communication with their parents about diabetes, and significant positive health-related behavior changes" (p. 22). They add that "Disease-related interactive games may also provide an excellent opportunity for patients to receive feedback on health choices, to rehearse self-care skills, and to access information about their illnesses in a fun context . . . In addition, the social nature of video game play encourages discussions with parents, teachers, and peers about health-related topics found in the games" (p. 27).

## Video-Game-Play Interventions

Despite the various benefits just detailed, parents and teachers are still more concerned than pleased with video-game play. A group of students, while working on a class presentation on video games, found themselves talking about their experiences:

When talking as a group about the effects of violent games on a person after play, Kevin described feelings which paralleled the statistical findings we were reading up on. Kevin told us of how he played many violent games with his siblings and friends throughout his life; he also spoke of how there were heightened feelings of anger and aggression after playing them. This sense of aggression and anger he blamed fully on the vivid depictions of violence in the games that he had been playing. After playing Grand Theft Auto, Kevin wanted to recreate the actions of his virtual character–to continue playing only this time in a real life setting. Now, he never actually did these things simply because he knows better, but it raises the point that violent video games instill a sense of greater aggression in the individual. Sure, adults can hold back on these violent urges, but kids are another story, they simply do not have the neural, physical, and social restraints necessary to redirect aggressive impulses when they are socialized in the opposite direction.

In a review article on video games and aggression, researchers in the Department of Criminology at the University of Melbourne point out that:

> To date, there have been no studies considering the clinical implications of the findings of violent video game research. Clinicians may be justified in arguing that the current body of research is too small and inconclusive to warrant such an exercise. However, the topical nature of the effects of violent video games and the increasing popularity and technological advancement of this media format suggest that it is timely for researchers to develop strategies for managing the negative effects reported in the literature. (Unsworth & Ward, 2001, p. 189)

These authors go on to recommend various cognitive-behavioural techniques as adaptable for the treatment of video-game-related aggressive behaviour. These include, "changing cognitive inferences and dysfunctional schemata, improving control of physiological arousal, and broadening the repertoire of coping responses (including problem solving, modeling, and rehearsal)" (2001, p. 189).

Likewise, Kubey and Csikszentmihalyi (2004) recommend steps in dealing with television addiction, but their recommendations also pertain to video-game addiction. They include things like raising the awareness of both the addicted person and the family members about what is happening without overreacting. Needless to say restricting access to video games can help, but at the same time attractive alternative activities need to be lined up. When the child/adult is playing a game limits on play time should be enforced, and game playing can be used as a reward for participating in other family responsibilities.

Although these things are fairly obvious, the first line of defense when guiding a child in their electronic game play is the rating system developed by the game industry. Like the movie and television industries, the video game rating system is called the Entertainment Software Rating Board (ESRB). "ESRB ratings have two parts: **rating symbols** suggest age appropriateness for the game, and **content descriptors** indicate elements in a game that may have triggered a particular rating and/or may be of interest or concern" (ESRB, 2005). Figure 4.4 is a table with ratings and sample games from the ESRB Web site.

### Figure 4.4 ESRB Ratings*

 **Early Childhood (EC):** Content may be suitable for ages 3 and older. Contains no material that parents would find inappropriate. Examples include *Finding Nemo* and *Sesame Street Compilation (Elmo's Letters and Numbers)*.

 **Everyone (E):** Content may be suitable for ages 6 and older. Titles in this category may contain minimal cartoon, fantasy or mild violence and/or infrequent use of mild language. Examples include *Mario Kart 64* and *NHL 2K2*.

 **Everyone 10+ (E10+):** Content may be suitable for ages 10 and older. Titles in this category may contain more cartoon, fantasy or mild violence, mild language, and/or minimal suggestive themes. Examples include *Civilization IV* and *Capcom TV Games.*

 **Teen (T):** Content may be suitable for ages 13 and older. Titles in this category may contain violence, suggestive themes, crude humor, minimal blood and/or infrequent use of strong language. Examples include *Tactics Ogre* and *Hack Infection.*

**Mature (M):** Content may be suitable for persons ages 17 and older. Titles in this category may contain intense violence, blood and gore, sexual content, and/or strong language. Examples include *Tabloid Beauties* and *Half-Life 1.*

 **Adults Only (AO):** Should only be played by persons 18 years and older. Titles in this category may include prolonged scenes of intense violence and/or graphic sexual content and nudity. Examples include *Grand Theft Auto: San Andreas* and *Leisure Suit Larry: Magna Cum Laude Uncut and Uncensored.*

 **Rating Pending:** Titles have been submitted to the ESRB and are awaiting final rating. (This symbol appears only in advertising prior to a game's release.)

To take full advantage of the ESRB rating system, it's important to check both the **rating symbol** (on the front of the game box) and the **content descriptors** (on the back of the game box).

Here is an example:

*Reprinted with permission from the Entertainment Software Rating Board.

Despite these steps toward creating a ratings system, a special report on video gaming in *The Economist* illustrated the confusion when applying rating guidelines to gaming versus movies. "Critics of gaming object to violence in games, even though it is common in movies. They worry about the industry's rating model, even though it is borrowed from the movie industry. They call upon big retailers (such as Wal-Mart) not to sell AO-rated games, but seem not to mind that they sell unrated movies that include far more explicit content" (2005, p. 55). Play has always been the work of childhood, and now digital and Internet

## Exercise 4.1.   Win, Play, or Lose: Before You Play, Know the Game

*Goal:* To help parents and kids understand the power and effects of playing interactive multimedia games.

*Directions:* Together choose 3 games and evaluate the social messages contained in each. Use the ESRB age rating system on page 144 in this chapter. Now fill in the rubric and then give the game your overall rating:

1 = Lose      2 = Play      3 = Win

| Name of Game | Game:<br>ESRB Rating ⎯<br>Your Rating ⎯ | Game:<br>ESRB Rating ⎯<br>Your Rating ⎯ | Game:<br>ESRB Rating ⎯<br>Your Rating ⎯ |
|---|---|---|---|
| *Market Strategy:*<br>1. What are these games selling?<br>2. What **is the point** of this game? | | | |
| 1. Who wins in this game?<br>2. How does the technology used in this game increase the offline effects? | | | |
| List 5 *positive social messages* reinforced as this game is played. | 1<br>2<br>3<br>4<br>5 | 1<br>2<br>3<br>4<br>5 | 1<br>2<br>3<br>4<br>5 |
| List 5 *negative social messages* reinforced as this game is played. | 1<br>2<br>3<br>4<br>5 | 1<br>2<br>3<br>4<br>5 | 1<br>2<br>3<br>4<br>5 |

*Examples of positive social messages:* cooperation, sustainability, building, win/win, helping others, sharing, problem-solving by consensus, shared power, learning healthy behaviors, respect for others.
*Examples of negative social messages:* competition, polluting, destruction, win/loose, harming others, stealing, autocratic power, modeling unhealthy behaviors, disrespect for others.

technology "are revolutionary in that they socialize children to interact with artificial intelligence on a mass scale from a very early point in their development" (Greenfield, 1996, p. 87). Unfortunately, nanno technology and special effects in the gaming world still add up to old news: video game content is no different than early media in that racist, sexist and harmful stereotypes abound, when we should (by now) know better. While there are clearly negative (social aggression) and behavioral (compulsive use) effects that occur as a result of playing some video games, there are also some positive effects emerging: primarily, an increase in attention and information processing speed, the ability for more mental focus or flow as in lucid dreaming, as well as the opportunity to interact with other gamers while learning real-world problem-solving strategies.

In the real world, kids want to buy games and parents want to know which games to buy. Exercise 4.1 offers one way to understand the social and psychological effects of playing video games so that families can make more informed choices when deciding which games to buy. First, it's essential to identify the marketing strategy: who's selling to whom and why? Next, be able to explain the point of the game. Finally, being aware of both positive and negative social messages encourages players to evaluate whether or not the game is worth playing with others. For example, when boys and girls play together, it is important that sexist themes are not prevalent.

# Chapter 5

# Hooking Up:
# Cyber Sex and Youth

*One of the paradoxes of U.S. culture is that sexual desire is used to sell everything from motorcycles to ice cream, while the sexuality of youth is denied.* (KELLER & BROWN)

*Cyber Sex . . . a pulsating network of switches, a polymorphous perversity of post-human pleasures safe as well as filthy . . . the epitome of disembodied pleasure, contact-free sex without the secretions in a zone of total autonomy. A safe environment free from the side effects and complications of transmittable diseases, conceptions, abortions, and the obligations of emotional need . . .*
(PLANT, 2001, P. 460)

B efore the Internet, sexuality was never so visible and accessible, especially to kids. If you believe the front-page news, cyber sex is turning our kids into sex fiends or victims of online sexual predators. Others believe that it's mostly hype and hysteria, a cover for not addressing the reality of young people's offline lives (Males, 2006). Whether we like it or not, cyberspace lets us all be voyeurs or participants in an expanding world of sexual diversity that ranges from everyday chat to beyond depravity.

We are not prepared for what kids are doing online. However, we do know what they're doing. Whether it's unbelievable blog evidence, an incriminating history on the Web browser, or stories on *Oprah,* it's hard to be quite so clueless anymore. Nevertheless, we still have real problems talking to young people about sex, and so they rarely come to us with their questions. So far, all we can come up with in the digital age are the same old fear-based lectures or worse, admonitions not to *do it.*

As a society we have let a lot slide when it comes to supporting our children's healthy sexual development. Incredibly, while we are so busy being shocked by kids' cyberspace sexual antics we conveniently ignore the fact that we're their role models!

Middle school kids and young teenagers express their sexuality online in astonishing ways, even in ways that they do not consider sexual at all: e-mail, IM, blogging, and all kinds of casual, coded, or explicit sexual chat, uploading seductive photos and cruising cyber sexuality in all its permutations, just like adults. The Internet hasn't really changed kids, they're just doing more of it sooner in more ways. Cyberspace has become an important place to experience relationships, intimacy, and power. Internet technology and media are central to youth culture, whose influence is often greater than the community (Taffel, 2005). They aren't going to give it up.

The trail blazed by cyberspace opened our eyes. It can't be OK for 11-year-olds to look at bestiality sex sites, can it? Parents often ask if "regular porn" online is OK. They usually mean the garden-variety porn in most print and film media. Young teens not only view cyber sex for their own arousal but they are experimenting with group virtual masturbation assisted by multitasking technology. Parents (and therapists and educators) are not sure what to do. Advice from the experts is just downright confusing. Spyware, censorship, and lock down don't appear to work. These tactics silence adolescents, disconnecting them further from support networks, just when they need it the most. Compared to other countries, we do not provide adequate sexuality information, support, and services to adolescents offline. It's no wonder we are at a loss when it comes to cyber porn or cell phone sex.

Cyberspace is the perfect place to hang out. Someone is always there online, but who? Some experts warn that online sexual activities lead to the sexploitation of children by cyber predators lurking in cyberspace (Begner, 2005; Freeman-Longo, 2000). Others remind us that communication technology has always been used for sexual purposes and it's not the Internet that's the problem, but the alienation of youth (Males, 2006; Tapscott, 2005).

Here's what's not working. Parents are advised to supervise all online activities but research suggests that such supervision is more than just ineffective. If this method has not worked in the past (50% of parents don't even monitor their children's TV watching consistently), why should we expect these tactics to be any different with the Internet? (Goodson et al., 2000; Greenfield, 2004a, 2004b; Gross, 2004). The PEW Internet and American Life survey finds that monitoring Internet use can give parents the illusion of control. The reality is that most kids over 14 can go wherever they want to online, at home or anywhere else (Choy, Hudson, Prits, & Goldman, 2003; Lenhart, 2005; Roberts, Foehr, & Rideout, 2005).

Instead of a confusing array of discipline strategies guaranteed to flop because parents can't follow through consistently or keep track of the discipline details, try using the simple metaphor of crossing the street. Parents already know how to teach their kids to cross the street safely. In addition, crossing guidelines also include where you're going and whom you're with. This metaphor can be developmentally applied to the Internet to illustrate how to figure out when children need total control online, when consistent supervision is indicated, and when young teenagers are ready to make their own choices online. The relationship between accountability and freedom in cyberspace is the same as offline; poor choices mean more training and more limits. Parents like this metaphor because it's simple and they can remember the details. Kids like it because it's so concrete and makes sense in their offline world too. Think about it: it works.

It's not just about Internet rules or cyber sex. Our concerns about young people's sexual experiences online are part of a much larger picture. Cyber culture author David Bell believes that the emerging cyber-sexual culture has rewired age-old questions about sex. It's a "complex cultural world with its own codes, norms, and modes of behavior-and maybe its own morality" (2001, p. 390). Further, Internet technology stimulates free expression, diversity, and global connections while reducing the power of censorship (Simon, 2001). Sexuality researchers (Denegri-Knott & Taylor, 2005; Lloyd, 2002; Shlain, 1998) acknowledge that erotic media has always proliferated and profited outside the mainstream, often in direct opposition to community norms and social convention.

Because kids do not get a clear message or enough support from adults about sex offline, they are pretty much on their own in cyberspace. Cyber sex activities have already expanded boundaries and sexual repertoires between genders, sexual identities, intimate relationships, cultures, and countries. These changes are migrating offline (Bell, 2001; Bernoff, Charron, Lonian, Stroh, & Flemming, 2003; Cooper et al., 2002; Greenfield, 2004a, 2004b; Joinson, 1998; Young, 2004). Is this how we want kids to learn about sexuality? Addressing the hot-button issue of young people's access to sexual expression online is the perfect opportunity for kids to take back their sexual health, but only if we know enough to help them understand some of the risks. To measure what you know and what you don't know, it's time to take the Cyber Sex Quiz. As you read the rest of this chapter, it's OK to come back to this quiz and change your answers.

## Exercise 5.1. Cyber Sex Quiz

1. Most adults feel _____and _____ when it comes to young people and sex.
2. Kids don't talk to adults about sex because:
3. List three ways kids experience cyber sexuality:
4. Why apply "crossing the street" discipline strategies to the Internet and cyber sex?
5. The top four risks to adolescent sexual health offline are:

    1)                          3)

    2)                          4)

6. Why?
7. Sex positive media messages are:
8. Sex negative media messages are:
9. Define these online activities, then label as Sex Positive + or Sex Negative –

    a. booty call

    b. bad sex

    c. identity tourism

    d. cyber affair

    e. compulsive sexual behavior

    f. online Sex Ed

    g. cyber porn

    h. trafficking in child porn

10. Explain why the three A's of cyber psychology (Access, Anonymity, and Autonomy) fuel kids' online sexual behaviors.

11. What are three healthy ways kids can express their sexuality online?

12. What are four risks to kids' healthy sexual development online?

13. Why are the five "Cyber Sex Reality Checks" essential before adults talk to kids about sex and cyber sex?

14. Explain how to use the Talking Tips for Making Effective Connections with Kids About Cyber Sex.

## Kids Are Doing *What* Online?

In cyberspace, kids appear to be in charge. At least they think they are, because no one is telling them anything different. Get ready. Here's an eye-opening view of what's up online:

Courtney is laughing when she shows you a photo on her cell phone that she posted to her blog site with the caption "cum." Courtney, age 13, entered therapy because her parents were concerned about her friendships and slipping grades. Courtney is earnestly trying to figure out how to have a life and raise her parents at the same time. "They just don't understand me" she tells you, but apparently 65 million adolescents on MySpace do.

Three girls hang out on a Friday night with their music cranked. The teens vie for space in front of the camera as several classmates, all boys, appear via Web cam. It's Friday night strip poker and the loser has to masturbate to orgasm in front of the camera.

A 20-something college grad, disillusioned and unemployed, spends much of the day gaming, surfing, and file-sharing on Dark.net. After three months of therapy, he admits to "being addicted to" hard-core porn online.

Are these and other cyber sex activities affecting young people's healthy development? The literature on child development may have some answers. For example, Courtney is only 13. Offline research shows that the earlier girls mature sexually, the more they are at risk of being victimized because their bodies are physically developed beyond their psychological and social abilities to deal with the positive and negative sexual attention they receive. In the same vein, most young boys do not receive the information they need when they begin to experience arousal and orgasm. We acknowledge and celebrate girls when they begin menarche but few support what it means for a young boy to experience his first wet dream. As a result, most young males look around for role models for what is acceptable behavior. At this point the mentors are media and cyberspace. Further, parents don't understand their sons' need for information and discussion around positive sexual expression, such as the right time and place, or why their discipline strategies are ineffective.

In the absence of parental involvement, it doesn't take much for the Friday night sleepover to head south. We know that peers influence each other and that it is difficult to resist a group of friends and fun. However, group sexual experiences, especially at young ages, increase the potential for adverse effects. Should these friends have a falling out, the IM history or party photos may be reinterpreted as sexual harassment. Taking your clothes off in front of a Web cam or online booty calls are one wised-up, angry parent away from public humiliation or a charge of child endangerment brought against the absentee parents. Adults are liable for what happens to underage kids in their homes even when they are not there. It's not kids with Web cams or the Internet that's the issue. It's all of the parents involved who think a group of young teenagers can be home alone on a Friday night.

While Internet addiction probably does not exist, compulsive behaviors online do. Jason's loneliness and disconnection from peers at this point in his life may be partially due to his early experiences with hard-core cyber sex. The Internet makes even the most graphic pornography easily available. International black market materials online mean child pornography and snuff films proliferate without risk of U.S. law enforcement and are a click away from what is considered "regular porn." Sex scripts that push the boundary of erotica from the mission position to violent and dehumanizing sexual acts are common. Exposure to violent or degrading cyber porn themes in the early stages of sexual development may permanently alter a person's arousal mechanisms and result in a sexual impulse control disorder (a paraphilia). Although all paraphilias are not harmful to the individual or between consenting adults, some are, such as pedophilia. Paraphilias are difficult to treat and remain a life-long problem because they are *not* curable.

## Some Facts for Confused Adults

At this point you should still be confused and concerned about what to do about kids' online sexual behaviors, and here's why. We do not have enough knowledge about adolescent sexuality and behavior because very little research is funded, primarily due to sociopolitical barriers (Boies, Cooper, & Osborne, 2004). We are afraid that straight talk and clear answers will make kids have sex, so parents and schools remain largely silent or are too controlling, while media sends the opposite message. Poverty, family turmoil, school failure, and community apathy, coupled with untreated psychological disorders all contribute to risks to our kids' healthy sexual development (Collins, 1997; DeAngelis, 2004).

The messages that parents, schools, and the media are sending to kids do not promote healthy sexuality. It is normal for adolescents to experience sexual desire and arousal, to be sexually curious, and to begin to seek intimacy. What do kids hear from adults? "Wait until marriage." Is this reasonable? Is this even reality? No.

### ADOLESCENT SEXUALITY OFFLINE

How long do they have to wait? Thirty years ago the period of adolescence comprised the 5 to 7 years after a person reached sexual maturity, now it's about 14! Here are some of the facts: menarche now occurs between ages 9 and 11, it takes longer to prepare for viable careers, and young people are delaying or avoiding marriage altogether (Moser, Kleinplatz, Zuccarini, & Reiner, 2004). How are we helping kids make sense of this reality and conflicting messages about sexuality and what should they do while they wait?

The reality of adolescent health in general makes waiting without knowledge and support dangerous. In this country we have little scientific knowledge about what is normal or age-appropriate sexual behavior for adolescents and so we can't help them adequately. Most importantly, for cyberspace sexuality, the concept of healthy, deviant, or harmful sexual experiences have no reference group either on- or offline (Cooper, 2002; Denegri-Knott & Taylor, 2005; Noonan, 1998; Remez, 2000). Ignorant or harmful stereotypes about sexuality prevail. All of these factors contribute to the fact that U.S. teens have the worst sexual health of industrialized nations. What are we doing about this? Read on and judge for yourself. According to the World Health Organization, the Sexuality Education Council of the United States, the Centers for Disease Control and Prevention, the National Institutes of Health, the American Psychological Association, the Kaiser Family Foundation, and Planned Parenthood, healthy sexual development for too many youth remains compromised and correlates to teen pregnancy, school drop-out rates, and problems maintaining sexual and reproductive wellness in adulthood. Here's why:

1. We don't teach kids the facts about sex. There is a lack of effective and comprehensive sexuality education in homes and in schools.
2. We don't teach young people the social skills necessary to negotiate consistent safer sex methods and as a result teenagers have three times the rate of sexually transmitted diseases as adults do.
3. Teens have no access to sexual medicine and health clinics in their communities. Young people lack access to and cannot afford reproductive health services and contraception.
4. Teens don't have access to adequate mental health treatment. Adolescents have a 1 in 3 chance of developing a clinically significant psychosocial problem, which often contributes to sexual risk behaviors.

If we want young people to make wise choices about their sexual experiences in cyberspace, what we teach them offline needs an overhaul. Currently the U.S. government funds only abstinence-based sex education in the schools. Abstinence-based curricula do not offer the comprehensive sexuality information that 75% of adults say they want for their children (Roberts, Foehr, & Rideout, 2005). High school family life and sex education classes avoid topics like birth control, masturbation, homosexuality, bisexuality, STD prevention, and diversity of sexual expression, cultural differences, fetishes, or paraphilias (Bearman, 2004; Edwards, 2003). Research shows that the government-sponsored, abstinence-based curriculum has failed in the prevention of teenage pregnancy and sexually transmitted diseases:

> When government severely restricts sex education in the United States, teens who have been kept largely sexually ignorant will be ill-prepared for the possible consequences of engaging in sex . . . Despite the concerns of society and parents, children do engage in sexual acts alone as well as with others . . . it is important to give positive sexual messages to children and to avoid associating sexuality with shame. In general, typical children appear to experiment with many different sexual behaviors during childhood and adolescence. An adult's focus on a particular behavior may have undesirable effects. Prohibitions may actually focus interests on the forbidden. Thus, admonitions may play a pivotal role in determining whether sexual experimentation remains exactly that or becomes more entrenched developmentally. (Moser, Kleinplatz, Zuccarini, & Reiner, 2004, p. 14)

When kids lack sexual negotiation skills, have questions, or are confused about their sexuality, it increases the risk of harm. For example, when young people are pressured by well-meaning adults to take "virginity pledges," they are more likely to feel shameful or hide what they are doing sexually, even online. Unfortunately, in order to remain virgins some teens are engaging in noncoital behaviors like unprotected oral and anal sex, which significantly increases their risk of contracting a sexually transmitted disease (Remez, 2000; Vlassoff, Singh, Darroch, & Carborne, 2004). While some reviews of abstinence-based health education in high school found that initiation of sexual intercourse was delayed for one year when compared to students who did not have this curriculum, when these teenagers did become sexually active they were much less likely to use protection (Bearman, 2004).

How can this be? High school sex educators report that they must teach students that the condom failure rate is 30%, due to breakage and incorrect use, rather than the condom success rate is 95% when used correctly (Bearman, 2004). Further, many teachers and counselors in schools are cautioned not to ask students about their sexual behaviors because there are few support systems in place to help them if they are reported (K. Sutton, personal communication, April 22, 2006). But not even California, the state with the largest school system both in the United States and worldwide, has any plans to educate students and parents about healthy Internet behaviors, much less cyber sexual ones. Joyce Wright, head of curriculum and instruction at the California Department of Education, acknowledges that there are no state-level training opportunities for teachers or workshops planned for parents or students that address Internet safety on a wide enough scale (Joyce Wright, personal communication, July 7, 2005).

If we want to address cyber sexuality, we need to get real about offline sexuality first. Comprehensive sexuality education curricula need an upgrade that reflects the social and sexual realities of adolescents. Even the word *sex* is confusing. To most parents and teens having sex involves coitus only. Many kids believe that they are abstinent and thus still virgins if they engage in oral or anal sex but not genital intercourse. Gay and bisexual sexual behaviors are pathologized. Questionnaires given to teenagers about sex rarely ask about noncoital behaviors, yet health clinics and schools around the country are reporting that even middle-school-age children are experimenting with a wider range of sexual behaviors, including oral and anal sex, same gender sexual exploration, and multiple partners (Remez, 2000). There is a lot kids and parents still don't know.

## ADOLESCENT SEXUALITY ONLINE

If we clearly are not doing enough offline to support healthy sexual development, is there any good news about sex online? Yes. Thanks to the Internet, sex ed and a whole lot more about sex are online. Not only are all government-sponsored and professional health organizations in this and most countries accessible via the net, any question can be asked and answered. Young people can now get this information when they really need it, even in the middle of the night, from their cell phone, at a party, or in an emergency. No topic is off limit, from "Am I normal?" to "Should I have sex to get this guy/or girl to like me?" to "I have this red spot on my genitals" or "I think I may have been sexually assaulted while I was passed out at a party. My parents will freak out, what can I do?" Before the Internet, teenagers relied on each other for this kind of help or didn't get any at all.

Few parents, teachers, and counselors are comfortable or knowledgeable enough to deal with adolescent sexuality. However, with the Internet, everyone can explore sex sites and compare the information. The Sexuality Education and Information Council of the United States (SEICUS) is a good place to start, but there are others. Find the messages that work for you and your adolescent and have frequent conversations about the topics presented. Go online together. Even kids who would not bring up their own sexual issues will often use the experience of "their friends" to test the waters with their own parents. So don't blow this opportunity.

Ending the silence and misinformation around sexual concerns brings this important area of young people's development into the open and helps to end the embarrassment and poor health choices that result from misinformation and stigma. Talk to sexuality experts online. Dr. Drew, at drdrew.com, from the original radio show *Loveline*, is a physician with a lot of clout and charisma. Teens listen because Dr. Drew gives clear, professional advice, focuses on personal responsibility and safety, and explains how to understand, respect, and promote healthy sexual development.

Experts like Dr. Drew, sexuality information sites like seicus.org and youth forums give young people information and support to guide sexual decision-making offline. But what about what Courtney, Sam, Jason, and other teenagers are doing? Switching genders, exploring different sexual identities, group sex with strangers, or your classmates: it's all available. Cyberspace offers us a window into the sex lives of young people, "a literal and metaphorical screen for representing two major adolescent developmental issues: sexuality and identity" (Subrahmanyam, Greenfield, & Tynes, 2004, pp. 651–652). While it's tempting to focus on the dangers of online sexuality, it's important to remember that one of the reasons we have not been very effective in helping kids avoid risk behaviors is that we did not know (or want to know) what they were really doing. Now that we do, it may be more than we can handle. Barrett Seaman, in his book *Binge: What Your College Student Won't Tell You* (2005), explains the "Online Booty Call":

> In the lexicon of the hanging-out/hooking-up culture is the booty call a more specific invitation than the ritualized random hook up?. Booty calls are often issued electronically through the campus instant messaging system because face-to-face encounters require work and commitment and no assurances of sexual favor. (p. 45)

Is it economical in terms of emotional cost to advertise or solicit sexual connection online? Are these cyber hook-ups meaningful and safe? Does access to a greatly enlarged online applicant pool of potential sex partners increase one's chances of finding satisfying sexual connections or is the digital dating ritual a recipe for only one night stands or a precursor to future problems with intimacy? We need to be very careful when drawing conclusions from these types of vignettes because we need to hear from more young people about how sexuality online affects them. Jeremiah shares another experience about hooking up in cyberspace:

> My name is Jeremiah but it used to be Hope. I am a Transgendered person. I am also diagnosed with Asperger's Syndrome. Asperger's Syndrome is a high-functioning form of autism, which is a developmental disorder that affects communication, social skills, social interactions, and sensory development. In the autism chat room, I learn how to communicate with other adults like myself, so I could go out into the real world and feel more comfortable meeting new people and making friends. The Internet has helped me to learn more about myself and my disability. As a result, I have become more comfortable as a transgendered person. I am learning to accept and respect myself both online and offline. Online other people with autism have made a difference in my life and I know I have made a difference in theirs.

Online, I can copy conversations. I have transferred what I learned about social interactions online to the outside world. One struggle I have faced online and offline is when people overstep my boundaries or when I overstep theirs. I particularly remember an autistic adult that tried to get sexual with me online and was asking me all my personal information. This made me very uncomfortable. He was really pressuring me and I made the mistake of giving him my phone number. Also, I think he might have been just pretending to have high-functioning autism. His behavior was very unacceptable. He got kicked out of the chat room because of it. With so many people overstepping boundaries online, I eventually found myself doing the same thing, engaging in sexual acts online, even with people outside of the autism blog. I found myself making sexual advances when the other person didn't expect it or consent to it. I lied about myself and described myself as someone I wasn't, at times changing genders and my weight and appearance. It is almost as if it was some sort of sick joke I was playing or something. This is not what I would normally do. I usually have manners and here I was making people uncomfortable by trying to get sexual with them in cyberspace. Now I have learned to be online in a way that isn't intrusive. Sometimes when I'm on the Internet I pretend I'm a fish hiding deep underwater making conversation with other fish underwater. I then go out into the real world and practice how to be with other people.

Jeremiah explained that there is very little that stops us from acting disingenuously or impulsively in cyberspace, especially when others model it. Remember it is not the fact that kids engage in sexual behavior (because they've already been doing this offline for generations) but it's about how technology expands the potential for problems. Dating and mating are different now and because there are many more ways to be sexual in cyberspace, sex ed becomes even more essential.

We've already learned that it is not easy to make assumptions about adolescents' sexual behaviors offline. The same is true online as well. Cybersex research is limited, anecdotal, or conducted with specific populations and not generalizable to adolescents. For example, studies that examine young people's cyber sex behaviors are often based on small samples of college-age youth and do not really advance understanding of other youth populations (Gross, 2004; Huffaker, 2004). Despite the lack of online adolescent sexuality research in this country, we are learning from research conducted in other countries. Here's what we know so far about online sexual behaviors of young people.

In Sweden, where there is no prohibition against asking young teenagers about their sexual behaviors, several studies have compared the relationship between youths' online pornography consumption and their offline sexual practices. A recent investigation of cyber sex habits found that adolescents who accessed cyber sex materials 1 to 3 times per day also engaged in offline sex two years earlier than the general youth population (at age 15 rather than 17). Swedish teens also reported that they initiated more kinds of offline sexual behaviors as a result of viewing different sexual scenarios online. Investigators found that youth who accessed online pornography tended to use condoms during vaginal sexual intercourse only. Swedish youth also reported a higher likelihood of engaging in unprotected anal sex as a result of viewing explicit anal sexual contact online, because cyber sex scenarios involving anal sex did not emphasize safer sex practices and there was no need to practice birth control (Haggstron-Nordin, Hanson, & Tyden, 2005).

Interestingly, when it comes to viewing cyber porn there is gender parity in Sweden. In 1996 researchers discovered that 98% of young men and 72% of women aged 18–24 viewed pornography online. More young women accessed online sex sites than 50 to 65-year-old men. However, several years later, researchers from Uppsala University investigated the sexual habits of 1,000 Swedish women aged 18–24. They found that 80% had consumed Internet pornography, and one third of these respondents believed that this had influenced their offline sexual behavior (Haggstron-Nordin, Hanson, & Tyden, 2005).

In this country, Internet cyber sex research is primarily limited to college students. Before 1998, researchers found that few students accessed sex sites online (Morahan-Martin & Shumacher, 1997). However, three years later Goodson and her colleagues (2000) conducted one of the first studies that examined the psychological correlates of sexual arousal of college students when viewing online sex sites. They found that 43% of these college students interviewed admitted to accessing sexually explicit materials online for sexual arousal. Also, Sylvain Boies (2004) from the University of Victoria in British Columbia and his colleagues from Johns Hopkins University School of Medicine recently surveyed 760 university students' online sexual habits. These researchers found that 64% of their sample acknowledged between 1 and 3 symptoms of problematic online sexual activities. These students defined problematic use as causing academic or interpersonal problems, psychological distress, an increasing need to engage in more online sexual activities, and a tendency to engage in cyber sex to alleviate boredom or depressed mood. The authors report,

> Young adults who use the Internet to meet needs relating to social support, environmental mastery . . . and to increase their knowledge of sexual matters and explore their sexuality, are *less* connected to offline life. This disconnection looks as if it increases with sexually focused Internet use. (p. 216)

However, the authors also caution that these results are limited to college students. It may well be that social isolation predicts more frequent cyber sex activities among users rather than the other way around. Additionally, we must remember that college students are not a representative sample of adolescent populations in the United States.

When it comes to sexual behavior in cyberspace, there is a pervasive but unexamined threat to kids' healthy sexuality and it's neither Internet porn or cyber predators. Sociologist Mike Males (2006) speaks out against the misguided hysteria that persists about protecting our children from online sexual predators and reminds parents that sex crimes, sexual assault, and sexual abuse are much more likely to occur in children's homes, communities, and churches than as a result of a pedophile's online lure . However, this does not mean that there are no risks to kids online, it's just not the one most parents think it is. The National Science Foundation's Digital Media Center at UCLA analyzed youth IM, e-mail, and blogs over the last five years and discovered such a disturbing degree of negative communication patterns that they believe it is likely to alter a young person's psychosexual development. "Online core issues like identity and sexuality become amplified and transformed" by social discourse that is combative and sexualized (2004a, p. 761). More pervasive and insidious than cyber predators, this type of conversation is clearly present offline but somehow it looks worse when captured verbatim online.

A good way for adults unfamiliar with the pervasiveness of sexualized culture online is to visit youth blogs and judge for themselves. Bad netiquette is contagious. In the exponential online world, Internet researchers Boies, Cooper, and Osborne (2004) discovered that kids' exposure to graphic sex does not appear to be as much of a problem as the social modeling occurring in everyday chat where sexist, racist, and angry conversations are commonplace (Greenfield, 2004a, 2004b). Linguists and psychologists have analyzed chat-room dialogue and find that adolescents are constructing their own cyber culture and language. In both monitored and unmonitored teen chat rooms the talk ranges from unsolicited sexual advances (want to *69 me?) to coded sexual allusions (who likes French?). Interestingly, many examples of online chat would be considered sexual harassment or bullying in face-to-face converstaions but is the accepted currency of discourse in cyberspace (Subraham, Greenfield, & Tynes, 2004). Bad netiquette is visible online, but why?

Anyone who works with youth and families knows the stressors young people encounter. Should we expect it to be any different online? Family violence, overt and covert forms of racism, various kinds of sexuality-bashing, bullying, sexual harassment, and date rape are all issues that adults have not addressed effectively enough with youth offline. In spite of these trends or perhaps because of them as any young person will tell you, there is also a good life online: many meaningful conversations, social encounters, altruism, and political activism present (Lloyd, 2002). Even if your own child is not on MySpace, open forums, browsers, and anecdotal evidence let us be a fly on the wall in cyberspace. Maybe we can learn something by hanging out where kids do.

## Sexual Messages in Media

Sex thrives online in the daily discourse of youth, so much that researchers believe this will change kids' sexual and social development by the force of critical mass, if nothing else. But another contender that has the power to change kids was born again online: digital media. The Internet is the connectivity that makes media so easy to digest. It's become such an essential part of young people's reality that few realize that it's *not* reality. All media, from ads, to music, to film, contain sexual messages but what exactly media says about sex is difficult to interpret apart from the technology that serves it up. Are these images and activities, many of them interactive, "live" and multisensory, going to rewire brains and sexual repertoires? Labeling young people's emerging or exploratory sexual behaviors as either healthy or harmful as a result of media's influence is difficult enough on ground but in cyberspace it's really tricky. However, in cyberspace we have an opportunity to understand kids' sexual behaviors online that co-occurs with media because so much of it is visible.

When clueless parents discover their kids' online booty calls or Web poker, they are shocked. Stories like Jeremiah's, Jason's, Sam's, and Courtney's illustrate how the Internet creates ways to express sexuality. Some of it's old stuff with a different wrapping, no longer hidden, shameful, or even private. If media promoted positive models of sexuality and relationships, taking the secrecy out of sexuality could be beneficial to adolescents. Maintaining sexual and relational intimacy is hard. Unfortunately sex as portrayed in most media is the antithesis of what works in reality. Let's start with the most basic sexual act: intercourse. Everything from hardcore pornography to Hollywood films both on- and offline rarely include safer sex practices or even dialogue about consent or protection. It gets in the way of the story line or the camera. Behavior analysts and the sexual health of adolescents suggest that teens are influenced by this model offline more than we like to admit (Moser, Kleinplatz, Zuccarini, & Reiner, 2004).

Besides the lack of safer sex, another disturbing model emerges in graphic sex scenes involving intercourse. Is it OK to be aroused by others who put their own health at risk for your sexual gratification? The actors in these films are real people. Even the sex industry admits that unprotected vaginal and anal intercourse pose significant health risks for sex workers and pays them more to engage in unsafe sex. Is this a good way to get off? The increasing sophistication of interactive media technology and greed will continue to expand kids' access to cyber porn, so we had better examine the messages in media and specifically sexual media more carefully. Roy Noonan (1998), research professor at New York University, captures the issue succinctly:

> Cyber sex is a compendium of the good, the bad, the beautiful, and the ugly. As such, one could argue that it is reflective of sex in real life, with the bad and the ugly often being the chief focal points for many people in the United States and elsewhere. Yet, the good and the beautiful are well represented in both arenas. The problem of course is in distinguishing between the two groupings because for too many people, there are simply no such distinctions. As a result, on the Internet, as in real life, it is left to the individual to navigate her or his way throughout the dizzying array of sex information and services available. As a result too, there are often those who seek to impose their own agendas and viewpoints on what others may view or the services to which others may have access. Therein lie the daunting qualities of the Internet and efforts to bring sanity to the sexual global village. (1998, pp. 143–144)

## CYBER SEX

How far will the cyber porn industry push the boundaries of sex, relationships, gender, and sexual identities? Are sexual materials that bend or break socially acceptable norms harmful if these are the first sexual materials adolescents are likely to view? The issues are expanding. The Internet Corporation for Assigned Names and Numbers (ICANN) has just approved the new domain ".XXX," where sexually explicit sites are asked to voluntarily move to this domain. However, ICANN admits that there is no way to effectively police, censor, or monitor the 15-billion-dollar cyber sex industry (Wagner, 2005).

With no limits and no way to monitor pornography online, we have to find effective ways to teach parents and kids how to evaluate "the good, the bad, the beautiful, and the ugly." While studies suggest that 50% to 75% of men and women worldwide view online porn, cyber sex research tends to investigate socially unacceptable activities like sexual offending, child pornography, or cyber affairs. As a result, we must not conclude that all cyber sex experiences are harmful. Sexual experiences online, in the absence of compulsive use and violent or exploitative cyber sex content, represent a healthy exploration of sexuality and connections with others

(Cooper & Griffin-Shelley, 2002; Noonan, 1998). For kids' sake we have to get better at separating out harmful from healthy exploration.

Central to understanding both healthy sexuality and kids' exposure to cyber porn is the concept of obscenity. We have laws that are supposed to protect children from the harm of these kinds of materials. In *Miller v. California* (1973), the Court, defining it as "appealing to prurient interests, depicting sexual conduct in a patently offensive manner, and lacking serious literary, artistic, political, and scientific value," ruled that obscenity was to be judged by contemporary community standards. What are contemporary community standards in an online and global community? When it comes to cyber porn the scope of available materials is almost beyond comprehension and certainly no community standards exist. For example, in some communities sexual behaviors like sex before marriage or anal sex are socially accepted while in other locations the same activities could be illegal or even result in death (Bhugra, 2000).

If there is no way to judge the harm of cyber porn in cyberspace by one community's standards then is censorship what we have left? Marjorie Heins, First Amendment attorney and author of *Not in Front of the Children: Indecency and Censorship and the Innocence of Youth* (2001) believes that all censorship is ineffective and does not allow young people the autonomy necessary to make good decisions about important issues. Adult-imposed restrictions leave young people ignorant and unable to problem solve later in life. Cyberspace enables diversity of sexual expression to proliferate and thus nullifies the power of censorship and authority (Simon, 2001).

Now what? If there is no way to judge obscenity, censor, or enforce standards in cyberspace, how do we protect kids from bad sexual experiences online? Once again we look to the child-development research. The data suggest that early exposure to adult-oriented, explicit sexual activities accelerates young people's sexual development often at the expense of other important areas of growth and thus parents should monitor their kids' access to online sexual materials (Brown, Cohen, Chen, Smailes, & Johnson, 2004; Roman, Martin, Gendall, & Herbison, 2003). How can this work when we already have mentioned that less than 50% of children younger than twelve are monitored by parents when on the Internet and supervision almost disappears as kids get older (Roberts, Foehr, & Rideout,

2005). Ironically, just when young people really need adults to stay connected, parents drop the ball and kids boogie into cyber space.

And boy, what a party! Web cams, cell phones, and iPods synchronize cyber sex to the party: text messages with guest lists, location, and intoxicants, e-mail photos of naked body parts, and yes, portable porn. Digitized cell service enables customers to *play with* a virtual sex partner on cell phones and/or Ipods (King, 2005). In Western Europe there are already 21 million digital cell phones offering sex, bringing in one billion dollars in yearly profits. Analysts project triple growth in the next three years as the market expands into North America (Bryan-Low & Pringle, 2005). Digital sex sells.

What's a parent to do? Take away the cell phone, hide the Web cam, ground the kids? Consider a mother driving a car full of seventh-grade girls talking to friends on their cell phones and to each other at the same time. The conversation is peppered with sexually graphic comments like "how wet" and "dude, you ran down the batteries in my vibrator." Should this mom say something and risk embarrassing her daughter? Parents and kids definitely need to talk more but not until you know what you are doing. Here's a good rule of thumb. If you get upset and can't keep your emotions cool don't say anything yet. If you haven't practiced what to say in these kinds of scenarios, then don't say anything yet. If you feel you don't know enough about adolescents' sexuality and their online lives, don't say anything yet until you become more informed about normal adolescent sexual development and cyber sexuality. If you think what you overhear or what you discover is awful don't say anything yet. (Exception: if their life is in danger.)

Because the adolescent stage of development encompasses such a range of maturity and readiness to be sexual there is no one-size-fits-all approach with any teenager. Teens like Jason, Courtney, and Sam need different strategies based on their psychosexual development and individual needs. But they all benefit from noncritical advice. At 13 Courtney tries to project an older image and is using Internet media to do it. Rather than censor her from this expression, Courtney can be encouraged to expand her identity and efficacy beyond the socially constructed view of females sexualizing their power in order to have any.

Sam, on the other hand, is using cyber porn for sexual arousal and experimenting with online booty calls. His solicitation for oral sex may be perceived as harassment, a joke, or a welcome invitation but he is too inexperienced to understand the difference. He has already become adept at hiding what he is doing from his mother. Sam would benefit from learning more appropriate sexual negotiation skills and also how to evaluate sexual and social messages in cyber porn so that he does not model negative ones offline.

The first step for parents is to connect more with their kids' everyday lives. This opens the door to dialogue about all difficult topics, not just sexual ones. Next, conversations between parents and kids must occur way before puberty. It's easier to have a discussion about sexual behaviors when your own child is not directly involved. Kids talk about sex all the time but rarely to adults, because few really listen without freaking out. A large part of being more effective with young people about sexual health is learning how to really communicate with kids about the messages and meaning in all media, especially pornography and cyber sex. Really communicating means listening to them, not lecturing, and not getting upset.

The exercise "Exploring Your Attitudes About Cyber Sex" lists some examples of the most common cyber sexual activities. Encourage your child or teen to be clear about what he or she really thinks, whether it's OK or not OK, at what ages. Including possible online and offline effects illustrates that the power of media extends beyond the media itself. Clarifying your attitudes about these cyber sex scenarios before you discuss their cyber sex behaviors goes a long way toward defusing emotional or judgmental reactions especially if there is disagreement.

## Cyber Sex Reality Checks

1. Keep your emotions cool and be cool.
2. Defer judgment.
3. Don't remain clueless. Get some clout. Become more informed about normal adolescent sexual development, media, and cyber sexuality.

## Exercise 5.2.  What Do You Really Think About Cyber Sex?

| Common Online Sexual Activities | OK | Not OK | Age Range | Possible Online Effects | Possible Offline Effects |
|---|---|---|---|---|---|
| *Sharing sexually explicit online materials with friends.* | | | | | |
| *Masturbating while viewing cyber pornography, alone: in a group:* | *alone* *group* | *alone* *group* | *alone* *group* | *alone* *group* | *alone* *group* |
| *Participating in sexually explicit online chat with friends.* | | | | | |
| *Participating in sexually explicit online chat with someone you have never met.* | | | | | |
| *Viewing unusual or deviant cyber sex sites.* | | | | | |
| *Viewing cyber sex sites with violent or demeaning content.* | | | | | |
| *Exploring different sexual identities online.* | | | | | |

4. Begin to talk with, and listen to, your kids about sex and cyber sex well before puberty by discussing facts and hypothetical scenarios. Include topics like knowing your body, appreciating your private sexual zones, menstruation, wet dreams, masturbation, sexual differences, solo verses group sexual experiences, gender roles,

sexual identities, sexual respect, waiting until all of you is ready not just your sexual organs, sexual negotiation and consent, sexual pleasure, sexual risk, and what it takes to maintain lifelong sexual health.

## BAD SEX

Now that you have some foundation in adolescent sexual health, sexual media, and pornography and have explored some of your attitudes about cyber sexuality together with your kids, it's time to convince them to avoid the real risks online. But first, here's a recap of what you've learned so far:

- We are not prepared for what kids are doing online because we don't know enough about what they are doing offline and we are poor role models.
- Kids are disconnected from adults and community. We've lost our clout so they tune us out.
- Cyberspace is a Power Point presentation of youth culture and sexuality.
- Parents already don't monitor kids' media use consistently; old rules like silence, judgment, and censorship do not give kids what they need to make healthy decisions.
- The status of adolescent sexual health in the U.S. is among the worst in developed nations.
- Kids aren't learning about sex from us, they're learning it online.

Most cyber sexual activities are not harmful but there are four kinds that do have the potential to harm young people's sexual development:

1. cyber affairs
2. compulsive cyber sexual behaviors
3. cyber child pornography
4. early and repeated viewing of deviant cyber pornography.

In 1999, before broadband and gender parity online, MSNBC surveyed 9,177 adults (86% male) about their online sex habits. Seventeen percent reported signs of sexual compulsivity online and 13% reported generalized psychological distress. But it was not clear whether theses individuals develop problematic sexual behavior as a result of their online activities or if pre-existing psychopathology was somehow triggered by online sexual experiences (Cooper, Scherer, Boies, & Gordon, 1999).

Social scientists from the University of Michigan suggested that adults who engaged in compulsive cyber sex activities one to three times per day were those with few offline social bonds and lack of engagement in a deviant lifestyle (Stack, Wasserman, & Kern, 2004). Investigators wondered whether the frequency of viewing cyber porn was a function of the addiction potential of the Internet or primarily a compulsive sexual behavior that had just migrated online. Adults who admitted they were behaviorally addicted to the Internet itself were compared to those who went online for sexually related purposes. Results suggest that the anonymity and disinhibition generated by the Internet fueled secondary addictions of a sexual nature, including self-reported, compulsive cyber sex activities, cyberstalking, and online infidelity.

Pamela Paul's book *Pornified: How Pornography Is Transforming Our Lives, Our Relationships, and Our Families* (2005) discussed the effects of Internet porn on society. According to Paul, Internet technology is partially responsible for the increase in file sharing of pornography materials depicting children. Paul asserted that the availability of child pornography via the Internet accounts for the increase in sexual offenses against children reported by the F.B.I. in the past five years. However, Paul's research focused only on men who admitted that their use of pornography caused problems in their lives. Her book did not include the opinions of women, men without cyber sexual problems, or couples.

Cyber affairs are another area of cyber sexuality that has harmful offline effects. Earlier research found that more men viewed cyber sex online but now the gender differences have largely disappeared. However, men and women do have different ways of expressing sexuality online. Men tend to explore sexual activities online for arousal while women engage in emotionally intimate cyber chat first that then progresses to sexual intimacy (Boies, Cooper, & Osborne, 2004; Subrahmanyam, Greenfield, & Tynes, 2004). Between 30% and 50% of these relationships eventually meet offline (Stack, 2004). Women who discovered their partners were having a cyber affair appear to experience more negative effects than men do when the tables are turned. Women felt devalued, excluded, and inadequate sexually when they compared themselves to their spouse's cyber sexual partner (Bridges, Bergner, & Hesson-McInnis, 2003).

By far the most urgent question regarding cyber sex is whether the use of child pornography increases child sexual exploitation and sexual offending either online or offline. The increased capabilities of file sharing of child pornographic materials appear to contribute to an increased risk of offline sexual offending for adults with a sexual interest in children (Begner, 2005; Freeman-Longo, 2000; Quale & Taylor, 2003; Thornburgh & Lin, 2002). In addition, Internet technology itself acts as a trigger for pedophiles to sexually exploit children because it enables them to groom multiple victims simultaneously. A massive distribution of sexually explicit materials on the web also increases the likelihood that children will be exposed to them and, because they are still maturing sexually, the potential for harm is increased. (Nichols & Nicki, 2004).

Does frequent use of cyber porn with sexually deviant content increase the risk of a young person developing a paraphilia? It's a reasonable assumption based on what we know about how paraphilias develop offline. Research suggests that early exposure to adult sexual experiences or pornography with violent, unusual, or dehumanizing content can disrupt the trajectory of a young person's sexual response. Because sexually explicit materials are so easy to access online there is a greater likelihood that children may repeatedly view these materials before their sexual repertoires mature enough so that their sexual development is not altered in harmful ways.

## HEALTHY SEXUALITY

Most online sexual experiences allow young people to explore their sexuality safely, practice being sexual, obtain accurate information about sexual health, and ask any kind of question. Boies and colleagues (2004) discovered that over 50% of college men and women reported satisfaction with their online sex lives. Eighty-nine percent of these college students stated they had benefited from their cyber sex experience and 50% said it increased their comfort with sexual issues. These young adults obtained sexuality information, experienced sexual pleasure, and initiated or maintained meaningful intimate relationships. In contrast to earlier research that suggested heavy Internet users were more likely to be socially isolated, the college students in this study reported good adjustment with offline friendships and family as well.

However, it remains to be seen how online sexual activities will eventually affect sexual intimacy offline, especially when today's first generation of digital teens become adults. Nevertheless, most adults agree that they want their children to learn how to make healthy decisions about their sexuality now and as they mature, in part to counter the negative messages in sexual media and their own challenges in sustaining adult sexual and relational intimacies. Cyberspace can be used to teach kids how to evaluate the difference between sex positive and sex negative media messages. Cyber sex is exciting. When it comes to adolescents and cyber sexuality, parents and educators are clearly not in control of what kids can do and see–but were we ever? Hopefully, cyber sexual expression will never replace the real thing but cyber sex options give the real thing a much needed upgrade and a reality check.

Adults are not experts in sexuality just because of sexual maturity. Effective dialogue between parents, educators, and kids means a lot more honesty and a lot less criticism about kids' lives. Remember, we're their role models and we are responsible for their well-being as it stands today. We have failed to educate young people adequately about one of the most important areas of their own development and this puts their futures at risk (and ours too). Effective connections and support for adolescent sexuality must acknowledge our limited capacity to make kids do what we want them to do by directives alone. Finally, effective conversations about sex online is the same as effective conversations about sex offline: facilitate opportunities for young people to learn all they can about theirs and others' sexualities in order to create sex positive identities in the context of nonexploitative sexual behaviors. Most importantly, use cyber sex and media culture to publicly reject sex negative influences online and offline, rather than the other way around. We've learned that healthy sexuality does not just happen. It is fragile in the face of ignorance, stigma, and bad sex, especially when we are young, but we can change that. In cyberspace we can promote positive sexuality, learn some simple crossing rules, and have more empathy for others. This may not save the planet but it will certainly help kids.

### Exercise 5.3. Talking Tips for Making Effective Connections with Kids About Cyber Sex

1. Pass the Cyber Sex Quiz.
2. Remember the "Cyber Sex Reality Checks"
3. Keep supervision strategies simple and developmentally appropriate; remember that you know how to teach kids to cross the street safely, use it as a strategy to help kids navigate their cyber lives.
4. To learn the difference between sex positive and sex negative messages, choose from a variety of print media, music lyrics, film ads, and of course cyber sex face pages (it's even better if kids find some of their own). Now, together with kids define sex positive messages (illustrating respect, mutuality, and pleasure) and sex negative messages (depicting exploitative or demeaning sexual acts). As you place some media examples in the sex positive pile and some media examples in the sex negative pile, expect debate and admit that some messages are mixed.
5. Don't get complacent in cyberspace because there's more to come. Internet technology will continue to change the way we interact online and this will continue to affect kids. Check out haptics and fog screens. Joining kids in cyberspace gives us clout and gives them guidance. It's a good tool for treating parental ignorance and the alienation of youth.

# Chapter 6

# Got Health Online?

How many of us use the Internet for health-related activities? According to the Pew Internet and American Life survey, 70 million people in the United States are online daily looking for health information, up 37% from five years ago (Rainie & Horrigan, 2005). Why is this important? Health is a big issue, one that impacts every person and every country. Like the other online activities discussed in previous chapters, new generations of technology will continue to allow easier access and integration of online and offline health services but, despite the fact that visiting an online health site now trumps in-person office visits by three to one, there is no plan to make cyber health options widely available; so it's up to the consumer (Choy, Hudson, Prits, & Goldman, 2003; Gillispie, 2007; Moraham-Martin, 2004). There are medical doctors and psychologists waiting: psychotherapy, consultation, AA, virtual reality interventions, support groups, and weight-loss seminars are all online and many are free. Family doctors prescribe medication and can conduct case consultation with other physicians around the world. People with diabetes can test their blood sugar levels and upload the results directly to their medical chart in the hospital from their blood-testing machine.

The stakes for health promotion online are high: we need to compare options for chemotherapy, we have a rare disease and want to know the research, or we want information to help a friend or family member. But as with most cyber issues, figuring out which online health sources are legitimate and which are not is confusing at best. Knowing where to go and what to avoid is essential to making good choices about health online, but like other cyber behaviors tackled in earlier chapters, the 70 million people who search for health in cyber space are on their own.

In the United States the cost of health care equals 18% of our GNP and is rising steadily, largely due to the number of people with preventable lifestyle diseases (e.g., diseases related to inactivity, substance use, sun exposure, poor nutrition, and stress). As our population ages, these chronic conditions will require more and more medical care. A recent report funded by the CDC and the U.S. Department of Health and Human Services (Hitti, 2005) revealed that 95% of health care dollars are spent on treating rather than preventing these diseases. We know the problem is growing, especially in regards to the un- or underinsured. The solution? While concerted efforts are being made toward an equitable and effective health care system, little will change for the average person any time soon. So, until then, why not look in cyberspace?

According to the Kaiser Family Foundation (2005), when we are actively engaged in promoting our health we get better faster, adhere to treatment, and maintain wellness goals. But there are problems with face-to-face health treatment. Many people do not access the care they need when they need it or they cannot afford treatment. Patients often feel marginalized by the health care system when they do access it. Health professionals report they do not have enough time to really listen to patients and patients say they feel rushed and thus frequently forget to ask important questions during their appointment (Chen & Siu, 2001). Internet health searches are one way to make better use of the health professional's time because questions and concerns can be organized ahead of time (Taylor & Leitman, 2001). The Pew Internet Health Survey (Choy et al., 2003) discovered that the Internet has had a positive impact on people's health in the following ways:

- Online health information positively affected our treatment decisions.

- We asked new questions and sought a second opinion.

- We changed our approach to maintaining health goals in a positive direction.

- We initiated positive changes in diet, exercise, and stress levels.
- We found online health information was helpful in coping with chronic conditions.
- We decided to consult a health professional as a result of information learned online.

## Who's Looking?

Do health professionals help their patients utilize the Web? Unfortunately no. Janet Morahan-Martin (2004) conducted a review of how Internet users find, evaluate, and use online health information around the world. Based on her cross-cultural research, she determined that very few professionals are using the Web effectively to help their patients. The sheer volume of online information can be overwhelming for the average person, but there are expanded opportunities for wellness online. Practitioners are just beginning to include some aspects of electronic communication in their clinical practice, and refer patients to specific sites for research and treatment data. Proponents of Internet-based health practice believe that the accessibility, convenience, and choice will eventually make health interventions in cyberspace a viable option in the health care industry (Fisher & Fried, 2003; Grohol, 1998; Morahan-Martin, 2004).

Here are three ways Morahan-Martin (2004) suggests that professionals can begin to incorporate the Internet into their practice and expand the health options for their patients:

1. Preview and then recommend good health sites for online patient education.
2. Promote and teach patients effective search and evaluation techniques.
3. Be involved in developing and promoting uniform standards for health, and mental health sites.

Are 70 million per day getting the health information or services that they're looking for? According to a national survey, the results are mixed. The Kaiser Family Foundation (2005a) found that those with the most health concerns use the Internet the least. Only 31% of seniors, aged 65 and older, use the Web as a health resource but over 75% of adults aged 50 to 64 do. For young adults the figure tops 80%. On this survey 76% of teens aged 15 to 17 used the Internet to look for health information about sexuality, drugs and alcohol, and mental illness.

Clearly many of us rely on the Web for health data but the risk of inaccurate or outdated information is very real. Not only is there no regulation of information on the Internet but no uniform search strategies are used. Morahan-Martin (2004) discovered that most people don't know how to scroll, screen, or judge the value of Internet sites. Even though good search tools and search guidelines for health data are available most people don't know how to employ them for health purposes. For example, the Pew health research team found that only 24% of new users and 48% of experienced users were aware that organizations paid to place their site at the top of search results. Most believe that the top listings were the most legitimate. However, Google stands behind its search engines and maintain that the top listings are the best fit for the search term entered (Choy et al., 2003).

Teaching health consumers how to navigate the Web for health-related activities may become one of the most important ways we use the Internet. Here is a summary of the potential benefits and risks to health online:

## The Benefits

- 24/7 access.
- Anonymity and privacy.
- Less stigma for help or information online.
- Knowledge is empowering.
- No f2f communication barriers.
- Information is free and easy to share with others.
- Autonomy online increases a person's willingness to be more detailed about symptoms and proactive about obtaining information for challenging health issues.

## The Risks

- Too much information becomes overwhelming.
- Most people "hit" the first listing and few go past first two pages when searching.
- Links and URL addresses are often not available or expire.
- Outdated, repetitive, inaccurate, and/or incomplete information predominate.
- There is a lack of information about data sources, organization mission, or affiliates.
- Scams with hidden agendas or commercialism are hard to separate from legitimate sites.

## HOW TO SEARCH

Morahan-Martin (2004) and others (Mathwick & Rigdon, 2004; Skinner & Zack, 2004; Newman, 2001) state that we know very little about how people look for health online. It is a disorganized system almost guaranteed to confuse patients with conflicting information. As a result, employing search strategies would improve our ability to help ourselves and inform our treatment providers. Perhaps the most effective method initially is to cast the net wide by directing consumers to the major international, national, university, and organizational Web sites. The World Health Organization and the International Society of Mental Health Online are good ones. The Centers for Disease Control and Prevention, the National Institutes of Health, and the National Institutes for Mental Health are other excellent sources to get you started. Major clearinghouses maintain Web sites that are updated regularly and these Web sites prominently display their organization mission statements, policies, and affiliates. A significant benefit of the larger organizations is that their links are continually reviewed for accuracy and most are operative.

After several major health sites have been reviewed, the next search strategy is to enter search terms. Broad search terms like "heart disease" or "depression" allow the consumer to find general information and then funnel down to the specifics with more detailed descriptions like "treatment after heart attack" or "most effective psychotherapy for depression." Another way to look for health information is to narrow the search from the beginning. This works best for specific problems or diagnoses like "Tourette's Syndrome" or "Adolescent Onset Diabetes." While there are several search engines, Google appears to be the way most of us begin. However, the U.S. Department of Health and Human Services has developed a search tool for consumers called Healthfinder (Healthfinder, 2005). The goal of this tool is to improve consumer access to selected health information from government agencies, nonprofit organizations, and research universities. More importantly, Healthfinder's mission is to inform, not advertise, so commercial enterprises are not included. Exercise 6-1 is a template for how to look for health information.

## Exercise 6.1. Best Search Strategies

1. Write down at least three health questions(s).
2. From your questions, isolate three single search terms and then the term with another descriptor that narrows your search. Examples below:

| Broad Search Terms | Narrow Search Terms |
|---|---|
| a. Depression | depression and medication |
| b. Heart attack | heart attack and recovery |
| c. Overweight | overweight and youth camps |

3. Spend at least 30 minutes searching; 15 minutes using an expanded search term and 15 minutes narrowing your search descriptor.
4. Use Healthfinder and Google as search engines and enter your broad health terms. Compare the results. Repeat with the narrow, paired health terms. Print out first pages for later review.
5. Identify and then access three major health-information clearing houses. Enter your broad and narrow terms. Are these results similar to Healthfinder and Google? Print out the first pages and compare to question 4.
6. Evaluate which terms, strategies, and results provided you with the most useable information. Bookmark some of your best site addresses under Favorites to return to later as needed.

7. Then use the "Criteria for Evaluating Health Information Web Sites" from Exercise 6-2 to evaluate your search results.

## BARRIERS TO GOOD HEALTH ONLINE

Clearly the e-health market has changed the way people participate in their health care. We want to learn about our psychological or medical conditions and comparison shop before we make a decision. We can now access databases, e-mail experts, and participate in some treatment online (Barnett & Scheetz, 2003; Fisher & Fried, 2003; Jones, 2000; Morahan-Martin, 2004), but it's important not to assume that the Internet affords more legitimacy or accuracy with health-related topics than we find offline. Here's what we are doing wrong when we look for health information online:

1. *No destination.* Most health searchers start to cruise with no destination or end goal in mind.
2. *No major health site.* Most people use a major search engine like Google rather than a specific health site.
3. *Search terms.* Most enter only one search term (often misspelled) to access data.
4. *Facts v. opinion.* Most people cannot tell whether a site posts facts (verifiable by legitimate research) or opinion by an author whose credentials are inflated or inaccurate.
5. *Different sites, same information.* When the same information is found on two different sites, people are more likely to believe it. However, research shows that the same information is likely to be syndicated, and can be repeated in many different, unrelated Web sites. In other words, just because information is found in different places online, it doesn't necessarily mean that it is accurate.
6. *Same site different information.* Because information online outdates rapidly, it is possible for divergent information to appear on a particular site without clarification of sources to the readers. Unsubstantiated health opinions and unverifiable health facts with no citations are common. Research suggests that most consumers cannot differentiate between health fact, health opinion, and commercial health sites.

Because providers are hesitant to direct their patients to the Internet, they underutilize it as a collateral resource. However, encouraging patients to find out all they can about their condition is good treatment and contributes to proactive health behaviors. This is one of the most powerful aspects of health online (UCLA Center for Communication and Policy, 2003). How to evaluate the accuracy of the resources and data you find online is another significant problem. The Health on the Internet Foundation Code of Conduct (HONcode) was established in 1995 as the first international society to help consumers evaluate the sources of online health information. In 29 languages, HONcode lists all known hospital health information Web sites anywhere in the world as part of an online resource to consumers. In addition, HONcode specializes in what it calls "cross-border talk," research conferences, and case consultation for health professionals and consumers in 72 countries. Any Internet health-based organization that wants to belong to HONcode must adhere to the Web standards devised by its board of directors, health professionals from 17 countries (2005). However, there is no system that is able to monitor or ensure HONcode members' compliance with the ethical guidelines that follow:

1. *Authority.* Differentiates between medical fact and opinion.
2. *Compatibility.* Works to support f2f relationships with other health providers.
3. *Confidentiality.* Web sites exceed legal jurisdictional health information privacy.
4. *Attribution.* Clear references, accurate HTML links, and updates of clinical information displayed at the bottom of page.
5. *Justifiability.* Claims regarding treatments are supported by evidence.
6. *Authorship.* Webmaster displays e-mail address clearly.
7. *Sponsorship.* Support for Web site clearly identified including identities of all commercial and noncommercial organizations.
8. *Honesty in Advertising.* If advertising is a source of funding, it will be clearly stated and presented to viewers in a manner that differentiates it from the original material created by the organization operating the site.

Even with the best online presence and Web design understanding the written text is a problem for many. Often the language is too technical or too simplistic for the average user. Sometimes, to decipher the research the reader needs a graduate degree. As a result, the Pew Internet research team estimated that the reading level of Web text should be at the sixth grade, the level of most daily newspapers! Interestingly, respondents of the Pew survey indicated that while technical jargon was often unintelligible on health-related sites, it increased the consumer's perception that the Web site provided accurate health information (Rainie & Horrigan, 2005), Ironically, 72% of health seekers stated that what they read online must be true because they read it online (Morahan-Martin, 2004).

Health consumers aren't the only ones who have a problem with health online. Clinicians report that health data gleaned from Web surfing or discussion forums over-simplify the issue. In some cases, the information available on the Internet is so misleading that it may even be harmful to a person's health. In the past, we had to make appointments to visit an expert, or telephone them, or go to the library. There are so many ways to obtain information and interact with others online that one can never be sure that the information, even if accurate, is clearly understood by the patient, further increasing the burden on the clinician and the risk to the consumer.

## How to Use Online Health Information

Along with increased access to the Web, there has been a shift in the way individuals consume healthcare in general. Many patients no longer passively accept their diagnosis and treatment as dictated by their providers without doing their homework (Alleman, 2002; King & Moreggi, 1998; Grohol, 1998). The more accurate the health data, the better chance patients have of using their appointment with a professional more effectively. For example, someone who finds the diagnostic criteria for depression online, or reviews medications and their side effects before their offline appointment, can become more knowledgeable in discussions with doctors.

### CONSUMER BEWARE

Internet researchers Storm King and Danielle Moreggi (1998) call the consumer the ultimate arbitrator online and much more in control of both treatment and information-gathering interactions than in f2f office visits. However, they warn that:

> There are thousands of open, unmoderated Internet forums that exist as self help, mutual aid groups. There is no way to stop members from disseminating misleading or false information concerning any aspect of the diagnosis and treatment of mental disorders. It is entirely on the shoulders of concerned mental health professionals to educate themselves about the psychology of online relationships and the accuracy of online data, in order to help clients who are involved online, as well as to offer an ethically correct service when involved themselves online. (p. 78)

What happens if a health provider suggests that a patient explore an online support group for adult children of alcoholics and the group discussion becomes combative? We know that online communication increases the possibility of being on the receiving end of cyber bullying, flaming, or ostracism. John Suler, a psychologist from Rider University in New Jersey and board member of the International Society of Mental Health Online (ISMHO), has studied Internet communication for the past 10 years. Suler admits that being on the receiving end of harassment in chat rooms or on discussion forums is common (J. Suler, personal communication, February, 2005). Several researchers from the University of Iowa compared online verses f2f conversations and discovered that the unique culture of cyberspace, the anonymity, the time-delay, the place–distortion, and the norm of disclosure, all contribute to the potential for increased conflict (Mallen, Day, & Green, 2003). These cyber psychological communication patterns are a concern for health professionals who want to refer their patients to online discussion boards or support groups. However, the same can be said for many offline collateral health experiences. Consumers and medical providers can determine together whether a patient is being helped or not.

Probably the biggest barrier to obtaining effective psychological services for many patients is access to services. Those who live in rural communities, who have certain phobias, who feel ashamed about their condition, or those with mobility limitations have real difficulty initiating offline treatment. Many patients may not be able to find a clinician in their community who is qualified in a particular area or who takes their insurance. Additionally, shift workers and first responders, like flight attendants, hospital workers, or police, would benefit from Internet therapy because it is accessible and available 24/7. Online 12-step programs and supportive group therapy are two examples of Internet-driven treatment modalities already available to the consumer online.

Some psychologists are developing real expertise conducting online treatment. Recently, David Lukoff (2002), professor of psychology at the Saybrook Graduate School and Research Institute in San Francisco, provided online mental health treatment to native peoples in a small Inuit village. According to Lukoff, health care providers in Alaska have always recognized the utility of the distance modality because of geographic, financial, and cultural barriers. A prototype of Lukoff's online treatment protocol (see Exercise 6.2) includes direct links to assessment measures, collateral providers for medication management, educational materials, indigenous support from a university in Connecticut 3,000 miles away, and access to a 12-step program (D. Lukoff, personal communication, May 5, 2005).

The case of John is a good example of how the Internet assists in the delivery of health services for those who cannot access the comprehensive care they might need. John is a 27-year-old fisherman living in Alaska and struggling with a dual addiction and chronic depression. Mental health counselors working with John in this rural community have received training online for culturally sensitive addiction treatment that includes cyber case consultation with a psychiatrist and an internist from a large city. With off-site collateral providers they have developed an online treatment plan that incorporates a culturally sensitive, multi-disciplinary approach, providing John with a system of interventions beyond the resources available on his island. An example of how the Internet can be used to provide comprehensive interventions is outlined in Exercise 6.2. Readers are encouraged to access several of these websites in order to experience

what it would be like to have an online component to one's offline
health care.

## Exercise 6.2. Sample Online Treatment Plan

1. Self Assessment for Substance Use, the Michigan Alcohol Screening
   Test (MAST) taken and self-scored online: http://www.ncadd-sfv.org/
   symptoms/mast_test.html
2. Based on offline intake data and online medical consultation between
   addiction specialists, an internist, and the Aleutian Village substance
   abuse counselors, John's treatment plan includes:
   a. A prescription for Zoloft. John accesses the National Institutes of
      Mental health where he learns about this medication as related to
      his diagnosis and treatment, the side effects, and possible treatment
      compliance issues: http://www.nimh.nih.gov/publicat/medicate.cfm
   b. Links to Alcoholic's Anonymous online 12-Step group: http://
      www.alcoholics-anonymous.org/?Media=PlayFlash
3. John is then asked to visit several sites for the Patient Education component of his treatment:
   a. a link to the National Clearinghouse for Alcohol and Drug Infor-
      mation where John can view videos and ebooks about a variety
      of medical and psychological topics related to addiction and email
      questions about his symptoms to clinicians: https://ncadistore.
      samhsa.gov/
   b. a link to the University of Utah Medical School for a mini turor-
      ial on the effects of alcohol on the liver: http://medlib.med.utah.
      edu/WebPath/TUTORIAL/DRUG/DRUG.html
4. Finally, to expand John's social support network, including recon-
   necting with his indigenous roots (Aleutian Indian), he logs on to the
   following sites and joins a listserv discussion group:
   c. The Four Worlds Institute for Human and Community Develop-
      ment, an international clearinghouse for Native peoples: http://
      www.4words.org/
   d. A site that focuses on the stories of the Aleutian tribes, University of
      Connecticut Web site: Arctic Circle: http://arcticcircle.uconn. edu/

Another concern that many clinicians express about the online
treatment modality in general is the adequacy of a patient's level of

participation. A study of online therapy found that the electronic form of therapeutic communication resulted in higher levels of participation than traditional offline methods of therapy. Susan Day and Paul Schneider (2002) conducted an experiment at the University of Illinois comparing distance verses f2f modes of therapy. Their findings suggest that when we participate more in our health treatment the benefits are increased as well.

Some researchers have demonstrated that those who are not comfortable with technology are the most reluctant to use the Internet as a method of finding health information, either for their own or a patient's benefit (Mallen et al., 2003; Ragusa & VandeCreek, 2003; Skinner & Zack, 2004). But even those who are experienced cyber searchers agree that it is easy to get lost in cyberspace or overwhelmed with too much information. Many health providers are inundated with materials that patients find on the Internet. Sometimes clinicians are asked to critique the information or to employ a particular intervention recommended because "it's on the Internet." However, some practitioners are beginning to teach their patients how to search the Web more effectively.

The Internet offers ways to connect with large databases and research at the click of a mouse. However, when does this amount of patient education become treatment? A medical doctor in California was successfully sued for not providing enough additional medical information about what could happen if the cancer patient decided against the recommended treatment. In other words, the standard of care upheld by this malpractice suit required that clinicians not only fully inform the patient about recommended treatment but also about the risks of not employing a particular treatment strategy (Clark, 1996). In terms of educating patients about their health problems, the Internet provides so much information that many patients are overwhelmed.

Web site data has a shelf life and often expires but usually no one erases the entry. As a result, it's possible for old Web sites to redirect you to other domains entirely without your awareness. For example, after a recent election was over, a well-known politician did not renew his domain registration, and his site was taken over by swingers with an invitation to participate (Hartlaub, 2004). Even the most well-meaning clinician and the most electronically sophisticated patients are not immune to the negative effects of too much information. When needing to find accurate data about one's health, retired or expired sites could be harmful. Even in the best of circumstances, if an organization or clinician lets their Web site expire inadvertently, a patient could assume that the new site was a legitimate affiliate of the original one.

When it comes to your privacy, identity theft is a downside of the digital age. The issue of blatant online identity theft goes beyond stealing an identity and into the area of how professionals create Web sites. Exaggerating one's credentials or expertise or blatantly misrepresenting one's background is easy to do online. It is easier for consumers to verify the credentials of someone in their community than in cyberspace.

While we know that the computer has helped us be more efficient, technology has created new kinds of risks in terms of protecting our privacy. In a report funded by the Pew Internet and American Life project, investigators found federal regulations outlined in HIPAA inadequate for most online transactions or online health service providers (Choy, Hudson, Prits, & Goldman, 2003). It appears that the communications revolution has increased, not reduced, the time it takes to receive health services online. As we all get more adept with the electronic systems of health delivery and communication, providers and consumers alike will learn how to safeguard their health information and their privacy online and obtain good health services just the way we have offline (Skinner & Zack, 2004).

## SOME GOOD NEWS

Despite technological glitches, privacy issues, ineffective online search strategies, and worries about the accuracy of Internet-based health information, there is good news. Online health searches have been shown to increase patients' motivation to improve their health. Increased treatment compliance is another way that Internet-based social support and the exchange of health information in cyberspace helps patients with chronic illness. In addition, interactive health information sites provide intensive individual and social support for those who need to change habits that contribute to illness or psychological distress (Skinner & Zack, 2004).

There is also a growing body of evidence that some medical and psychological problems can be treated successfully online. Virtual reality (VR) via Internet technology is an effective treatment component either as a stand-alone modality or as part of an offline treatment plan. VR as an effective change agent helps those who suffer from specific phobias, depression, obesity, male erectile disorders, and cognitive disorders, including rehabilitation from traumatic brain injury and posttraumatic stress. With VR we can experience visual and sensory immersion that facilitates the process of change. VR has been used to hypnotize patients (Patterson, Tininenko, Schmidt, & Sharar, 2004). Soon haptic feedback, or the sensation of touch, will be added to the audio and visual immersion of the healing VR environment (Feintuch, Raz, Hwang, Josman, Katz, Kizony, Rand, et al., 2006).

Group and individual psychotherapy are also effectively conducted online. Patients dealing with smoking cessation, weight loss, eating disorders, headaches, panic attacks, posttraumatic stress, pathological grief, maintaining physical exercise goals, tinnitus, diabetes, bed wetting, and post-cancer and heart attack recovery reported benefiting from online psychotherapy. (Ritterband, Gonder-Frederick, Cox, Clifton, West, & Borowitz, 2003). Studies suggested that effectiveness of online health interventions may be greatest for those who are either reluctant to participate in treatment due to stigma or for those who are unable to access health services for financial or mobility reasons. A central component of any intervention regardless of the clinical issue or therapeutic modality is the relationship between the patient and the health provider. Sometimes face-to-face disclosure is difficult, especially initially. Using the Internet as a first contact is both private and reduces initial anxiety.

As experts in wellness and disease, health practitioners are in a good position to guide their patients toward adjunct online health services. They can ensure that patients become familiar with the search tools and strategies outlined in this chapter. Streamlining search techniques and providing criteria to evaluate the accuracy of improving the online health information will help providers and consumers use their time together more efficiently. In the future, it may be unethical for health providers not to offer Web search strategies for patients as well as recommend health-education Web sites. But it is also important to teach their patients how to evaluate online information. Research shows that professionals need training in online searches as much as their patients do. Similar to the HONcode principals, the World Health Organization, the American Medical Association, and the Medical Library Association agree that the best health searches start with developing sound strategies and then implementing the criteria for evaluating the data presented on the Web sites. "A Short List of Good Health Web Sites," is included here to assist both the consumer and health provider when looking for accurate and timely health information online.

We can get healthy online. The information and the services are already there waiting to improve the health of individuals who may not have the mobility, financial resources, or ability to obtain what they need. The trick is to log on, know what you need to find out, have a search strategy, evaluate what you read, and then use what you learn or experience to improve yours or a loved one's health.

## A Short List of Good Health Websites

### Major National Health Organizations

| | |
|---|---|
| www.nih.org | National Institutes of Health |
| www.cdc.org | Centers for Disease Control and Prevention |
| http://medlineplus.gov | National Medical Library Association |
| www.pubedcentral.nih.gov | PubMed Central, National Institutes of Health free archive of biomedical and life sciences journal literature |

www.healthfinder.gov U.S. Department of Health and Human Services

## Major National Mental Health Organizations

www.nimh.org National Institute of Mental Health
www.apa.org American Psychological Association
www.psych.org American Psychiatric Association
www.aamft.org American Association of Marriage and Family
www.naswdc.org National Association of Social Workers
www.rider.edu Professional development for clinicians and educators
www.psychcentral.com John Grohol's professional resources for clinicians and consumers
http://www.apna.org/ American Psychiatric Nurses Association
http://www.schoolcounselor.org/ American School Counselor Association
http://www.fenichel.com Dr. Michael Fenichel, Cyberpsychology Theory

## Web Sites Health Facts and Stats

www.commerce.gov U.S. Department of Commerce
www.kff.org The Henry J. Kaiser Family Foundation
www.pew.org The Pew Internet and American Life Project
www.annenbergpublicpolicycenter.org Annenberg Public Policy Center of the University of Pennsylvania
www.cyberlaw.org Stanford University Center for Internet and Society
www.seicus.org Sexuality Education and Information Council of the United States

## INTERNATIONAL RESOURCES

www.ismho.com International Society of Mental Health Online, comprehensive resources for providers and consumers of online mental health

www.cybertherapy.info          European Union: A Telemedicine and
                               Portable Virtual Reality Environment, for
                               clinical psychologists in Europe
www.psychologyonline.co.uk     British Isles: A privately owned interactive
                               treatment clinic utilizing Internet counseling

# Chapter 7

# Evolving in Cyberspace

**W**hat kind of cyber rules do we need in the future? The Internet will continue to bring together media and communications in our lives. Entertainment and scientific media will lead the way. Computers implanted in our bodies will change the way we think, feel, and behave down to the cellular level. The influence of the screen is already so powerful that severely burned patients can self-hypnotize as a way to manage excruciating pain (Patterson, Tininenko, Schmidt, & Sharar, 2004). Imagine future technology that allows us to bypass the screen altogether as our bodies become the computer with subcutaneous chips. Want to get a sense of what's ahead? Go to video-game trade shows. Are you hassled but too busy to get to a therapist for some relaxation training? Try Interactive Institute's "Brainball," where you learn how to control your emotions by viewing your brain waves on the screen. Be calm and control the ball or stay stressed and lose the ball, and the game. Whether we want to relax or become aroused, the human experience in all its permutations will continue to fuse with Internet technology.

## Cyber Rules for the Future

Remember, advances in nanotechnology will double the storage capacity of computer chips every two years, making computers smaller, faster, and smarter. How? Primarily with the development of interactive effects like haptics and 3D submersible screens. Can't get to Machu Picchu? Thanks to haptic technology, you can feel the contours of a rock wall built by the Incas. Wish you were an astronaut or a dancer? Insert yourself into a Fog Screen and have a go. Soon we will become accustomed to technology that integrates multisensory effects so effortlessly that media and the Internet will become one experience reality. Biofeedback devices that attach sensors to fingertips and Fog Screens incorporate more and more physicality into the cyberspace experience. Your body can be a paintbrush or you can create a digital dance, which then becomes a painting. Or create a picture where each stroke is an image *and* a sound that sings back to you.

As more of our senses are combined with our online experiences, the distinctions between online and offline will disappear. Physicians can already perform lazer surgery at a distance. Even cuddling is computerizeable. "Interactive Pillows" designed by Interactive Institute create a digital cushion, woven with electro-luminescent wire and linked wirelessly to the Web, so you can hug your pillow and its counterpart glows, no matter where it is located (Wired NextFest, 2005). The Institute of Advanced Media Arts and Sciences has added biosensors to mobile phones that decode tactile and olfactory data that can then be transmitted to others. You can reach out, touch, and now *smell* someone too.

Don't worry about losing your cell phone, palm, iPod, or Blackberry—just remember to get dressed. University of Michigan engineers designed "nano-materials . . . fabrics containing solar cells, electronic circuits, and polymer batteries that generate and store electricity. Garments double as wearable power sources" (Wired NextFest, 2005, p. 34). How about never forgetting other important things like your social security number, medical data, or keys? There are already scannable computer chips imbedded in body tissue. A variety of security devices will soon be available to the public to address privacy and security concerns. Facial recognition software like "Face Detection" by Mitsubishi Electric Research Labs opens doors and starts the car with a mug shot.

## IS TECHNOLOGY MAKING US SMARTER?

If we are having difficulty figuring out the effects of text messaging or cyber sex on our lives, what about when most of us get used to being able to cuddle with, wear, dance, fly, smell, or *be in* the online experience? Psychologists Robert Sternberg and David Preiss (2005) already think old-fashioned texting is making us smarter:

> writing relates progressively less to the cultivation of expression on paper and more to effective computer use . . . this change restructures the writing process as planning and reviewing with word processors involves more cognitive effort than does working in longhand. (p. xiii)

As a result of computer and Internet use, children are achieving higher scores on measures of nonverbal problem-solving ability, primarily in the visuospatial areas. Digital research scrientists at UCLA proposed that playing and learning online improves children's overall cognitive ability because it teaches them cognitive flexibility and increases their information processing speed (Maynard, Subrahmanyam, and Greenfield, 2005). On the screen, kids' ability to rotate and transform objects mentally while simultaneously texting engages both hemispheres of the brain, increasing their attention, concentration, and memory capabilities so essential for learning.

# Making Sense of It

Canadian philosopher and communications theorist Marshall McLuhan got it even before the Internet: "In the electric age, we wear all mankind as our skin." He is most famous for the adage "the medium is the message" but he also coined the terms *global village* and *surfing*, in relation to sifting through lots of information (2005; n.d.). Even before today's interactive media, McLuhan realized that media shapes interpretation of the message and as a result changes the messenger. More recently, John Vivian and Peter Maurin (1997) examined Internet media through semiotics, which is the creation and meaning of the message, and through the process of sending and receiving messages.

Chaos theory offers a heuristic within which to view the overall human-machine effects and interactions. Chaos, or complexity theory, emerged like the Internet, from the cross-fertilization of many disciplines, including mathematics, physics, biology, and climatology. Chaos and the Internet share these basic characteristics:

- The system contains a large number of different elements.
- The many components are organized into various interrelated structures.
- The components are connected through physical links, energy interchanges, or some form of communication links.

As the interactive effects of multimedia communication become increasingly complicated, we will be less able to measure of predict with any accuracy its effects on our lives at any one point in time. Kids, most of whom live solidly in the here and now, have no problem embracing new technologies and not worrying about the ramifications of living and loving online. But adults have always been less trusting of the new. With the thousands of choices within and between Internet media becoming more complex and dynamic every year, even experts' predictions and research findings will continue to contradict each other. Perhaps that's the point: the Internet eschews complacency and control.

## GETTING IT

First, here are the answers to Exercise I.1.

1. How many Americans are online daily?
   70 million according to the Pew Internet and American Life Survey.
2. People who report more time online feel more connected to others.
3. 2 out of 10 kids are online every day.
4. What is the age when children start to use Internet media?
   9 months according to the Kaiser Family Foundation Research in 2005.
5. List three reasons that people say and do things online that they would not do offline: 1. autonomy 2. anonymity 3. access
6. List the four components to the cyber rules problem-solving model:
   a) Knowledge.
   b) Understanding the criteria that defines problem use.
   c) Assessing your online use.
   d) Comparing online behaviors with offline effects.

7. Explain Friedman's concept of "the world is flat" and what this has to do with online behaviors and offline effects. <u>Power is shared and continually co-constructed by the masses and censorship and control are not dictated by a top down approach.</u>

Douglas Rushkoff (1996) suggests that if we want to understand technology and media, we just need to see what kids are doing with it. The energy, creativity, and culture of youth embodies the push/pull of media: deeply engaging, a little over the top if we're not careful, but rejuvenating, resisting structure, and reinventing itself. Today's cyber culture does have self-correcting mechanisms. It runs on the twin engines of human and silicon-based intelligence. But the Internet is more than a giant user domain controlled by digerati, it is also a collective unconscious and a co-constructed global consciousness. Parents, teachers, and clinicians may be justifiably concerned with children's sophisticated and barely controllable media lives, but from the perspective of the child or teen this is how their world works.

Although interpreting the dynamic of the interaction between humans and media technology defies rigid and hierarchical ways of thinking and problem solving, this does not mean that there are no principals governing the system. The Cyber Rules Problem Solving Model discussed in the Introduction measures what you know, offers some criteria to define unhealthy Internet use, and then assesses whether or not you have a problem with what you are doing online. The metaphor of Crossing the Street in Cyber Space provides guidelines for healthy Internet use and sex positive netiquette. Whether you meet your mate online, confront a cyber compulsion, or creatively expand your consciousness through Internet connections remember that the three cyber psychological constructs of access, anonymity, and disinhibition can lead to both positive and negative outcomes. Remember, old rules and pejorative morals don't transfer to the horizontal power grid in cyber space. For example, the hysteria about kids' sex and nudity on blogsites is spawning "content moderators". These smut checkers are primarily hired by websites to appease parents from the Midwest where, supposedly the morals are more intact. These censors are paid $15.00 an hour to sift through 200 images a minute to decide what gets booted and what doesn't. For example a bare bottom is zapped, but a bottom with a 1/8 inch thong is ok. Confusion abounds with "nigga" (ok) and "nigger" (not ok) or apple pie, not ok (the apples and crust look like too much skin) (Angwin, 2006). If we keep trying to control or censor communication online, kids will hide what they are doing, and we will remain disconnected from young people, and thus our future.

By the time you get to the end of this book we want to be sure you got cyber rules clearly enough to share it with others (who may be clueless the way you once were). Here it is again, short and simple:

*The Problem isn't:*
The Internet (web cams, cell phones, MySpace, FaceBook, cyber porn. . . .).
Kids (their manners or morals).

*The Problem is:*
Young people are disconnected from adults.
Kids find connection and power in cyberspace that they don't have offline.
Bad sex and sex negative media messages, on- and offline.
Greed, selfishness, and ignorance.

## CYBER RULES

- The Internet is the power that got away.
- Online the world is flat.
- Netiquette basics: what you do online is not private; watch the anger, and know and practice positive sexuality and communication in cyberspace.
- Kids live online and most of it's good.
- On the Internet we can be the same, different, better, and worse.
- Kids aren't doing anything that adults aren't doing online.
- Don't ignore your offline problems and don't put them online because they'll get worse.
- We can use the metaphor of crossing the street safely to guide young people's Internet behaviors at the right ages, at the right time, with just the right amount of supervision.

- Sex ed gets a much-needed overhaul and upgrade in cyberspace.

- If you ignore these cyber rules now, new generations of Internet technology will exponentially expand the negative effects of certain Internet activities.

The Internet is a way to change some things that have really needed to change: The disenfranchisement of youth, bad sex, the abuse of power. In the past we have used communication technology to maintain the status quo, which has only really worked for those in charge. The Internet has changed the rules of the game. We're all on first. The Internet lets us examine ourselves and each other more closely. Kids know the game. If we listen more and criticize less, they'll let us play too. It just doesn't work to lecture without looking at ourselves first. We hope that this book has helped you think through and beyond the screen and to use the Internet to expose and change what hasn't worked offline for a long time. If you are still confused after reading this book ask any kid to help you. Let's follow the advice of Cornell West. Let's use the Internet to be great, for ourselves, each other, and the planet.

# References

A law too far. (2004, June 30). *San Francisco Chronicle*, p. B 8.

Achbar, M. (Producer/Director). (2003). *The corporation* [Motion Picture]. Canada: Big Picture Media Corporation.

Ackerman, D. (2004). *An alchemy of the mind*. New York: Scribner.

Addict (2005). My reason for being an addict . . . *The Parent Report*. Retrieved May 16, 2005, from http://www.theparentreport.com/resources/ages/preteen/kids_culture/130.html?view_annotation=8093

Adersson, G., Bergstrom, J., Carlbring, P., & Lindefors, N. (2005). The use of the Internet in the treatment of anxiety disorders. *Current Opinion in Psychiatry, 18*, 73–77.

Alexander, C. N., Davies, J. L., Dixon, C. A., Dillbeck, M. C., Ortzel, R. M., Muehlman, J. M., & Orme-Johnson, D. W. (1990). Higher stages of consciousness beyond formal operations: The Vedic psychology of human development. In C. N. Alexander & E. J. Langer (Eds.) *Higher stages of human development: Adult growth beyond formal operations*. New York: Oxford University Press.

Alleman, J. R. (2002). Online counseling: The Internet and mental health treatment. *Psychotherapy: Theory/Research/Practice/Training, 39*(2), 199–209.

American Psychiatric Association. (2000). *Diagnostic and statistical manual of mental disorders* (4th ed.). Washington, DC: Author.

American Psychological Association. (ed). APA statement on services by telephone, teleconferences, and Internet. Retrieved October 26, 2004, from http://www.apa.org/ethics

Amichai-Hamburger, Y. (2005). Internet minimal group paradigm. *CyberPsychology & Behavior, 8*(2), 140–142.

Anderson, C. A., & Dill, K. E. (2000). Video games and aggressive thoughts, feelings, and behavior in the laboratory and in life. *Journal of Personality & Social Psychology, 78*(4), 772–790.

Anderson, C. A., Berkowitz, L., Donnerstein, E., Huesmann, L. R., Johnson, J. D., Linz, D., et al. (2003). The influence of media violence on youth. *Psychological Science in the Public Interest, 4*(3), 81–110.

Ang, A. (2005, July 4). China treats addicted video game players. *Associated Press*. Retrieved July 4, 2005, from http://news.yahoo.com/s/ap/20050704/ap_on_hi_te/china_kicking_the_net&printer=1;_ylt=Ai5Kd JHE1aADSImlJqaI2RVk24cA;_ylu=X3oDMTA3MXN1bHE0BHN1YwN 0bWE

Angwan, J. (2006, May 16). A problem for hot web outfits: Keeping pages free from porn. *The Wall Street Journal*, A1, 9.

Anonymous (2005). My Addiction – Parents take note! *The Parent Report*. Retrieved May 16, 2005, from http://www.theparentreport.com/resources/ages/preteen/kids_culture/130.html?view_annotation= 6854

APA Practice Directorate. (2005, April 13). Secure your practice with the new "HIPAA Security Rule Online Workbook." Retrieved April 13, 2005, from http://www.apapractice.org/apo/insider/hipaa/hipaa_security_ rule?workbook.html

Associated Press (2004, November 19). Woman sues Internet dating agency after marriage turned violent. *ABC13TV*. Retrieved on December 18, 2004, from http://abclocal.go.com/ktrk/news/nat_world/111904_ APnat_internet.html

Associated Press (2005, Aug. 19). Online Resource Available For Teens With Cancer. WJACTV.com. Retreived September 3, 2005, from http://www.wjactv.com/health/4873363/detail.html

Atari (2005). *My Little Pony PC Play Pack: The Buz*. Retrieved May 17, 2005, from http://www.atari.com/us/games/my_little_pony_pp/pc

Aviram, I., and Amichai-Hamburger, Y. (2005). Online infidelity: Aspects of dyadic satisfaction, self-disclosure, and narcissism. *Journal of Computer-Mediated Communication, 10*(3), article 1. http://jcmc.indiana.edu/vol10/issue3/aviram.html

Badagliacco, J. (1990). Gender and race differences in computing attitudes and experience. Special Issue: Computing: Social and policy issues. *Social Science Computer Review, 8*(1), 42–63.

Bahney, A. (2006, March 9). Don't talk to invisible strangers: Parents fear Web predators. *The New York Times*, p. G1–2.

Bailenson, J. N., Blascovich, J., Beall, A. C., & Loomis, J. M. (2003). Inter-personal distance in immersive virtual environments. *Personality & Social Psychology Bulletin, 29*(7), 819–833.

Ballstadt, C., Hopkins, E., & Peterman, M. (1993). *Letters of love and duty.* Toronto: University of Toronto Press.

Bargh, J., & McKenna, K. (2004). The Internet and social life. *Annual Review of Psychology, 55,* 573–590.

Bargh, J. A., McKenna, K. Y. A., & Fitzsimons, G. M. (2002). Can you see the real me? activation and expression of the "true self" on the internet. *Journal of Social Issues, 58*(1), 33–48.   .

Barnett, J. E., & Scheetz, K. (2003). Technological advances and telehealth: Ethics, law, and the practice of psychotherapy. *Psychotherapy: Theory, Research, Practice, Training, 40*(1/2), 86–93.

Barnett, J. E., & Zur, O. (2005). Telehealth: Clinical, ethical, and legal issues online course. Retrieved September 29, 2005, from http://www.drzur. com/cgi-bin/test/drz04.cgi?telehealthclinicalethicalandlegalissuesonline

Baron, R., & Byrne, D. (1994). *Social psychology: Understanding human interaction.* Boston: Allyn and Bacon.

Barrett, D. (2001). *Trauma and dreams.* Cambridge, MA: Harvard University Press.

BBC News (2001). Delhi children make play of the net. *BBC News Sci/Tech.* Retrieved May 17, 2005, from http://news.bbc.co.uk/1/hi/sci/tech/ 1502820.stm

Beard, K. (2005). Internet addiction: A review of current assessment techniques and potential assessment questions. *CyberPsychology & Behavior, 8*(1), 7–14.

Bearman, D. (2004, March). The relationship between virginity pledges in adolescence and STD acquisition in young adulthood. Study presented at the National STD Prevention Conference, Philadelphia, PA.

Beck, J. C., & Wade, M. (2004). *Got game: How the gamer generation is reshaping business forever.* Boston: Harvard Business School Press.

Bedigian, L. (2005). Professor James Paul Gee shows the world the importance of video games. *GameZone.* Retrieved July 12, 2005, from http://pc.gamezone.com/news/07_03_03_06_17PM.htm

Begner, D. (2005, January 31). The making of a molester. *The New York Times Magazine,* pp. 26, 61.

Bell, D. (2001) Cybersexual. In David Bell and Barbara Kennedy (Eds.) *The cybercultures reader.* New York: Routledge, pp. 392–395.

Benigno, S. F. (2001). The blue desk chair. *Folks Online.* Retrieved May18, 2005, from http://www.folksonline.com/folks/ts/2001/whiz.htm

Bernoff, J., Charron, C., Lonian, A., Stroh, C., & Flemming, S. (2003). From discs to downloads. Retrieved from Forrester Research Group June 8, 2005, from http://www.forrester.com/ER/Research/Report/Summary/ 0,1338,16076.html

Bertolini, R., & Nissim, S. (2002). Video games and children's imagination. *Journal of Child Psychotherapy, 28*(3), 305–325.

Bharat, M., Merkel, C., & Bishop, A. (2004, December). The Internet for empowerment of minority and marginalized users. *New Media and Society, 6*(6), 781–802.

Bhugra, D. (2000). Disturbances in objects of desire: cross-cultural issues. *British Association of Sexual and Relationship Therapy,* Vol.15, No.1, 67–78.

Bianchi, A., & Phillips, J. G. (2005). Psychological predictors of problem mobile phone use. *CyberPsychology & Behavior, 8*(1), 39–51.

Bier, M. (1997). *Assessing the effect of unrestricted home Internet access on the underserved community: A case study of four east central Florida families.* Unpublished Dissertation from Florida Institute of Technology.

Bischof, W. F., & Boulanger, P. (2003). Spatial navigation in virtual reality environments: An EEG analysis. *CyberPsychology & Behavior, 6*(5), 487–495.

Bittanti, M. (2005, June). *'Making sense of Manhunt' or 'Why we play: The seductions of violent entertainment'.* Paper presented at the biannual meeting of Digital Game Researcher Association, Vancouver, BC.

Blackmore, S. (2003). *Consciousness: An introduction.* London: Oxford University Press.

Blechman, H. (1997). Introducing my parents to the online world. *Folks Online.* Retrieved May 20, 2005, from http://www.folksonline.com/ folks/ts/story7/story7.htm

Boies, S., Cooper, A., & Osborne, C. (2004). Variations in internet-related problems and psychosocial functioning in online sexual activities: Implications for social and sexual development of young adults. *Cyber Psychology and Behavior, 7*(2), 207–230.

Bolton, A., & Fouts, G. (2005, June). *Individual differences in violent video game play.* Paper presented at the biannual meeting of Digital Game Researcher Association, Vancouver, BC.

Borland, John (2004). New swap shop for Napster founder. *CNET News.com.* Retrieved Oct. 20, 2005, from http://news.com.com/New+swap+ shop+for+Napster+founder/2008-1082_3-5475465.html

Bowker, A., & Gray, M. (2004). An introduction to the supervision of the cybersex offender. *Federal Probation, 68*, Iss. 3, 3–6.

Boyer, M. (1996). *Cybercities: Visual perception in the age of electronic communication.* Princeton: Princeton Architectural Press.

Bridges, A., Bergner, R., & Hesson-McInnis, M. (2003). Romantic partners' use of pornography: It's significance for women. *Journal of Sex and Marital Therapy, 29,* 1–14.

Brown, J., Cohen, P., Chen, H., Smailes, E., & Johnson, J. (2004). Sexual trajectory of abused and neglected youth. *Journal of Developmental Behavioral Pediatrics, 25,* 77–82.

Brown, K., & Hamilton-Giachritsis, C. (2005). The influence of violent media on children. *The Lancet, 365*(9476).

Bryan-Low, C., & Pringle, D. (2005, May 12). Sex cells: Wireless operators in Europe, Asia find that racy cell phone video drives a surge in broadband use. *The Wall Street Journal,* pp. B1, B2.

Burkell, J. (2004). Health information seals of approval: What do they signify? *Information, Communication & Society, 7*(4), 491–509.

California Psychological Association (2004, February). *Expertise series.* Division of Clinical and Professional Practice. Sacramento, CA: Author.

Calvert, C. (2000). *Voyeur nation: Media, Privacy, and peering in modern culture.* Boulder CO: Westview Press.

Calvert, S., Rideout , V. J., Woolard, J. L., Barr, R. F., & Strouse, G. A. (2005). Age, ethnicity, and socioeconomic patterns in early computer use: A national survey. *American Behavioral Scientist, 48*(5), 590–607. Retrieved May 7, 2005, from http://cdmc.georgetown.edu/papers/age_ethnicity_ and_socioeconomic_patterns.pdf.

Calvert, Sa., Mahler, B., Zehnder, S., Jenkins, A., & Less, M. (2003). Gender differences in preadolescent children's online interactions: Symbolic modes of self-presentation and self-expression. *Applied Developmental Psychology, 24,* 627–644.

Center for Media Education. (1997, May). *Alcohol and tobacco on the Web: New threats to youth.* Retrieved March 13, 2001, from http://www.cme. org/children/marketing/execsum.html

Center for Media Education. (1998). *Interactions: CME's Research Initiative on Children and New Media.* Retrieved March 13, 2001, from http://www. cme.org/interactions/index_interact.html

Center for Media Education. (n.d). *Deception.* Retrieved March 13, 2001, from http://www.cme.org/children/marketing/deception.pdf

Chen, X., & Siu, L. (2001). Impact of the media and the Internet on oncology: Survey of cancer patients and their physicians in Canada. *Journal of Clinical Oncology, 1,* 4291–4297.

Chiero, R. (1998). *Teachers' professional uses of computers and perceptions of their value for work productivity.* Dissertation from the Claremont Graduate University and San Diego State University.

Chipman, S. F. (2003). Gazing yet again in to the silicon chip: The future of computers in education. In Harold F. O'Neil Jr. & Ray S. Perez (Eds). *Technology Applications in Education: A Learning View,* Mahwah, NJ: Lawrence Erlbaum Associates.

Choi, D., & Kim, J. (2004). Why people continue to play online games: In search of critical design factors to increase customer loyalty to online contents. *CyberPsychology & Behavior, 7*(1), 11–24.

Chou, T. J. & Ting, C. C. (2003). The role of flow experience in cyber-game addiction. *CyberPsychology & Behavior, 6*(6), 663–675.

Choy, A., Hudson, Z., Prits, J., & Goldman, J. (2003, November). *Exposed online: Why the new federal health privacy regulation doesn't offer much protection to Internet users.* Report of the Pew Internet and American Life Project. Institute for Health Care Research and Policy. Washington, DC: Georgetown University.

Clark, W. (1996). *Legal aspects of chemical dependency treatment.* Paper presented at annual meeting at the University of California, San Francisco, CA.

CNET News.com Staff (2005, May 9). Cell phones to ring in slight growth. *CNET News.com,* Retrieved Oct. 20, 2005, from http://news.com. com/Cell+phones+to+ring+in+slight+growth/2100-1039_3-5700417.html

Cole, J., Suman, M., Schramm, P., Lunn, R., Aquino, J.S., Firth, D., et al. (2003). *The UCLA Internet report: Surveying the digital future: Year three.* Los Angeles: UCLA Center for Communications Policy, Retrieved July 21, 2004, from www.ccp.ucla.edu

Collins, C. (1997, February). *Dangerous inhibitions: How America is letting AIDS become an epidemic of the young.* Monograph presented by Center for AIDS Prevention Studies, University of San Francisco and Harvard AIDS Institute, Occasional paper #3, pp. 1–42.

Cooper, A. (Ed.). (2002). *Sex and the Internet: A guidebook for clinicians.* New York: Brunner-Rutledge.

Cooper, A., Delmonico, D., & Berg, R. (2002). Cybersex users, abusers, and compulsives: New findings and implications. *Sexual Addiction and Compulsivity: Journal of Treatment and Prevention, 7,* (1–2), 5–30.

Cooper, A., & Griffin-Shelley, E. (2002). *Online sexual activity: Continuum complete International Encyclopedia of sexuality,* 1290–1386.

Cooper, A., Scherer, C., Boies, S., Gordon, B. (1999). Sexuality on the Internet: From sexual exploration to pathological expression. *Professional Psychology: Research and Practice, 30*(2), 154–164.

Cooper, J., & Weaver, K. (2003). *Gender and computers: Understanding the digital divide.* New York: Lawrence Erlbaum.

Crane, J. (2005, June 30). Internet bullying hits home for teen: Anonymous attacks a growing concern. *The Boston Globe.* Retrieved July 15, 2005, from http://www.boston.com/news/local/articles/2005/06/30internet_bullying_hits_home_for_teen

Csikszentmihalyi, M. (1990). *Flow: The psychology of optimal experience.* New York: Harper and Row.

Curtis, P. (1992) *Mudding: Social phenomena in text-based virtual realities.* Proceedings of Directions and Implications of Advanced Computing (DIAC'92) Symposium, Berkeley, California, May 2–3, 1992. Also published in *Intertek, 3,* 26–34. Also available as Xerox PARC technical report CSL–92–4.

Daily Market and Media Intelligence (2004, December 17). *Digging deep for online personals sites and user data from Nielsen//NetRatings.* Retrieved December 17, 2004, from http://www.centerformediaresearch.com/cfmr_brief.cfm?fnl=040611

Day, S. & Schneider, P. (2002) Psychotherapy using distance technology: A comparison of face-to-face, video, and audio treatment. *Journal of Consulting Psychology,* Vol. 49, No. 4, 499–503.

DeAngelis, T. (2004, December). Taking action for children's mental health. *Monitor on Psychology, 35*(11), 38–41.

Deirmenjian, J. (2000). Hate crimes on the Internet. *Journal of Forensic Science, 45*(5), 1020–1022. Retrieved January 13, 2005, from http://journals.astm.org/PDF/JOFS/JFS4551020/JFS4551020.pdf

Denegri-Knott, J., & Taylor, J. (2005). The labeling game: A conceptual exploration of deviance on the Internet. *Social Science and Computer Review, 23*(4), 39–47.

Derrig-Palumbo, K., & Zeine, F. (2005). *Online therapy.* New York: Norton.

Dickey, C., & Summers, N. (2005). A female sensibility. *Newsweek International Edition.* Retreived October 4, 2005, from http://www.msnbc.msn.com/id/9378641/site/newsweek/

*Digital childhood: A research agenda on human development & technology* (2000). Retrieved May 5, 2005, from http://www.decadeofbehavior.org/digitalchild/

Discovery Channel (2005). *JumpStart Toddlers 2000*. Retrieved Aug. 1, 2005, from http://school.discovery.com/

Downing, J. (2004). Psychotherapy practice in a pluralistic world: Philosophical and moral dilemmas. *Journal of Psychotherapy Integration, 14*(2), 123–148.

Drew, B., & Waters, J. (1986). Video games: Utilization of a novel strategy to improve perceptual motor skills and cognitive functioning in the non-institutionalized elderly. *Cognitive Rehabilitation, 4*(2), 26–31.

Ebrey, P. (1993). *Chinese civilization: A sourcebook* (2nd ed.) New York: Free Press.

Eckerson, W. (1992). Users enthused about electronic meetings. *Network World, 9*(24), 43.

Edwards, M. (2003). SIECUS Reports, *Sexuality Information and Education Council of the United States, 31*(4), 4–35.

Engelberg, E., & Sjoberg, L. (2004). Internet use, social skills, and adjustment. *CyberPsychology & Behavior, 7*(1), 41–47.

Ermi, L., & Mayra, F. (2005, June). *Fundamental components of the gameplay experience: Analysing immersion.* Paper presented at the biannual conference of the Digital Game Researcher Association, Vancouver, BC.

ESRB (2005). *ESRB Game Ratings: Game Rating & Descriptor Guide.* Retrieved July 16, 2005, from http://www.esrb.org/esrbratings_guide.asp

Everton, R. W., Mastrangelo, P.M., & Jolton, J. A. (2005). Personality correlates of employees' personal use of work computers. *CyberPsychology & Behavior, 8*(2), 143–153.

Federal Communications Commission (2003). *Children's Internet Protection Act.* Retrieved May 15, 2005, from http://www.fcc.gov/cgb/consumer-facts/cipa.html

Feintuch, U., Raz, L., Hwang, J., Josman, L., Katz, R., Kizony, D., Rand, A., et al. (2006, April). Integrating haptic-tactile feedback into a video-captive-based Virtual Environment for rehabilitation. *CyberPsychology and Behavior, 9*, Iss. 2, 129–132.

Fenichel, M., Jones G., Meunier, V., & Walker-Schmucker, W. (2005). *ISMHO clinical case study group: Half a decade of online case study.* Message posted to International Society for Mental Health Online. Retrieved October 10, 2005, from http://fenichel.com/csg6.shtml

*Few parents have the information they need to educate their children about safe sex,* (2004, April). Retrieved June 7, 2005, from http://www.guttmacher.org/media/nr/2004/04/29/index.html

Filtering software, better but still fallible (2005, June). *Consumer Reports,* 36–38.

Final Stand Records (2005). *Media*. Retrieved Oct. 17, 2005, from http://www.finalstandrecords.com/media.htm

fire-belly (2005, July 31). *Technology: Chinese gold farming and you*. Retrieved August 12, 2005, from http://erikumenhofer.blogspot.com/2005/07/technology-chinese-gold-farming-and.html

Fisher, C. B., & Fried, A. L. (2003). Internet-mediated psychological services and the American Psychological Association ethics code. *Psychotherapy: Theory, Research, Practice, Training, 40*(1/2), 103–111.

Fisher, W. A., & Barak, A. (2001). Internet pornography: A social psychological perspective on Internet sexuality. *The Journal of Sex Research, 38*(4), 312–323.

Flanagan, J. (2003, July 15–21). Learning history for conversations with a preschooler. *Downtown Express, 16*(7). Retrieved May 18, 2005, from http://www.downtownexpress.com/DE_12/learninghistory.html

Fox, S., Anderson, J., & Rainie, L. (2005). *The future of the Internet: In a survey technology experts and scholars evaluate where the Internet is headed in the next ten years*. Washington DC: Pew Internet and American Life Project.

Franklin, R. (2005). *Hate Directory*. Retrieved Oct. 17, 2005, from http://www.bcpl.net/~rfrankli/hatedir.pdf

Freeman-Longo, R. (2000). Children, teens, and sex on the Internet. *Sexual Addiction and Compulsivity, 7,* 75–90.

Freud, S. (1932). *New Introductory Lectures on Psychoanalysis*. Retrieved February 1, 2006, from http://en.wikiquote.org/wiki/Sigmund_Freud#New_Introductory_Lectures_on_Psychoanalysis_.281932.29

Friedland, L. (2005, Winter). Psychologists, robotics, and the new technology. *The Amplifier Media Psychology Newsletter* (pp. 3, 6). Washington DC: American Psychological Association.

Friedman, T. (2005). *The world is flat: A brief history of the twenty-first century*. New York: Farrar, Straus, and Giroux.

Funk, J. B., Pasold, T., & Baumgardner, J. (2003). How children experience playing video games. *ACM International Conference Proceeding Series, Vol. 38. Proceedings of the second international conference on entertainment computing*. Pittsburg, PA: Carnegie Mellon University.

Gackenbach, J. I. (1988). The psychological content of lucid dreams. In J. I. Gackenbach and S. P. LaBerge (Eds.), *Conscious mind, sleeping brain: Perspectives on lucid dreaming*. New York: Plenum.

Gackenbach, J. I. (1991). A developmental model of consciousness in sleep: From sleep consciousness to pure consciousness. In J. I. Gackenbach and A. Sheikh (Eds.), *Dream images: A call to mental arms*. New York: Baywood.

Gackenbach, J. (1998). Introduction to psychological aspects of Internet use. In J. Gackenbach (Ed.), *Psychology and the Internet* (pp. 1–25). San Diego, CA: Academic Press.

Gackenbach, J. I. (2005). *Video game play and lucid dreams: Implications for the development of consciousness.* Paper under editorial consideration.

Gackenbach, J. I., & Bosveld, J. (1989). *Control your dreams.* New York: Harper & Row.

Gackenbach, J. I., & Preston, J. (1998, April). *Video game play and the development of consciousness.* Poster presented at the third biannual meeting of the Science of Consciousness, University of Arizona.

Gaggioli, A., Mantovani, F., Castelnuovo, G., Wiederhold, B., & Riva, G. (2003). Avatars in clinical psychology: A framework for the clinical use of virtual humans. *CyberPsychology & Behavior, 6*(2), 117–125.

Galbreath, N., Berlin, F., & Sawyer, D. (2002). Paraphilias and the Internet. In A. Cooper (Ed.), *Sex and the Internet: A guidebook for clinicians* (pp. 187–205). New York: Brunner-Rutledge.

Garfield, B. (2005, April 8). An impending period of transitional chaos for media. *NPR's on the media.* Retrieved May 29, 2005, from http://www.npr.org/templates/story/story.php?storyId=4583366

Garos, S., Bleckley, M., Beggan, J., & Frizzell, J. (2004). Intrapsychic conflict and deviant sexual behavior in sex offenders. *Journal of Offender Rehabilitation, 40,* Iss. 1–2, 23–40.

Gee, J. (2005, June). *Learning is the engine that drives good video games.* Invited address to the biannual meeting of Digital Game Researcher Association, Vancouver, BC.

Gee, J. (2003). *What video games have to teach us about learning and literacy.* New York: Palgrave MacMillan.

Geist, C. (1997). Introduction. *Videotopia.* Retrieved July 11, 2005, from http://www.videotopia.com/intro.htm

Gerchener, K. (2003). Online dating grows up. *CBS Market Watch,* Retrieved December 17, 2004, from http://www.eharmony.com/core/eharmony?cmd=community-dating-grows

Gillispie, J.F. (2007). Cyber shrinks: Expanding the paradigm. In J.I. Gackenbach (Ed.), *Psychology and the Internet: Intrapersonal, Interpersonal, and Transpersonal Implications* (2$^{nd}$ edition). San Diego: Academic Press.

Glicksohn, J., & Avnon, M. (1997). Explorations in virtual reality: Absorption, cognition and altered state of consciousness. *Imagination, Cognition and Personality, 17*(2), 141–151.

Global Market Insite (2005). *GMI Poll: Video Gaming Gaining Ground in Populous India and Mexico and Continuing to Grow Worldwide.* Retreived August 17, 2005, from http://www.gmi-mr.com/gmipoll/press_room_wppk_pr_05182005.phtml

Goertzel, Ben (1998). Chapter 12: World wide brain: Self-organizing internet intelligence as the actualization of the collective unconscious. In J. I. Gackenbach (Ed.) Psychology and the Internet: Intrapersonal, Interpersonal, and Transpersonal Implications. San Diego: Academic Press, p. 293–320.

Goldberg, C. (2005, December 12). "We feel your pain . . . and your happiness too": The human brain's source of empathy may play a role in autism too. *The Boston Globe,* n.p.

Goldstein, J. (2003). People @ play: Electronic games. In H. van Oostendorp (Ed.), *Cognition in a Digital World* (pp. 25–45). Mahwah, NJ: Lawrence Erlbaum.

Goldstein, J., Cajko, L., Oosterbroek, M., Michielsen, M., Van Houten, O., & Salverda, F. (1997). Video games and the elderly. *Social Behavior & Personality: An International Journal, 25* (4), 345–352.

Goodson, P., McCormick, D., and Evans, A. (2000). Sex on the Internet: College students' emotional arousal when viewing sexually explicit materials on-line. *Journal of Sex Education and Therapy, 25*(4), 252–260.

Goodwin, E. (2003, May 15). *"Little blue light–Franz Kafka,"* Littlebluelight. Retrieved December 15, 2004, from http://www.littlebluelight.com/lblphp/intro.php?ikey=12

Green, C. S. & Baveller, D. (2003). Action video game modifies visual selective attention. *Nature, 423,* 534–537.

Greenfield, D. (1999). *Virtual addiction: Sometimes new technology can create new problems.* Paper presented at the annual convention of the American Psychological Association Annual convention.

Greenfield, D. (2004). Cybersex: Crossing the line online. *Virtual-Addiction.com.* Retrieved June 22, 2004, from http://www.virtual-addiction.com/a_cybersex.htm

Greenfield, P. M. (1996). Video games as cultural artifacts. In P. M. Greenfield & R. R. Cocking (Eds.), *Interacting with video: Advances in applied developmental psychology,* Vol. 11 (pp. 85–94). Norwood, NJ: Ablex Publishing.

Greenfield, P. M. (1998). The cultural evolution of IQ. In U. Neisser (Ed.), *The rising curve: Long term gains in IQ and related measures* (pp. 81–123). Washington, DC: American Psychological Association.

Greenfield, P. (2000). Digital childhood: A research agenda on human development & technology. Webcast retrieved July 14, 2001, from http://www.dacadeofbehavior.org/digitalchild

Greenfield, P. (2004). Developmental considerations for determining appropriate Internet use guidelines for children and adolescents. *Applied Developmental Psychology, 25,* 751–762.

Greenfield, P. (2004a). Developmental considerations for determining appropriate Internet use guidelines for children and adolescents. *Applied Developmental Psychology, 25,* 751–762.

Greenfield, P. (2004b). Inadvertent exposure to pornography on the Internet: Implications of peer-to-peer file-sharing networks for child development and families. *Journal of Applied Developmental Psychology, 25*(6), 741–750.

Greenfield, P. M, Brannon, C., & Lohr, D. (1996). Two-dimensional representation of movement through three-dimensional space: The role of video game expertise. In P. M. Greenfield & R. R. Cocking (Eds.), *Interacting with video. Advances in applied developmental psychology* (pp. 169–185). Norwood, NJ: Ablex Publishing.

Greenfield, P. M., & Cocking, R. R. (Eds.) (1996). *Interacting with video: Advances in applied developmental psychology,* Vol. 11. Norwood, NJ: Ablex Publishing.

Griffiths, M. (1998). Internet addiction: Does it really exist? In J. Gackenbach (Ed.), *Psychology and the Internet* (61–73). San Diego: Academic Press.

Griffiths, M. D., Davies, M. N. O., & Chappell, D. (2003). Breaking the stereotype: The case of online gaming. *CyberPsychology & Behavior, 6*(1), 81–91.

Griffiths, M. D., Davies, M. N. O., & Chappell, D. (2004). Online computer gaming: A comparison of adolescent and adult gamers. *Journal of Adolescence, 27,* 87–96.

Grohol, J. (1998). Future clinical directions: Professional development, pathology, and psychotherapy on-line. In J. Gackenbach (Ed.), *Psychology and the Internet* (pp. 111–138). San Diego, CA: Academic Press.

Grohol, J. (1999). Best practices in etherapy. Legal and licensing issues. Retrieved from http://psychcentral.com/best/best4htm

Grohol, J. (2005, April 16). *More spin on Internet addiction disorder.* Retrieved from http://psychcentral.com/blog/archives/2005/04/16/internet-addiction-disorder

Gross, E. (2004). Adolescent Internet use: What we expect, what teens report. *Journal of Applied Developmental Psychology, 25*(6), 633–649.

Grossman, D. (1995). *On killing: The psychological cost of learning to kill in war and society.* Boston: Little, Brown.

Grossman, L. (2005, May 23). The out of the X box. *Time Magazine* (Canadian Edition), *165*(21), 30–39.

Grossman, L. (2005, May 23). Inside Bill's new X-box. *Time Magazine, 165*(21), 30–39.

Gunter, B., & McAleer, J. (1997). Does advertising affect children? In Editors? *Children and television* (2nd ed., pp. 132–148). London: Routledge.

Haggstron-Nordin, E., Hanson, U., & Tyden, T. (2005). Associations between pornography consumption and sexual practices among adolescents in Sweden. *International Journal of STD & AIDS, 16*(2), 102–108.

Harman, J. P., Hansen, C. E., Cochran, M. E., & Lindsey, C. R. (2005). Liar, Liar: Internet faking but not frequency of use affects social skills, self-esteem, social anxiety, and aggression. *CyberPsychology & Behavior, 8*(1), 1–6.

Harris, R. J. (1999). *A cognitive psychology of mass communication* (3rd ed.). Mahwah, NJ: Lawrence Erlbaum.

Hartlaub, P. (2004, October 28). Pop culture: Click on a former candidate's web site, you never know what you'll find, from Pokemon to hooking up. *San Francisco Chronicle:* Datebook, p. E1, 3.

Health Canada (2002). *Safety and safe use of cellular phones.* Retrieved May 14, 2005, from http://www.hc-sc.gc.ca/english/iyh/products/cell-phones.htm

Health on the Internet Foundation Code of Conduct (2005, September 28). *HON code of conduct (HONcode) for medical and health web sites.* Retrieved April 11, 2005, from http://www.hon.ch/HONcode/conduct.html

Healthfinder (2005). *A Service of the national health information service center,* U.S. department of Health and Human Services. Retrieved November 1, 2005, from http://wwwheatlthfinder.gov

Heins, M. (2001). *Not in front of the children: Indecency and censorship and the innocence of youth.* New York: Hill and Wang.

Heller, Bob (2005, May). *Chatbots and learning communities: Applications and opportunities.* Paper presented at the annual Transformational Networks meeting, Edmonton, Alberta.

Henderson, L. (2005, June). *Video games: A significant cognitive artifact of contemporary youth culture.* Paper presented at the biannual meeting of Digital Game Researcher Association, Vancouver, BC.

Hewitt, H. (2004). *Blog: Understanding the information reformation that's changing your world.* Nashville, TN: Thomas Nelson.

Hill, C. (1987). Affiliation motivation: People who need people but in different ways. *Journal of Personality and Social Psychology, 52,* 1008–1018.

Hills, P., & Argyle, M. (2003). Uses of the Internet and their relationships with individual differences in personality. *Computers in Human Behavior, 19*(1), 59–70.

Hitti, M. (2005). Twenty-five steps to better health. Retrieved May 17, 2006, from http://www.cbsnews.com/stories/2006/05/17/health/webmd/main1624635.shtml

Hobbs, D. L. (2002). A constructivist approach to web course design: A review of the literature. *International Journal on E-Learning, 1*(2), 60–65.

HONcode (2005, April 11,2005). *HON code of conduct (HONcode) for medical and health web sites.* Retrieved April 11, 2005, from http://www.hon.ch/HONcode/conduct.html

Honeycutt, C. (2005). Hazing as a process of boundary maintenance in an online community. *Journal of Computer-Mediated Communication, 10*(2), article 3. Retreived Oct. 12, 2005, from http://jcmc.indiana.edu/vol10/issue2/honeycutt.html

Hopper, J. (1996). *Editorial standards for web advertising.* Retrieved March 13, 2001, from http://www.jimhopper.com/ads–pre.html

Høybyea, M. T., Johansen, C., & Tjørnhøj-Thomsen, T. (2005). Online interaction. Effects of storytelling in an Internet breast cancer support group. *Psycho-Oncology, 14,* 211–220.

Hu, Y., Wood, J. F., Smith, V., & Westbrook, N. (2004). Friendship through IM: Examining the relationship between instant messaging and intimacy. *Journal of Computer Mediated Communication, 10*(1), Retrieved October 6, 2005, from http://jcmc.indiana.edu/vol10/issue1/ hu.html

Huffaker, D. (2004). *Gender similarities and differences in online identity and language use among teenage bloggers.* Unpublished manuscript, Georgetown University, Washington, DC.

Hughes, R., & Hans, J. (2001). Computers, the Internet, and families. *Journal of Family Issues, 22*(6), 776–790.

Hunt, H. (1995). *On the nature of consciousness: Cognitive, phenomenological, and transpersonal perspectives.* New Haven, CT: Yale University Press.

Huntemann, N. (Producer/Director) (2000). *Game over: Gender, race & violence in video games* [Documentary Film]. United States: Media Education Foundation.

International Society for Mental Health Online. (2000, January 9). *Suggested principles for the online provision of mental health services online, Version 3.11*. Retrieved October 10, 2005, from http://www.ismho.org/suggestions.htm

International Society for Mental Health Online. (2005). *Mission statement of ISMHO*. Retrieved May 13, 2005, from http://www.ismho.org/mission.htm

It's My Life (2005a). *What would your dream bedroom look like?* Retrieved May 16, 2005, from http://pbskids.org/itsmylife/family/kids/you_said_it_dream_bedroom.html

It's My Life (2005b). *What do you like best and/or least about being home alone?* Retrieved May 16, 2005, from http://pbskids.org/itsmylife/family/homealone/you_said_it.html

Jackson, D. N. III, Vernon, P. A, & Jackson, D. N. (1993). Dynamic spatial performance and general intelligence. *Intelligence, 17*(4), 451–460.

Jackson, L., von Eye, A., Biocca, F., Barbatsis, G., Fitzgerald, H., & Zhao, Y. (2003). Personality, cognitive style, demographic characteristics and Internet use. Findings from the HomeNetToo project. *Swiss Journal of Psychology, 62*(2), 79–90.

James, L. K., Lin, C. Y., Steed, A., Swapp, D., & Slater, M. (2003). Social Anxiety in Virtual Environments: Results of a Pilot Study. *CyberPsychology & Behavior, 6*(3), 237–243.

Johnson, S. (2005). *Everything bad is good for you: How today's popular culture is actually making us smarter*. New York: Riverhead Books.

Joinson, A. (1998). Causes and implications of disinhibited behavior on the Internet. In J. Gackenbach (Ed.). *Psychology and the Internet* (43–58). San Diego: Academic Press.

Joinson, A. I. (2007). Disinhibition and the Internet. In J. I. Gackenbach (Ed.), *Psychology and the Internet: Intrapersonal, Interpersonal, and Transpersonal Implications* (2nd ed.), San Diego: Academic Press.

Jones, S. G. (1998). Cybersociety: Revisiting computer-mediated communication and community (pp. 185–205). Thousand Oaks, CA: Sage Publications.

Jones, S. G. (2000), Virtual culture: Identity and communication in cyber society. S. Jones (Ed.). *Cybersociety 2.0* (pp. 185–205). Thousand Oaks, CA: Sage Publications.

Jones, S., Clarke, L. N., Cornish, S., Gonzales, M., Johnson, C., Lawson, J. N. et al. (2003, July 6). *Let the games begin: Gaming technology and entertainment among college students*. Washington, DC: Pew Internet and American Life Project.

Kaiser Family Foundation (2002, December 10). *See no evil: How Internet filters affect the search for online health information.* Retrieved April 12, 2005, from http://www.kff.org/entmedia/2002110a-index.cfm

Kaiser Family Foundation (2005a, January). *eHealth and the elderly: How seniors use the Internet for health.* Retrieved April 11, 2005, from http://www.kff.org/entmedia/entmedia011205pkg.cfm

Kaiser Family Foundation (2005b, April 11). *A study of entertainment, media, and health.* Retrieved April 11, 2005, from http://www.kff.org/entmedia/index.cfm

Kaltiala-Heino, R., Lintonen, T., & Rimpela, A. (2004). Internet addiction? Potentially problematic use of the Internet in a population of 12–18 year old adolescents. *Addiction Research and Theory, 12*(1), 89–96.

Karmiloff-Smith, A. (1992). *Beyond modularity: A developmental perspective on cognitive science.* Cambridge, MA: MIT Press.

Kaufman, G., & Phua, V. C. (2003). Is ageism alive in date selection among men? Age requests among gay and straight men in Internet personal ads. *Journal of Men's Studies, 11*(2), 225–235.

Keller, S., & Brown, J. (2002). Media interventions to promote responsible sexual behavior. *The Journal of Sex Research, 39*, Iss. 1, 1–10.

Kiesler, S., Bozena, Z., Lundmark, V., & Kraut, R. (2000). Troubles with the Internet: The dynamics of help at home. *Human-Computer Interaction, 15*, 323–351.

King, D. (2005, August 11). Hot, steamy and now downloadable: Aural sex shimmies into the podcast as 'podnography' trend takes off. *The San Francisco Chronicle,* D10.

King, S., & Moreggi, D. (1998). Internet therapy and self help groups–the pros and cons. In J. Gackenbach (Ed.), *Psychology and the Internet* (pp. 77–110). San Diego, CA: Academic Press.

King, S., & Moreggi, D. (in press). Internet self-help and support groups, the pros and cons of text-based mutual aid. In J. I. Gackenbach (Ed.), *Psychology and the Internet: Intrapersonal, Interpersonal, and Transpersonal Implications* (2nd ed.), San Diego: Academic Press.

Kirriemuir, J. (2005). Survey of games used in education. *The Education Arcade Forum,* Retrieved May 18, 2005, from http://www.educationarcade.org/index.php?name=PNphpBB2&file=viewtopic&t=69

Kirschner, P., & van Bruggen, J. (2004). Learning and understanding in virtual teams. *CyberPsychology & Behavior, 7*(2), 135–139.

Klien, B. (2005, September). Book Review. *Clinical Social Work Journal, 33*(3), pp. 374–377.

Koch, W., & Pratarelli, M. (2004). Effects of intro/extraversion and sex on social Internet use. *North American Journal of Psychology, 6*(3), 371–382.

Koocher, G., & Morray, E. (2000). Regulation of telepsychology: A survey of State Attorneys General. *Professional Psychology Research and Practice, 31*(5), 503–508.

Krantz, J. H., Ballard, J., & Scher, J. (1997). Comparing the results of laboratory and World-Wide Web samples on the determinants of female attractiveness. *Behavior Research Methods, Instruments & Computers, 29*(2), 264–269.

Kraut, R., Kiesler, S. & Boneva, B. (2002). Internet paradox revisited. *Journal of Social Issues, 58*(1), 49–74.

Kraut, R., Lundmark, V., Patterson, M., Kiesler, S., Mukopadhyaya, T., & Scherlis, W. (1998). Internet paradox: A social technology that reduces social involvement and psychological well-being. *American Psychologist, 5*, 1017–1031.

Kraut, R., Olson, J., Banaji, M., Bruckman, A., Cohen, J., & Couper, M. (2004). Psychological research online: Report of board of scientific affairs' advisory group on the conduct of research on the Internet. *American Psychologist, 59*(2), 105–117.

Kraut, R., Patterson, M., Lundmark, V., Kiesler, S., & Scherlis, W. (1998). Internet paradox: A social technology that reduces social involvement and psychological well-being? *American Psychologist, 53*, 1017–1031.

KSSTANK (2005). Response to 'Aryan justice a hate crime'. Retrieved Oct. 17, 2005, from http://www.finalstandrecords.com/forum/viewtopic.php?t=898

Kubey, R., & Csikszentmihalyi, M. (2004). Television addiction is no mere metaphor. *Scientific American (Special Edition), 14*(1), 48–55.

Kuhn, D. (1999). A developmental model of critical thinking. *Educational Researcher, 28*(2), 16–26.

Kusahara, M. (2001). The art of creating subjective reality: An analysis of Japanese digital pets. *Leonardo, 34*(4), 299–302. Retrieved May 14, 2005, from http://wos01.isiknowledge.com/CIW.cgi

Langer, E. (1996). *Mindfulness.* New York: Perseus Books.

Langer, E. (1989). *The power of mindful learning.* New York: Perseus Books.

Larsen, R. J. & Buss, D. M. (2005). *Personality psychology: domains of knowledge about human nature* (2nd ed.). NY: McGraw Hill.

Lawlor, J. (2005, May 11). Diary details violent urge. *The Flint Journal First Edition.* Retrieved May 18, 2005, from http://www.mlive.com/news/fljournal/index.ssf?/base/news-29/111582483914190.xml

Lazar, J., & Preece, J. (2003). Social consideration in online communities: Usability, sociability, and success factors. In H. van Oostendorp (Ed.), *Cognition in a Digital World* (pp. 127–151). Mahwah, NJ: Erlbaum.

Leaders, S. (2005, August 6–12). Breeding evil? *The Economist, 376*(8,438), p. 9.

Lebo, H., & Wolpert, S. (2004, January 14). First release of findings from the UCLA world internet project shows significant 'digital gender gap' in many countries. *UCLANEWS.*

Lee, E., & Leets, L. (2002). Persuasive storytelling by hate groups online: Examining its effects on adolescents. *American Behavioral Scientist, 45*(6), 927–957.

Lee, J., Jackson, H., Pattison, P., & Ward, T. (2002). Developmental risk factors for sexual offending. *Child Abuse & Neglect, 26*(1), 73–92.

Lee, W., Tan, T., & Hameed, S. (2005). Polychronicity, the Internet, and the Mass Media: A Singapore study. *Journal of Computer-Mediated Communication, 11*(1), 1–17.

Lenhart, A. (2005, March 17). Protecting teens online. *Report from the Pew Internet and American Life Project: Teens Online.* Retrieved on June 7, 2005, from http://www.pewinternet.org/PPF/r/152/report_display.asp

Lenhart, A. (2005, March 17). Protecting teens online. *Report from the Pew Internet and American Life Project: Teens Online.* Retrieved on June 7, 2005, from http://www.pewinternet.org/PPF/r/152/report_display.asp

Leon, D. T., Rotunda, R. J., Sutton, M., & Schlossman, C. (2003). Internet forewarning effects on ratings of attraction. *Computers in Human Behavior, 19*(1), 39–57.

Lessig, L. (2005, May). The second conference on online deliberation: Design, research, and practice. Paper presented at the annual meeting of Stanford University Center for Internet and Society, Stanford, CA.

Lewis, R. (2004). Communications technology in the developing nations. *Journal of Computer Assisted Learning, 20*, pp. 159.

Levy, S. & Stone, B. (2006, April 3). The new wisdom of the Web. *Newsweek,* p. 53.

Lloyd, B. T. (2002). A conceptual framework for examining adolescent identity, media influence, and social development. *Review of General Psychology, 6*(1), 73–91.

Lorber, J., & Satow, R. (1975, July). Dropout rates in mental health centers. *Social Work, 20*(4), pp. 308–312.

Los Angeles County District Attorney's Office (2005a). Comprehensive IM Shorthand List. *Protecting Our Kids.* Retrieved May 17, 2005, from http://da.co.la.ca.us/pok/poklist.htm

Los Angeles County District Attorney's Office (2005b). Instant Messaging, Chat Rooms, ICQ–Do you know who your kid's talking to? *Protecting Our Kid's*. Retrieved May 17, 2005, from http://da.co.la.ca.us/pok/im.htm

Lukoff, D. (2002). *Navigating the mental health Internet*. Retrieved January 26, 2005, from http://www.internetguides.com/nmhi/navhome.html

Maheu, M., Whitten, P., & Allen, A. (2001). E-health, Telehealth, and telemedicine: A guide to start-up and success. New York: Jossey-Bass.

Malec, J., Jones, R., Rao, N., & Stubbs, K. (1984). Video game practice effects on sustained attention in patients with craniocerebral trauma. *Cognitive Rehabilitation, 2*(4), 18–23.

Males, M. (2006). Grown-ups get a grip. Retrieved May 5, 2006, from http://home.earthlink.net/~mmales/yt-myspa.htm

Males, M. (2003). Kids, talk to your grown-ups. Retrieved May 5, 2006, from http://home.earthlink.net/~mmales/yt-bully.htm

Males, M. (1994). Media violence does not cause societal violence. In W. Barbour (Ed.), *Mass Media: Opposing Viewpoints* (pp. 130–134). San Diego, CA: Greenhaven.

Mallen, M., Day, S., & Green, M. (2003). Online verses face-to-face conversations: An examinations of relational and discourse variables. *Psychotherapy: Theory, Research, Practice, Training, 40*(1/2), 155–163.

Martin, P., & Petry, N. (2005). Are non-substance related addictions really addictions? *American Journal on Addictions, 14*(1), 1& 3.

Mathwick, C., & Rigdon, E. (2004). Play, flow, and the online search experience. *Journal of Consumer Research, 31*(2), 324–333.

Mattes, C., Nanney, R., & Coussons-Read, M. (2003). The online university: Who are its students and how are they unique? *Journal of Educational Computing Research, 28*(2), 89–102.

Matthews, T. D. (1999). A world wide web-based research project. *Teaching of Psychology, 26*(3), 227–230.

Maynard, A. E., Subrahmanyam, K., & Greenfield, P. (2005). Technology and the development of intelligence: From the loom to the computer. In R. J. Sternberg & D.D. Preiss (Eds.), *Intelligence and technology: The impact of tools on the nature and development of human abilities* (pp. 29–53). Mahwah, NJ: Lawrence Erlbaum.

Maynard, A. E., Subrahmanyam, K., & Greenfield, P. M. (2005) Technology and the development of intelligence: From the loom to the computer. In Robert Sternberg and David Preiss (Eds.), *Intelligence and Technology: The Impact of Tools on the Nature and Development of Human Abilities* (p. xiii-xxii). Mahwah, NJ: Lawrence Erlbaum.

McCloskey, B. (2005, January 12). Holiday traffic. *Media Posts Email Insider*. Retrieved January 12, 2005, from http://www.mediapost.com/dtls_dsp_EmailInsider.cfm?fnl=050112

McGinnis, J. M. (2006). National Priorities in disease prevention. National Academy of Science, Electronic Journal Issues in Science and Technology.

McKenna, K., & Bargh, J. (1998). Coming out in the age of the Internet: Identity "demarginalization" through virtual group participation. *Journal of Personality and Social Psychology, 75*, 681–694.

McKenna, K.Y.A., Green, A. S., & Gleason, M. E. J. (2002). Relationship formation on the Internet: What's the big attraction? *Journal of Social Issues, 58*(1), 9–31.

McLaughlin, M., Osborne, K., & Ellison, N. (1997). Virtual community in a telepresence environment. In S. G. Jones (Ed.), *Virtual culture: Identity and communication in cybersociety* (pp. 146–168). London: Sage.

McLean, A. (2005, Feb. 12). Sweet dreams for gamers: Video games prompt more lucid dreams, says Grant MacEwan prof. *Edmonton Journal*. Retrieved Feb 12, 2005, from http://www.canada.com/edmonton/edmontonjournal/news/culture/story.html?id=9d1c053b-16e5-4f1e-ad7c-f893509c952c

McLuhan, M. (n.d.). Retrieved May 29, 2006, from http://en.wikipedia.org/wiki/Marshall_McLuhan#Hot_and_cold_media

McLuhan, M. (2005). *Frequently asked questions: On "The Medium is the Message."* Retrieved Sept. 27, 2005 from http://www.marshallmcluhan.com/faqs.html

Metzl, J. (2004). Voyeur nation? Changing definitions of voyeurism. *Harvard Review of Psychiatry, 12*, 127–131.

Meunier, L. (1996). *Computer background of men and women*. Retrieved May, 1998, from http://lists.cmhc.com/research/1997/0626.html. Note: This item was no longer available online on March 17, 2001.

Miller v. California (1973). 413 U.S. 15.

Moody, E. (2001). Internet use and its relationship to loneliness. *CyberPsychology & Behavior, 4*, 393–401.

Moore, G. (2005). A prediction made real improved billions of lives. Retrieved October 14, 2005, from http://www.intel.com/technology/silicon/mooreslaw/

Morahan-Martin, J. (2004). How Internet users find, evaluate, and use online health information: A cross-cultural review. *CyberPsychology & Behavior, 7*(5), 497–510.

Morahan-Martin, J., & Shumacher, P. (1997). Incidents and correlates of pathological Internet use. Paper presented at the 105th Annual Convention of the American Psychological Association, Chicago, IL.

Morahan-Martin, J., & Schumacher, P. (2000). Incidence and correlates of pathological Internet use among college students. *Computers in Human Behavior, 16*, 13–29.

Morahan-Martin, J., & Schumacher, P. (2003). Loneliness and social uses of the Internet. *Computers in Human Behavior, 19*(6), 659–671.

Morgan, C., & Cotton, S. (2003). The relationship between Internet activities and depressive symptoms in a sample of college freshmen. *Cyberpsychology & Behavior, 6*(2), 133–142.

Moser, C., Kleinplatz, P. J., Zuccarini, D. & Reiner, W. G. (2004). Situating unusual child and adolescent behaviors in context. *Child and adolescent psychiatry clinics of North America: Sex and gender issues, 13*(3), 569–589.

Murray, J. (2005, June). *The future of electronic games: Lessons from the first 250,000 years*. Keynote address at the biannual meeting of Digital Game Researcher Association, Vancouver, BC.

Nelson, M. (1997). *Community and media influences of adolescent sexual abstinence*. Dissertation Abstracts International: Section B: The Sciences and Eng Vol 58 (5-B0 Nov 1997, 2721pp).

Newman, R. (2001, March). Not a question of for or against. *Monitor on Psychology, 32*(3). Retrieved October 11, 2004, from http://www.apa.org/monitor/mar01/pp.html

Ng, B., & Wiemer-Hastings, P. (2005). Addiction to the Internet and online gaming. *CyberPsychology & Behavior, 8*(2), 110–113.

Ng, Elaine, & Detenber, B. (2005). The impact of synchronicity and civility in online political discussions on perceptions and intentions to participate. *Journal of Computer-Mediated Communications, 10*(3). Article 4. Retreived on Oct. 12, 2005, from http://jcmc.indiana.edu/vol10/ issue3/ng.html

Nichols, L., & Nicki, R. (2004). Development of a psychometrically sound Internet addiction scale: A preliminary step. *Psychology of Addictive Behaviors, 18*(4), 381–384.

Nickelson, D. (2001, August 24) Psychology online: Current issues in behavioral telehealth. Message posted to http://www.fenichel.com/ismhopanel2001.shtml

Nicovich, S. G., Boller, G. W., & Cornwell, T. B. (2005). Experienced presence within computer-mediated communications: Initial explorations on the effects of gender with respect to empathy and immersion.

*Journal of Computer-Mediated Communications, 10*(2), Retreived October 12, 2005, from http://jcmc.indiana.edu/vol10/issue2/ nicovich.html

Nie, N., Simpser, A., Stepanikova, I., & Zheng, L. (2004). Ten years after the birth of the Internet: How do Americans use the Internet in their daily lives? *Stanford Center for the Quantitative Study of Society,* Retreived May 18, 2005, from http://www.stanford.edu/group/siqss/SIQSS_Time_Study_04.pdf

Nielsen//NetRatings (2004). Online games claim stickiest web sites, according to Nielsen//NetRatings. Retreived October 4, 2005, from www.internetadsales.com/ modules/news/article.php?storyid=1470

Noonan, R. (1998). The psychology of sex: A mirror of the Internet. In J. Gackenbach (Ed.), *Psychology and the Internet.* San Diego: Academic Press, 143–166.

Norris, P. (2000). *Digital Divide? Civic engagement, information poverty and the Internet worldwide.* Cambridge: Cambridge University Press. Retrieved July 20, 2004, from http://ksghome.harvard.edu/~.pnorris.shorenstein.ksg/Books/Digital%20Divide.htm

Nowak, K. (2004). The Influence of Anthropomorphism and Agency on Social Judgment in Virtual Environments. *Journal of Computer Mediated Communication, 9*(2). Retrieved October 7, 2005, from http://jcmc.indiana.edu/vol9/issue2/nowak.html#ninth

Nowak, K. L., Watt, J., & Walther, J. B. (2005). The influence of synchrony and sensorymodality on the person perception process in computer-mediated groups. *Journal of Computer-Mediated Communication, 10*(3), article 3. Retrieved October 12, 2005, from http://jcmc.indiana.edu/vol10/issue3/mowak.html

NUA Internet Surveys. (2001, February 27). *Yahoo: African Americans lead in US Internet growth.* Retrieved March 17, 2001, from http://www.nua.ie/surveys/?f=VS&art_id=905356501&rel=true

NUA Internet Surveys. (2001, March 12). *Yahoo: US leads in web rankings.* Retrieved March 17, 2001, from http://www.nua.ie/surveys/?f=VS&art_id=905356544&rel=true

Nussbaum, E. (2004, January 11). My so-called blog. *The New York Times.* Retrieved July 15, 2005, from http://www.nytimes/2004/01/11/magazine11blog.html

O'Connell, R., Price, J., & Barrow, C. (2004). *Emerging Trends Amongst Primary School Children's Use of the Internet.* Research report from the Cyberspace Research Unit. Retrieved March 9, 2006 from http://www.uclan.ac.uk/host/cru//does/emerging_trends_full_report_060204.pdf.

O'Keefe, B. (2000). *Summary and synthesis: Digital kids.* Retrieved July 14, 2001 http://www.dacadeofbehavior.org/digitalchild/workgroupsumms.html

Offit, A. (1995). Are you ready for virtual love. . .? A psychiatrist looks at cybersex. Retrieved May, 1998, from http://web2.airmail.net/walraven/cosmo.html. Note: This item was no longer available online on March 8, 2001.

Okita, S. (2004). Effects of age on associating virtual and embodied toys. *CyberPsychology & Behavior, 7*(4), 464–471.

Ono, H., & Zavodny, M. (2003). Gender and the Internet. *Social Science Quarterly, 84*(1), 111–121.

Ottoskin (2005). Response to 'Non-whites in NHL.' Retrieved October 17, 2005, from http://www.finalstandrecords.com/forum/viewtopic.php?t=1002

Page, B. J., Jencius, M. J., Rehfuss, M. C., Foss, L. L., Dean, E. P., Petruzzi, M. L., Olson, S. D., and Sager, D. E. (2003). PalTalk online groups: Process and reflections on students' experience. *Journal for Specialists in Group Work, 28*(1), 35–41.

Patterson, D., Tininenko, J., Schmidt, A., & Sharar, S. (2004). Virtual Reality hypnosis: A Case Report. *International Journal of Clinical and Experimental Hypnosis, 52*(1), 27–38.

Paraphilia. (2005) *Psychology Today.* Retrieved May 29, 2005, from http://cms.psychologytoday.com/conditions/paraphilias.html

Parker, T. S., & Wampler, K. S. (2003). How bad is it? Perceptions of the relationship impact of different types of Internet sexual activities. *Contemporary Family Therapy: An International Journal, 25*(4), 415–429.

Paul, P. (2005). *Pornified: How pornography is transforming our lives, our relationships, and our families.* New York: Times Books.

Peck, I., & Peck, R. (2005). How traditional Chinese medicine views the human body in relation to disease process. *The Pain Practitioner, 15*(1), 21–22.

Phua, V. C., Hooper, J., & Vazquez, O. (2002). Men's concerns with sex and health in personal advertisements. *Culture, Health & Sexuality, 4*(3), 355–363.

Plant, S. (2001). Coming across the future. In Bell, D., & Kennedy, B. (Eds.). *The Cybercultures Reader.* pp. 460–467. New York: Routledge.

Poole, B. (1997). *Education for an information age: Teaching in the computerized classroom.* Madison, WI: WCB Brown and Benchmark.

Preece, J., Noonecke, B., & Andrews, D. (2004). The top five reasons for lurking: Improving community experiences for everyone. *Computers in Human Behavior, 20*(2), 201–223.

Preston, J. M. (in press). Mediated environments: Interfaces, transparency and intelligence augmentation. In J. I. Gackenbach (Ed.), *Psychology and the internet: Intrapersonal, interpersonal and transpersonal implications* (2nd ed.). San Diego, CA: Academic Press.

Preston, J. M., & Nery, R. (2004, November). Video game play, spatial skills, balance, and consciousness experiences. Personal Communication.

Quan-Haase, A., Cothrel, J., & Wellman, B. (2005). Instant messaging for collaboration: A case study of a high-tech firm. *Journal of Computer-Mediated Communication. 10*(4), article 13. Retrieved October 12, 2005, from http://jcmc.indiana.edu/vol10/issue4/quan-haase.html

Quayle, E., & Taylor, M. (2003). Model of problematic Internet use in people with a sexual interest in children. *Cyberpsychology and Behavior, 6*(1), 93–106.

Quindlen, A. (2001, February). Too busy to have a life of your own? There's always the vicarious voyeurism of reality TV. *Newsweek, 26,* 74.

Ragusa, A., & VandeCreek, L. (2003). Suggestions for the ethical practice of online psychotherapy. *Psychotherapy, Research and Practice, 40*(1/2), 94–102.

Rainie, L., & Horrigan, J. (2005, January 25). *A decade of adoption: How the Internet has woven itself into American life.* PEW Internet and American Life Project. Retrieved from http://www.pewinternet.org/PPF/r/148/report_display.asp

Rainie, L. (2005, March 30). Freedom to connect conference. *PEW Internet and American Life Project.* Retrieved July 11, 2005, from http://www.perinternet.org/pp/

Rainie, L., & Horrigan, J. (2005, January 25). *A decade of adoption: How the Internet has woven itself into American life.* PEW Internet and American Life Project. Retrieved from http://www.pewinternet.org/PPF/r/148/report_display.asp

Rainie, L., & Kalsnes, B. (2001, October 10). *The commons of the tragedy.* Pew Internet & American Life Project. Retrieved December 16, 2004, from http://www.pewinternet.org/pdfs/PIP_Tragedy_Report.pdf

Rainie, L., & Kohot, L., (2000). *Tracking online life: How women use the Internet to cultivate relationships with family and friends.* Washington, DC: Pew Internet & American Life Project. Retrieved July 19, 2004, from http://www.pewinternet.org/pdfs/Report1.pdf

Reid, E. (1994). *Cultural formations in text-based virtual realities.* Master's Thesis, Cultural Studies Program, Department of English, University of Melbourne. Retrieved March 11, 2001, from http://www.crosswinds.net/~aluluei/cult-form.htm

Remez, L. (2000). Oral sex among adolescents: Is it sex or abstinence? *Family Planning Perspectives, 32*(6), Nov/Dec., 298–304.

Reynolds, C., & Picard, R. (2004). Ethical evaluation of displays that adapt to affect. *CyberPsychology & Behavior, 7*(6), 662–666.

Rideout, V. J., Vandewater, E. A., & Wartella, E. A. (2003). *Zero to six: Electronic media in the lives of infants, toddlers and preschoolers.* The Henry Kaiser Family Foundation. Retrieved May 8, 2005, from http://www.kff.org/entmedia/loader.cfm?url=/commonspot/security/getfile.cfm&PageID=22754

Ridings, C. M. & Gefen, D. (2004). Virtual Community attraction: Why people hang out online. *Journal of Computer-Mediated Communication, 10*(1), article 4. Retreived October 15, 2005, from http://jcmc.indiana.edu/vol10/issue1/ridings_gefen.html

Ritterband, L., Gonder-Frederick, L., Cox, D., Clifton, A., West, R., & Borowitz, S. (2003). Internet interventions: In review, in use, and into the future. *Professional Psychology, Research and Practice, 34*(5), 527–34.

Riva, G. (2005). Virtual reality in psychotherapy: A review. *CyberPsychology & Behavior, 8*(3), 220–230.

Roberts, D., Foehr, U., & Rideout, V. (2005). *Generation M: Media in the lives of 8-18 year-olds.* The Henry Kaiser Family Foundation. Retrieved March 24, 2005, from http://www.kff.org/entmedia/entmedia030905pkg.cfm

Roberts, D., Foehr, U., & Rideout, V. (2005, March). *Generation M: Media in the lives of 8–18 year olds.* Kaiser Family Foundation Study. Menlo Park, CA.

Robinett, W. (2003). Foreword. In M. J. P. Wolf & B. Perron (Eds.), *The Video Game Theory Reader* (pp. vii-xix). New York: Routledge.

Rohde, L. (2005, Jan. 11). Study advises limiting children's use of mobile phones. IDG News Service. Retrieved May 14, 2005, from http://www.networkworld.com/news/2005/0111studyadvis.html

Roland, W. (1999). *The age of information from telegraph to Internet.* Toronto, Canada: Key Porter Books.

Roman, S., Martin, J., Gendall, K., & Herbison, G. (2003). Age of menarche: The role of some psychosocial factor, *Psychological Medicine, 35,* 933–039.

Rouse, S., & Haas, H. A. (2003). Exploring the accuracies and inaccuracies of personality perception following Internet-mediated communication. *Journal of Research in Personality, 37*(5), 446–467.

Rushkoff, D. (1996). *Playing the future.* New York: Harper Collins.

Rushkoff, D. (2005, May 23). Everything bad is good for me too. *Douglas Rushkoff.* Retrieved May 26, 2005, from http://www.rushkoff.com/2005_05_01_archive.php

Russell, P. (1989/1995). *The global brain awakens*. Palo Alto, CA: Global Brain.

Ruvinsky, J. (2003, April). Haptic technology simulates the sense of touch–via computer. Paper retrieved September 12, 2005 from http://news-service.stanford.edu/news/2003/april2/haptics-42.html

Salanova, M., Llorens, S., Cifre, E., Martinex, I., & Schaufeli, W. (2003). Perceived collective efficacy, subjective well-being, and task performance among electronic work groups: An experimental study. *Small Group Research, 34*(1), 43–73.

Sanders, C., Field, T., Diego, M., & Kaplan, M. (2000). The relation of Internet use to depression and social isolation among adolescents. *Adolescence, 35*, 237–241.

Santrock, J., Woloshyn, V., Gallagher, T., DiPetta, T., & Mariini, Z. (2004). *Educational Psychology* (First Canadian Edition). Toronto: McGraw-Hill Ryerson.

Schafer, J. A. (2002). Spinning the web of hate: Web-based hate propagation by extremist organizations. *Journal of Criminal Justice and Popular Culture, 9*(2), 69–88.

Schiano, D. (1997). Convergent methodologies in cyber–psychology: A case study. *Behavior Research Methods, Instruments, and Computers, 29*(2), 270–273.

Seaman, B. (2005). *Binge: What your college student won't tell you*. Hoboken, New Jersey: John Wiley & Sons.

Seepersad, S. (2004). Coping with loneliness: Adolescent online and offline behavior. *CyberPsychology & Behavior, 7*(1), 35–39.

*Sex education in America*, (2004). A Report from National Public Radio, the Kaiser Family Foundation, and Harvard University, John F. Kennedy School of Government. Menlo Park, CA: The Henry J. Kaiser Foundation.

*Sex education: Needs, programs, and policies*, (2004, April). Slide and lecture presentation, the Allan Guttmacher Institute.

Shaffer, R. J., Jocokes, L. E., Cassily, J. F., Greenspan, S. I., Tuchman, R. F. & Stemmer, P. J. (2001). Effect of interactive metronome training on children with ADHD. *The American Journal of Occupational Therapy, 55*(2), 155–166.

Shaw, L., & Gant, L. (2002). In defense of the Internet: The relationship between Internet communication and depression, loneliness, self-esteem, and perceived social support. *Cyber Psychology and Behavior, 5*(2), 157–71.

Shlain, L. (2006). *Leonardo's brain: The right/leftr roots of creativity*, New York: Viking Press, The Penguin Group.

Shlain, L. (1998). *The alphabet verses the goddess: The conflict between word and image*. New York: Viking Press, The Penguin Group.

Simon, G. (2001). Cyberporn and censorship: Constitutional barriers to preventing access to Internet pornography by minors. *The Journal of Criminal Law and Criminology, 8*(5), 1015–1033.

Skinner, A., & Zack, J. (2004). Counseling and the Internet. *American Behavioral Scientist, 48*(4), 434–446.

Skinner, A., & Zack, J. (2004). Counseling and the Internet. *American Behavioral Scientist, 48*(4), 434–446.

Smith, A., & Williams, K. (2004). R U there? Ostracism by cell phone text messages. *Group Dynamics: Theory, Research, & Practice, 8*(4), 291–301.

Smith, D. (2001, May). One-tenth of college students are dependent on the Internet, research finds. *Monitor on Psychology, 32*(5). Retrieved May 1, 2001, from http://www.apa.org/montor/may01/internetdep.html

Special Report Video Gaming (2005, August 6–12). Chasing the dream. *The Economist, 376*(8438), 53–55.

Spooner, T., & Rainie, L. (2004). African-Americans and the Internet. *Pew Online Life Report.* Retrieved July 21, 2004, from www.pewinternet.org

Srivastava, L. (2005). Mobile phones and the evolution of social behaviour. *Behaviour & Information Technology, 24*(2), 111–129.

Stack, S., Waserman, I., & Kern, R. (2004). Adult social bonds, and the use of Internet pornography. *Social Science Quarterly, 85*(1), 75–89.

Staldt, G. (2005, June). *Hit the man: Fascination of death and violence in computer games.* Paper presented at the biannual meeting of Digital Game Researcher Association, Vancouver, BC.

Starr, P. (2004). *The creation of the media.* New York: Basic Books.

Stern, D. (2004). *The present moment in everyday life.* New York: Norton.

Stern, S. E., & Handel, A. (2001). Sexuality and mass media: The historical context of psychology's reaction to sexuality on the Internet. *The Journal of Sex Research, 38*(4), 283–291.

Sternberg, R. J., & Preiss, D. (2005). Preface. In Robert Sternberg and David Preiss (Eds.), *Intelligence and Technology: The Impact of Tools on the Nature and Development of Human Abilities* (p. 29–53). Mahwah, NJ: Lawrence Erlbaum.

Stickgold, R., Malia, A., Maguire, D., Roddenberry D., & O'Connor, M. (2000). Replaying the game: Hypnagogic images in normals and amnesics. *Science, 290*(5490), 350–353.

Stoddart, T., & Niederhauser, D. (1993). Technology and educational change. *Computers in the Schools, 9*(2/3), 5–22.

Strassberg, D. S. & Holty, S. (2003). An experimental study of women's Internet personal ads. *Archives of Sexual Behavior, 32*(3), 253–260.

Straus, N. (1997). The fourth blow to narcissism and the Internet. *Literature and Psychology, 43* (1–2), 96–109.

Subrahmanyam, K., Greenfield, P., Kraut, R., & Gross, E. (2001). The impact of computer use on childrens' and adolescents' development. *Applied Developmental Psychology, 22,* 7–30.

Subrahmanyam, K., Greenfield, P., Kraut, R., & Gross, E. (2002). The impact of computer use on children's and adolescents' development. In S. L. Calvert, A. B. Jordan, and R. R. Cocking (Eds.), *Children in the digital age: Influences of electronic media on development* (p. 3–33). Westport, CT: Praeger.

Subrahmanyam, K., Greenfield, P., & Tynes, B. (2004). Constructing sexuality and identity in an online teen chat room. *Applied Developmental Psychology, 2,* 651–66.

Suler, J. (2004). The online disinhibition effect. *Cyberpsychology and Behavior, 7,* 321–326.

Sullivan, B. (2005, April 29). Kids, blogs and too much information. *MSNBC.* Retrieved May 7, 2005, from http://www.msnbc.msn.com/id/7668788

Suzuki, L. K., & Kato, P. M. (in press). *Psychosocial support for patients in pediatric oncology: The influences of parents, schools, peers, and technology.* Retrieved July 13, 2005, from http://www.cdmc.ucla.edu/downloads/SuzukiKato2003.pdf

Taffel, R. (2005). *Breaking through to teens.* New York: The Guilford Press.

Tao, L., & Boulware, B. (2002). Issues in technology: E-mail: instructional potentials and learning opportunities. *Reading & Writing Quarterly, 18,* 285–288.

Tapscott, D. (1998). *Growing up digital: The rise of the net generation.* San Francisco: McGraw-Hill.

Tapscott, D. (2004, March 29). *Keynote presentation: Annual international corporate citizenship conference.* Paper presented at Center for Corporate Citizenship, Boston College.

Tapscott, D. (2005, February). The Telephonosaurus. *The Wall Street Journal,* February 22. Retrieved from http://online.wsj.com/articles/O.SB110902664738560249html

Tashima, K. T., Harwell, J. I., Fiebich-Perez, D. K., & Flanigan, T. P. (2003). Internet sex-seeking leads to acute HIV infection: A report of two cases. *International Journal of STD & AIDS, 14*(4), 285–286.

Taylor, H. & Leitman, R. (2001). Study reveals big differences in attitudes towards health care systems in 10 countries. *Health Care.* 1:2.

Terdiman, D. (2004, Sept. 10). Beware of bots bearing messages. *Wired News*. Retrieved May 18, 2005, from http://www.wired.com/news/culture/0,1284,64888,00.html?tw=wn_tophead_4

The Education Arcade (2003). History and direction. *The Education Arcade*, Retrieved May 18, 2005, from http://www.educationarcade.org/modules.php?op=modload&name=Sections&file=index&req=viewarticle&artid=3&page=1

The Parents Information Network (2003). *Internet Filtering Software*. Retrieved May 15, 2005, from http://www.pin.org.uk/filtering/

Thompson, L., & Coovert, M. (2003). Teamwork online: The effects of computer conferencing on perceived confusion, satisfaction and post discussion accuracy. *Group Dynamics, 7*(2), 135–151.

Thornburgh, D., & Lin, H. (2002). *Youth, pornography, and the Internet*. Washington DC: National Academy Press.

Tips for telepsychology. (2005, January). *Board of Psychology Update, 12, 2*.

Tomas, D. (2001). The technophilic body. In D. Bell and B. Kennedy (Eds.), *The cybercultures reader* (pp. 175–189). New York: Routledge.

Topkis, L. (2002). Therapy via instant messenger. Tech TV Vault. Retrieved May 18, 2005, from www.techtv.com/news/internet/story/0,24195,3389035,00.html

Tunnard, R. (2002). Communities of information and the geography of cyberspace: New visualizations of world order. Unpublished manuscript Tufts University, Fletcher School of Law, Boston MA.

Turkle, S. (1995). Chapter 7: Aspects of the self. From *Life on the Screen: Identity in the Age of the Internet* (pp. 177–209, 310–312). New York: Simon and Schuster.

Turkle, S. (June 16, 1997). Interview on CBC's Nightwatch.

Turkle, S. (2005). *The cyberanalist*. Retrieved February 4, 2005, from http://www.edge.org/digerati/turkle

Tyler, T. R. (2002). Is the Internet changing social life? It seems the more things change, the more they stay the same. *Journal of Social Issues, 58*(1), 195–205.

Tynes, B., Reynolds, L., & Greenfield, P. (2004). Adolescence, race, and ethnicity on the Internet: A comparison of discourse in monitored vs. unmonitored chat rooms. *Applied Developmental Psychology, 25*, 667–684.

Ubelacker, S. (2005, March 3). Virtual game helps burned kids beat pain. *Globe and Mail*.

UCLA Center for Communication and Policy. (2003, February). *The UCLA internet report, year three: Surveying the digital future.* Retrieved September 15, 2004, from http://www.ccp.ucla.edu

Underhill, C., & Olmsted, M. (2003). An experimental comparison of computer-mediated and face-to-face focus groups. *Social Science Computer Review, 21*(4), 506–512.

UNESCO (2003). Education in and for the information society. UNESCO Report, Paris. Retrieved November 1, 2005, from http://www.unesco.org/wsis

Unsworth, G., & Ward, T. (2001). Video games and aggressive behaviour. *Australian Psychologist, 36*(3), 184–192.

USA Today (1997). *Computer access lags for minority students.* Retrieved March 17, 2001, from http://www.usatoday.com/life/cyber/tech/cta505.htm

U.S. Department of Health and Human Services. (2005 April 12). Healthfinder: Your guide to reliable health information. Retrieved on April 12, 2005, from http://www.healthfinder.gov

Valkenburg, P. M., Schouten, A. P., & Jochen, P. (2005). Adolescents' identity experiments on the internet. *New Media & Society, 7*(3), 383–402.

Van Mierlo, J., & Van den Bulck, J. (2004). Benchmarking the cultivation approach to video game effects: A comparison of the correlates of TV viewing and game play. *Journal of Adolescence, 27*(1), 97–111.

Varela, F. (Ed.). (1997). *Sleeping, dreaming, and dying: An exploration of consciousness with The Dalai Lama.* Boston: Wisdom Publications.

Vazire, S., & Gosling, S. (2004). E-Perceptions: Personality impressions based on personal websites. *Journal of Personality and Social Psychology, 87*(1), 123–132.

Ventura, M. (2005). The 8-minute cure. *Psychotherapy Networker,* July/August, 56–102/104.

Vivian, J., & Maurin, P. (1997). *The media of mass communication* (Canadian Edition). Scarborough, Ontario: Allyn & Bacon.

Vlassoff, M., Singh, S., Darroch, J., & Carborne, E. (2004, December). *Assessing costs and benefits of sexual and reproductive health interventions.* Occasional Report #11. New York: The Allan Guttmacher Institute.

Voiskounsky, A. E., Mitina, O. V., & Avetisova, A. A. (2004). Playing online games: Flow experience. *PsychNology Journal, 2*(3), 259–281.

Wagner, J. (2005, July). .XXX domain gets ICANN nod. Retrieved June 10, 2005, from http://www.internetnews.com/xSP/article.php/3509511

Wallace, P. (2001). *The psychology of the Internet.* New York: Cambridge University Press.

Walther, J. (1999, August). Communication addiction disorder: Concern over media, behavior and effects. Paper presented at the annual meeting of the American Psychological Association, Boston, MA.

Wang, P., Bergland, P., & Kessler, R. (2000). Recent care of common mental disorders in the United States. *Journal of General Internal Medicine, 15*(5), 284–285. Retrieved September 13, 2005, from http://www.blackwell-synergy.com/links/doi/10.1046/j.1525-1497.2000.9908044.x

Warschauer, M. (2003). Demystifying the digital divide. *Scientific American, 289*(2), 1–6.

Wastlund, E., Norlander, T., & Archer, T. (2001). Internet blues revisited: Replication and extension of an internet paradox study. *CyberPsychology & Behavior, 4*(3), 385–391.

Weisskirch, R., & Murphey, L. (2004). Friends, porn, and punk: Sensation seeking in personal relationships, Internet activities, and music preference among college students. *Adolescence, 39*(154), 189–202.

West, C. (Speaker). (2004). *Democracy matters.* Compact Disc Recording No. 207. San Francisco, CA: The Commonwealth Club of California.

What the research tells us. (2005). SIECUS Reports. Retrieved May 31, 2005, from http://www.communityationkit.org/pdfs/Learning_The_Basics

Whittaker, J. (2004). *The cyberspace handbook.* New York: Routledge.

Whitty, M. T. (2003). Pushing the wrong buttons: Men's and women's attitudes toward online and offline infidelity. *CyberPsychology & Behavior, 6,* 569–579.

Widyanto, L., & Griffiths, M. (in press). *Internet addiction: Does it really exist? (Revisited).* New York: Academic Press.

WII. (2003). The wireless internet opportunity for developing countries. World Times, Inc., Boston, MA. Retrieved from http://www.w2i.org

Wildermuth, S. M. (2004). The effects of stigmatizing discourse on the quality of on-line relationships. *CyberPsychology & Behavior, 7*(1), 73–84.

Williams, D., & Skoric, M. (2005). Internet fantasy violence: A test of aggression in an online game. *Communications Monograph, 72*(2), 217–233.

Wingfield, N. (2005, Feb. 22). Web's addictive Neopets are ready for big career leap. *Wall Street Journal* (Eastern edition), B1. Retrieved May 14, 2005, from Proquest through Athabasca University.

Wingfield, N. (2005, July 26). Guess what's hiding in your videogame; Flap over grand theft auto highlights wide availability of 'secret' added content. *Wall Street Journal* (Eastern Edition), D1.

Wired NextFest (2005, June). NextFest. *Wired*, pp. 1–41.

Witmer, B., & Singer, M. (1998). Measuring presence in virtual environments: A presence questionnaire. *Presence*, 7(3), 225–240.

Wolak, J., Mitchell, K., & Finkelhor, D. (2003). Escaping or connecting? Characteristics of youth who form close online relationships. *Journal of Adolescence*, 26(1), 105–119.

Wood, R. T. A., Griffiths, M. D., Chappell, D., & Davies, M. N. O. (2004). The structural characteristics of video games: A psycho-structural analysis. *CyberPsychology & Behavior*, 7(1), 1–10.

Worling, J., & Langstrom, N. (2003). Assessment of criminal recidivism risk with adolescents who have offended sexually. *Trauma, Violence, and Abuse*, 4(4), 341–361.

WritingFix (nd). Three ways to use writingfix with students . . . if you're a teacher. *WritingFix*. Retrieved May 16, 2005, from http://www.writingfix. com/three_ways_to_use_WritingFix.htm

Yang, B., & Lester, D. (2003). National character and Internet use. *Psychological Reports*, 93(3–1), 940.

Yee, L. (2006, March/April). Violent video game legislation protects children. *The California Psychologist*, 39(2).

Young, K. (1996, August). Internet addiction: The emergence of a new clinical disorder. Paper presented at the 104th annual meeting of the American Psychological Association, August 15, 1996. Toronto, Canada.

Young, K, (1998). *Caught in the net: How to recognize the signs of Internet addiction and a winning strategy for recovery*. New York: John Wiley & Sons, Inc.

Young, K. (1999). The research and controversy surrounding Internet addiction. *Cyberpsychology & Behavior*, 2(5), 381–383.

Young, K, (2004). *Caught in the net: How to recognize the signs of Internet addiction*. New York: John Wiley & Sons.

Young, K. (2005a). *A therapist's guide to assess and treat Internet addiction: An exclusive guide for practitioners*. Retrieved July 25, 2005, from http://secure4. mysecureorder.netadditction/other/therapist_guide.htm

Young, K. (2005b). An empirical examination of client attitudes towards online counseling. *Cyberpsychology & Behavior*, 8(2), 172–177.

Young, R. (2005c). *Primitive processes on the Internet*. Retrieved February 4, 2005, from http://www.shef.ac.uk/uni/academic/N-Q/psysc/staff/ rmyoung/papers/prim.html

Yuen, N., & Lavin, M. (2004). Internet dependence and shyness. *CyberPsychology & Behavior*, 7(4), 379–383.

Yum, Y., & Hara, K. (2005). Computer-mediated relationship development: A cross cultural comparison. *Journal of Computer-Mediated Communication, 11*(1), 11–19.

Zickmund, S. (1997). Approaching the radical other: The discursive culture
of cyberhate. In S. G. Jones (Ed.), *Virtual culture: Identity and communication
in cybersociety* (pp. 185–205). London: Sage.

Zigurs, I., Poole, M. S., & DeSanctis, G. L. (1988). A study of influence
in computer-mediated group decision making. *MIS Quarterly, 12*(4),
625–644.

# Index